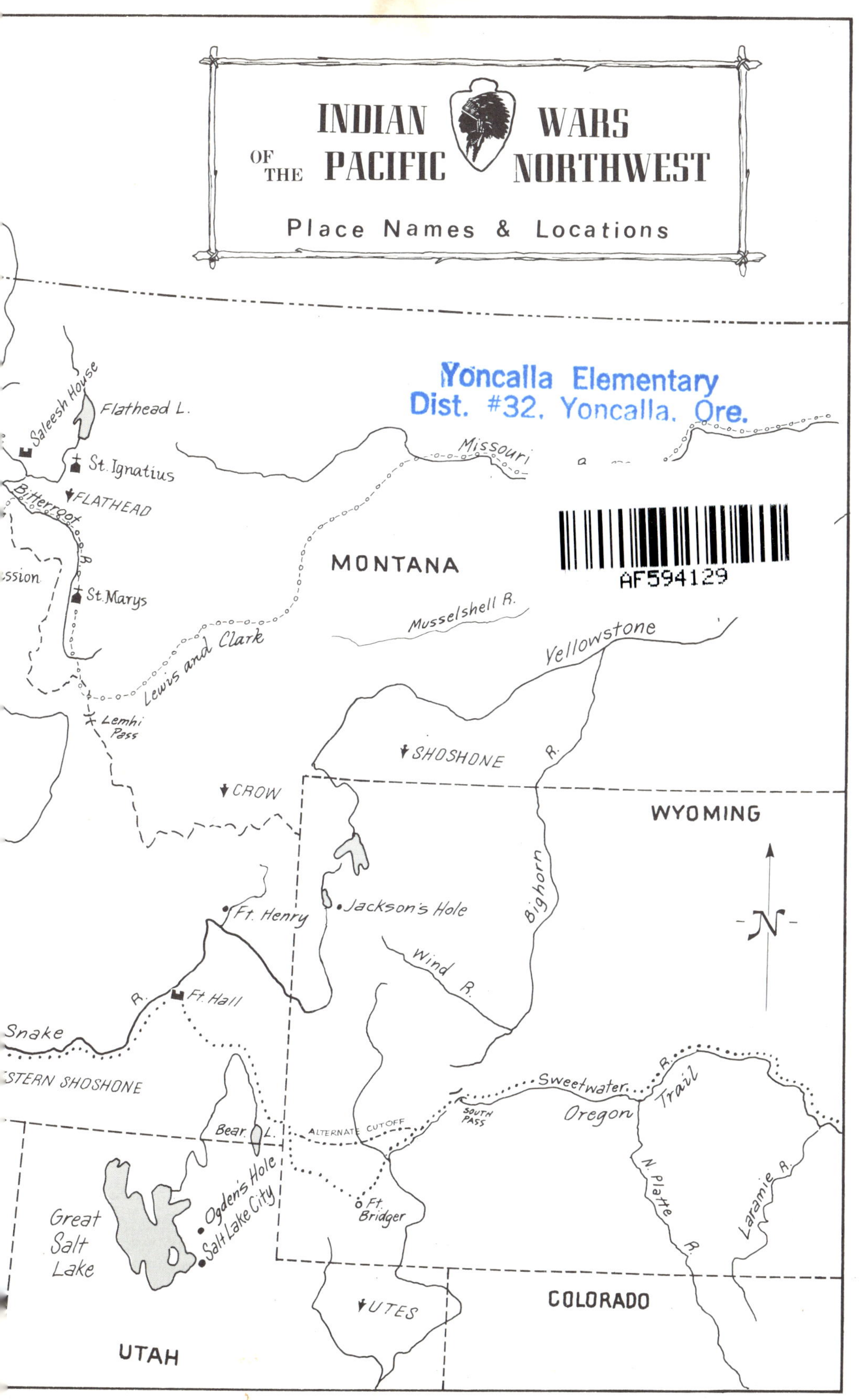
INDIAN WARS OF THE PACIFIC NORTHWEST
Place Names & Locations
Saleesh House
Flathead L.
St. Ignatius
FLATHEAD
Bitterroot R.
St. Marys
Lewis and Clark
Lemhi Pass
Missouri
MONTANA
Musselshell R.
Yellowstone
SHOSHONE
R.
CROW
WYOMING
N
Bighorn
Ft. Henry
Jackson's Hole
Wind R.
Snake R.
Ft. Hall
Sweetwater R.
Oregon Trail
SOUTH PASS
ALTERNATE CUTOFF
Bear L.
N. Platte R.
Laramie R.
Great Salt Lake
Ogden's Hole
Salt Lake City
Ft. Bridger
UTES
COLORADO
UTAH

INDIAN WARS
of the Pacific Northwest

INDIAN WARS
of the Pacific Northwest

RAY HOARD GLASSLEY

Cayuse War, 1848
Rogue River Wars, 1850s
Yakima War, 1853-56
Coeur d'Alene War, 1857
Modoc War, 1873
Nez Perce War, 1877
Bannock War, 1878
Sheepeater War, 1879

BINFORDS & MORT, *Publishers*
Portland • Oregon • 97242

Indian Wars of the Pacific Northwest

LIBRARY OF CONGRESS CATALOG CARD NUMBER: 72-77590
ISBN: 0-8323-0014-4

Printed in the United States of America

SECOND EDITION 1972

INTRODUCTION

To ACQUIRE an adequate understanding of the Pacific Northwest Indian wars, it is essential that something be known of the various races and tribes, with their customs and characteristics. Ethnologists, generally, classify North American Indians racially by linguistic groups. About 55 stocks are now recognized, the number varying from 52 to 61 according to the individual authority. Some of these have not only survived but increased, others are almost extinct, while still others have completely vanished.

Fourteen are represented in the States of Washington, Idaho and Oregon, with some overlapping into Western Montana, Northern California, and Southern British Columbia. In addition there are three whose habitats were British Columbia and Southeastern Alaska, who occasionally entered the Puget Sound area for war or barter, and whose influence was left on the cultures encountered, These three were the Athabaskan, Haidan, and Tsimishian. Of the three, the Haidan, represented by the Haida Indians of Vancouver Island and the adjacent mainland, seem to have had more frequent contacts within present day United States than any other of those living outside the boundaries of our country.

Those living within the limits of the region with which this book is concerned, or extending across its borders, were the Shastan, Takelman, Chinookan, Chimakuan, Wakashan, Yakonan, Weitspekan, Kakapuyan, Waiilatpuan, Shoshonian, Salishan, Lutuamin, Kitunahan, and Sahaptian. Of these, six are relatively unimportant as far as our Indian wars are concerned. They are the Yakonan, Weitspekan, Chimakuan, Takelman, Kitunahan, and Wakashan. The Kitunahan stock is represented only by the Kootenay of Southern British Columbia and Northeastern Washington. *Kootenai* is the spelling favored by the Canadians. The Chimakuan has only one survivor of its linguistic stock, the Quileute of the Olympic Peninsula. The Wakashan includes the Kwakiutl and Nootkah, two strictly British Columbia tribes, and the Makah tribe of the Olympia Peninsula.

Thus eight stocks remain for our consideration. They are the Shastan, represented by the Shastas of Northern California and Southern Oregon, the Rogue River Indians being the more important Shastan tribe in Oregon; the Waiilatpuan, known to us as the Cayuses; the Chinookan, by the Chinooks. It must be remembered that after the white man came most of the Columbia River Indians were known locally as Chinooks, but this was incorrect because the Chinooks proper constituted a tribe living at the mouth of the Columbia River. The Kalapuyan survives in the Kalapooia Indians.

There is a great variation in the spelling of Indian names. This author has found thirteen different spellings for Kalapooia. Every explorer, trader, and trapper, spelled Indian words according to his individual phonetic understanding. The Shoshonian includes the Bannocks, also spelled Bannacks; the Shoshonee, also spelled Shoshone and Shoshoni; and the Paiutes, also spelled Piutes. There is confusion about this latter name also, because at one time, the term Paiute was applied to most Shoshonian tribes. The Lutuamin stock is composed of the Klamath and Modoc tribes, and the Sahaptian of the Yakimas, Umatillas, and Walla Wallas. The largest number of tribes belonged to the Salishan linguistic group, among which were the following: Chehalis, Clallam, Colville, Flatheads, Kalispels or Pend Oreilles, Lillooets, Lummi, Nespelim, Nisqualli, Okanogan, Puyallup, Quinaielt, Sanspoil, Shuswap, Spokan or Spokane, Bella Coolas, and Thompson Indians, a few of which were not resident in the lands now comprising the United States.

There were many other tribes, some known by several names and often without regard to accuracy. Settlers often arbitrarily gave a designation to Indians in no wise conforming to the facts. In the interest of clarity we must say something about it.

We hear of The Dalles Indians. They were Wascopum or Wascos; and the Celilos, Teninos, John Days, and Warm Springs Indians were either the same as Wascos or affiliated with them. We also hear of the Clatsops and the Nehalem, Tillamook, and Nestucca tribes. These were all allied to the Chinooks, spoke the Chinook tongue, with some dialectic differences, and lived southward from the mouth of the Columbia River for about 150 miles. Mention was made of the Cascade Indians, the Des-Chutes tribe, and the Snakes, because they were thus identified by the territories where they resided.

The Nez Perce were Sahaptians and represented the very highest degree of Indian intelligence. Their home was east of the Cayuse and Walla Walla country. The Palouse were allies of the Cayuses. The Klickitats, also Sahaptian, lived along the Columbia River in South Central Washington and east of Mt.

Adams. The Snohomish were on Puget Sound north of Seattle; the Chimakuan were on the east coast of the Olympic Peninsula; the Skonomish lived south of the Chimakuan, as did the Quinaults. The Cowlitz tribe occupied the country drained by the river named for them in southwest Washington and east to the Cascades of the Columbia; the Coeur d'Alenes were east of the Spokanes.

You may have read of the Simcoes and the Cowichan, the latter being a Salish tribe which sometimes made excursions to Puget Sound. The Multnomahs were the most enterprising and progressive of the various bands living along the Columbia River. They also inhabited both sides of the Willamette for about twenty miles upstream from its confluence with the Columbia. Their territory on the Columbia itself, and on both banks, was roughly between the Kalama River and the Sandy River. They were occasionally known as the Waukaississe. The Chemeketas were a band of the Kalapooias. Molallas lived on the western slopes of the Cascades from the Columbia River south to the Klamath River. The Rogue River Indians previously mentioned as belonging to the great Shasta nation and speaking that language, were a troublesome lot. They lived north of the Siskiyou Range in the valleys of several rivers in southwestern Oregon. The Umpquas were in the valley of the river of the same name between the Cascades and the Pacific Ocean. You may read elsewhere than in this book of the Siwash. It is not a true tribal name but a corruption of the word Salish, and was usually used in derogation of any slovenly tribe.

Having done with identification, we should briefly explain some of the customs and characteristics. To begin with, many tribes were peaceful people, others war-like and predatory. For example, the Flatheads were constantly harassed by the Blackfeet, who came from just east of the Rocky Mountains into the Flathead country to loot, kill and enslave. Incidentally, while many tribes practiced head flattening, the Flatheads never did so. It is merely another of the unpredictable errors in nomenclature which we find in Indian ethnology. Many tribes were alternately peaceful and war-like. Most of them had slaves and that was often the cause for inter-tribal hostilities. Racial alliances were strong.

The houses of the Salish and many of the southern tribes were long, rectangular, and with roofs sloping downward to the rear walls. Those of many northern tribes were square, some of them 60 feet in each dimension and all with an independent framework and an outer shell. Whatever the tribe, several families occupied a house, each family with its own fire which was usually in a corner of the family section instead of in the center, but with some notable exceptions. Raised platforms were built along the sides and equipped with mats for sleeping. In wintertime other mats were suspended between family sections to help conserve heat.

Food varied according to the location of the tribes. Generaally, wild game, fish, berries, roots, including the staple camas, and the seeds of many wild plants occupied places in the larder. Eulachon, the candle-fish, were caught for the oil they contained. Oil was used in almost every dish. Those living near the ocean supplemented their diet with shell-fish, and an occasional porpoise or whale. Pacific Coast Indians were the only North American Indians with the exception of one small tribe in Florida, who did not cultivate crops, nature in its wild state being sufficiently bountiful.

The natives were very ingenious in fashioning household utensils. Included in the list were stone mortars, wooden troughs of all sizes for preparing food, dug-out dishes, usually of alder because that wood imparted none of its flavor to food, and folding boxes, cleverly manufactured. A kerf or dado, commonly called a groove, was cut at whatever point a fold was to occur, the edges of the box beveled, and the fitted joints sewed or pegged into place.

Northwest Pacific Indians had stone hammers, knives, drills, chisels, pile-drivers and wedges, but no axes. They used adzes, utilizing a blade of shell, bone, or stone. Occasionally a blade of copper was used.

Their weaving was remarkable, particularly for its intricate patterns. Basketry, belts, nets, and hats, the latter only for keeping off the rain, were woven from the inner bark of cedar. Fishing nets were made from nettle fibers. Blankets were woven of mountain goat wool and from the wooly coat of one breed of dog.

The Indians were ingenious fishermen, constructing weirs and traps in addition to their nets; harpoons, and bone and thorn hooks. Canoes were of two types. The northern tribes constructed them with both bow and stern raised, while those of the southern tribes had a vertical stern and a projecting bow. All sizes were made, from the eight foot canoe to carry one man to huge craft up to 70 feet in length and holding from 50 to 60 men. Sometimes sails were used and they were of two kinds, either made of mats or of very thin boards lashed to a framework.

Their arms were bows and arrows, spears, knives, and bludgeons. They built snares and deadfalls to trap game.

Languages and dialects varied greatly. Often the speech of one tribe was unintelligible to another, in which case sign language was used.

The first traders came. Metal tools and implements thus came into Indian possession. And firearms and ammunition and the epidemic diseases of the white man. The Chinook jargon was developed. It was a mixture of Indian, English, and French words and other words made by combining parts of the three. Gradually all tribes and traders, and later the settlers, used this jargon for communication.

THE last of the Indian wars of the Pacific Northwest was fought close to a century ago. Those wars have been adequately recorded, either separately or geographically by States as well as in the general histories. However, no one has heretofore compiled the story of all of them into a single history.

The period from the early 1840's to 1879 was filled with danger and death from the warring tribes and is replete with the struggles incident to the settlement of new territory. Blame for hostilities did not always rest with the Indians.

These struggles brought out the best and the worst traits in men, white and Indian alike. Their history is sometimes poignant, sometimes tragic, and occasionally humorous. The author hopes that his factual story will prove to be interesting reading as well as helpful to those seeking an authentic record.

RAY HOARD GLASSLEY

ACKNOWLEDGMENT

THE author gratefully acknowledges many sources of aid in the preparation of this history. The staffs of the Oregon Historical Society Library and the Portland Library Association have always been cooperative and helpful. Particular gratitude is expressed to Mrs. Donald Stewart of Vancouver, Washington, for the loan of family documents. Mrs. Stewart is the daughter of the late John W. Redington, who in his young manhood was a scout with the Federal troops through three of the wars and who left a wealth of first-hand material which added much new detail to previously published accounts of these conflicts. Alfred B. Meacham, a Superintendent of Indian Affairs for Oregon and Chairman of the Peace Commission to the Modocs, was the maternal grandfather of Mrs. Stewart. In a few instances the Indians of today, descendants of those who participated in some of the wars, have been willing to enlighten me from their points of view.

In assembling the material, I have read widely for many years both current and out-of-print books dealing with the Indian wars. Through cooperation of the United States War Department, I had access to documents, reports, statistics, and various related contemporary matters in the Pacific Northwest. I have incorporated material from Army rosters, military orders, various diaries, and personal letters, as well as material from the complete files of *The Spectator* and *The Statesman* in the library of the Oregon Historical Society. I have received help from many other sources, directly and indirectly, and while it is not possible to mention each by name, I am none the less appreciative.

R. H. G.

CONTENTS

"These wars, in a large sense, were wars of destiny, perhaps inseparable from the process of quieting the Indian title to the soil."

—Charles H. Carey
General History of Oregon

INDIAN WARS
of the Pacific Northwest

Governor George Abernethy

"George Abernethy . . . on December 10, 1846, sent a message to the legislative assembly, suggesting that consideration be given to surveying the boundaries of Indian villages for the purpose of preventing white men from encroaching." (page 7)

Chief Tamayhas of the Cayuse

"On November 29, 1847, several of the Indians, including Tamayhas, went to the Whitman dwelling under pretext of asking for medicine, and started the attack. Tamayhas struck Dr. Whitman twice with a tomahawk and gunfire started." (page 10)

THE KETTLE BOILS

GROWING TENSION

INDIAN warfare was something based on surprise. Except in major battles it was a procedure of sneak and attack. It was a process of attrition which followed a general pattern. Almost never did an attack occur at night, dawn being the favored time. Of course it brought tragedy in many forms, occasionally amusing incidents, and much wasted effort in futile pursuit. It was a hodge-podge of stealth, noise, disorganization and military precision.

Until 1842 the few settlers in the lower Columbia and Willamette Valleys had been spared Indian warfare. The advent of white people had not reached the point at which the native tribes feared appropriation of the lands. True, there had been incidents around the borders of the roughly defined Oregon Country resulting in the killing of white men, but these had robbery for the motive rather than that of excluding whites from the territory.

In 1828 a party under Jedediah Smith of the Rocky Mountain Fur Company, coming up the coast from California, was attacked at a crossing of the Umpqua River near present-day Scottsburg. Of the 13 men in the group, nine were killed and all furs stolen. The other four eventually reached the settlements, Smith arriving at the Hudson's Bay Company post at Vancouver and wintering there. When weather permitted, the Hudson's Bay Company sent a punitive expedition against the murderers and regained most of the furs. Another of the four was John Turner, who, upon his second entrance into Oregon, underwent a duplicate of his 1828 experience, this time when crossing the Rogue River. In that encounter four men were killed but Turner again escaped. He, with two others, George Gay and William J. Bailey, reached Fort Vancouver and the fourth found safety on Sauvie Island. Smith was killed by an Indian arrow in May, 1831, on the Cimarron River in the Great Plains country.

Also in 1837 a cattle company headed by Ewing Young went to California to bring livestock back to Oregon. Turner, Gay and Bailey were members of Young's group. These three men longed for vengeance and upon the return journey and four days before reaching the Rogue River, Gay and Bailey shot an Indian and threatened an Indian boy. Of course that circumstance called for reprisal. In spite of a double guard the Indians attacked. Young's horse was killed and Gay was wounded but guns were more powerful than bows and arrows and the Indians fled.

There were two reasons for the peaceful conditions among the colonists in the Columbia and Willamette Valleys. First, the Hudson's Bay Company knew how to control Indians. The natives wanted to trade and that was possible under Company regulations only if the Indians remained at peace. True, the British at Fort Vancouver flogged natives who committed depredations and made it a point to apprehend such culprits to the degree that capture and punishment were sure. Indians had a higher regard for the British than for the Americans because the former did not work in their fields but utilized native labor, while even the American missionaries toiled hard and long at their crops. Indians looked on with contempt because with them labor was performed by their women or their slaves. Then, too, Americans often caused trouble by unprovoked attacks on the natives, which was not true of the British. That fact is amply proved by resultant wars in United States territory, whereas Western Canada never suffered from similar occurrences.

The second reason for the safety of the early settlers lay in the fact that disease had greatly weakened the tribes of the two valleys, though to the north, south, and east there were strong hostiles who usually stayed in their own territories—attacking only travelers who were passing through, if at all. Peripatetic American traders heightened the dangers by furnishing liquor to the Indians.

Gradually settlement extended to the middle reaches of the Columbia River Valley and the natives began to chafe at the intrusion of the settlers. Marcus Whitman established his mission at Waiilatpu, near Walla Walla, and Reverend Henry H. Spalding engaged in similar activity not far away at Lapwai. Travelers and prospective colonists stopped at such places and the Indians became aware of the increasing infiltration of whites. Reverend Samuel Parker, another missionary, promised the tribes that they would be paid for land settled by the "Bostons," which was the term applied to Americans. In fact, many similar promises were made based largely upon hope that a procrastinating Federal Congress would do something about it. When payment was not forthcoming, scattered settlers were ordered off the lands. Some of them left, others stayed, often taking the consequences of loss, or property damage, or worse. Occasionally someone was permitted to remain as was the case with Reverend Spalding, for whom the Indians had some regard. But unrest was increasing and suspicion filled the air.

In 1842 Dr. Elijah White, who was Government Agent, secured the agreement of the Nez Perce Indians to a code of regulations and the following spring the Cayuses also agreed. Such accomplishments were helpful in that they postponed hostilities until the white population had increased.

Chief Cockstock was head of a Wascopam or Dalles Indian tribe. He was a trouble rouser, quarrelsome and arrogant. In 1844 he staged a series of depredations at Oregon City and its surrounding localities, which caused Government Agent White to offer a reward of $100 for the Chief's capture. Part of the offer included a provision that when captured he would be tried by either the Cayuses or the Nez Perces according to Indian law. However, in attempting the capture, Chief Cockstock was killed and two white men died of wounds from poisoned arrows. The Indians had several ways for poisoning their arrows but the general practice was as follows: A rattlesnake would be captured and tethered to a stake; then the liver of a deer or a bison would be fastened to a stick and the liver thrust toward the snake; the rattler would sink his fangs into the liver impregnating it with its venom. This process would be repeated two or three times until the supply of venom was exhausted; then the arrowheads would be stuck into the liver and the moist film on them permitted to dry. Thus when a person was wounded the wound would be infected by the arrow.

All Indian troubles were not generated by Indians. Often white men were over-willing to take advantage of the natives. Such a policy was short-sighted for retaliation was the inevitable result.

A band of Indians living on the Tualatin Plains killed an old ox for food. White men in the neighborhood compelled them to give eight horses and a rifle as compensation.

A group of Indians from the country near Whitman's Mission formed an expedition to California for the purpose of buying cattle. Enroute they were stopped by a gang of California bandits. A fight ensued at the end of which the Indians had captured 22 horses from the highwaymen. When the Indians reached the settlements the horses were claimed by white men who alleged that the horses had been stolen from them. The Indians argued their right of ownership under the circumstances; the whites used poor judgment, and in the end a young chief was killed. Many Americans considered the Indians legitimate targets for superior arms or numbers, and that attitude was eventually to cost dearly.

In 1846 Jesse Applegate headed a surveying party of 15 men for the purpose of determining the probability of a good right-of-way for building a road to serve Southwestern Oregon and the entire Willamette Valley, and culminating at Ft. Hall in what is now Idaho. In the course of their survey they met a large party which two weeks earlier had suffered the loss of their horses to thieving Indians at the Rogue River. That was a common practice of the Rogues as well as with the Klamaths and the Modocs, who often waylaid travelers. This incident led to retaliation in the course of which several Indians and two white men were killed.

The Spectator, published at Oregon City, in its issue of November 26, 1846, recited the story of an attack by Klamath Indians on an emigrant train northbound from California, in which two white men were killed and another wounded.

The pyramiding of incidents, provoked and unprovoked, throughout the Oregon Country, advanced the day when formal armed conflict ensued. To these episodes must be added a second reference to the sale of hard liquor to Indians. For some pathological reason Indians could not absorb alcohol. Temperance societies were formed and laws were passed prohibiting the sale of liquor to the natives.

In 1846 the boundary between British territory and the United States was fixed but that circumstance had no influence on the natives except for the remote effect of Indian preference for the British. However, the United States Government had done nothing to aid or protect its settlers. Assistance had long been sought and it might be well, perhaps, to review that situation in the light of its impact on both natives and settlers.

In 1820 Congressman John Buchanan Floyd had presented a bill in Congress calling for the occupation of the Columbia River country. His bill was promptly and ably sponsored in the Senate by Thomas Hart Benton of Missouri, who was always the unwavering advocate of the needs and rights of Oregon. But Southern Congressmen ridiculed the bill, and knowing nothing about the Oregon country, minimized its importance by saying that the only section fit for occupancy was a narrow strip along the seacoast; that all the rest was either mountain or desert. The bill passed.

In 1823 Senator Baylies of Massachusetts announced as his conviction that the natural boundary of the United States was the Pacific Ocean. That same year a group of 80 farmers and craftsmen of Maryland sent a petition to Congress asking it to pass legislation causing the occupation of the Oregon Country so that they might migrate. The Maryland petitioners were followed by a group of 3000 from Massachusetts who likewise memorialized Congress. Another petition came from Louisiana, those people asking for a grant of forty square miles in Oregon where they might settle. But Kentucky's Breckenridge laid down the dictum that migration should be suppressed.

Two more years passed, then the ubiquitous subject came up again. This time Senator Dickerson of New Jersey said that the United States had never adopted a system of colonization and that he hoped it never would. He then followed that statement with another reciting that Oregon could never become one of the United States.

Many, many other Congressmen had their respective turns either for or against acquisition. The years dragged on. Missionaries came to Oregon expecting United States occupation. Settlers began trekking the long trail firm in their belief that it would not be a great while until their new homes would be a part of the United States. Even the Indians learned of the probability and expected that result.

More long years passed until, in 1839, Senator Lewis F. Linn, junior senator from Missouri, introduced a bill calling for the occupation of the Columbia River territory, coupled with a plea for grants of land to settlers as suggested by the missionary Jason Lee. Immediately half the members of Congress presented objections. Many wanted to know what the United States wanted with a territory so far away. But Benton was there to aid his younger colleague and with his traditional eloquence said, "Is it demanded what do we want with this country so far from us? I answer by asking in my turn, 'What do the British want with it, who are so much farther off?' They want it for the fur trade; for a colony; for an outlet to the sea; for communication across the continent; for a road to Asia." He continued with the defense of Oregon and ended his speech with further reference to Britain, saying, "to command the commerce of the North Pacific Ocean and open new channels of trade with China, Japan, and Polynesia, and with the great East. They want it for these reasons and we want it for the same; because it adjoins us, belongs to us, and should be possessed by our descendants." The argument continued without decision. American newspapers ridiculed the idea of colonizing Oregon, one of them calling it "the maddest enterprise that has ever deluded foolish man." But when the British press said it could not and would never be done, the American public and its Congress bristled with the old "show me" attitude.

In the midst of all this debate Senator Linn died, but his effort had already produced its first fruits. The good fight had been won whether Oregon's opponents knew it or not. As a corollary, the boundary question became a major issue and President James K. Polk was elected on the campaign slogan of "54-40 or fight," by which he demanded all of Oregon northward to latitude 54 degrees 40 minutes. Then, in 1846 as stated, the boundary was fixed by treaty at the 49th parallel. But that year and the next were to pass without the advent of United States troops or the building of forts to protect the territory and its increasing immigration. Of course the Mexican War was in progress and while troops had been recruited for service in the Oregon Country, they were sent instead to Mexico. The fact that war had been declared against Mexico was unknown to the officials of the provisional government in Oregon for a long time after the event, else there might have been less disquietude in the Pacific Northwest.

In 1847 5000 people crossed the plains from Missouri to the Oregon Country, which under the Provisional Government included present-day Washington, Oregon, and Idaho, with an indefinite overlap into Western Montana. These immigrants brought their flocks and herds, they crossed rivers on rafts made from the beds of their wagons. Where important cities stand today, herds of buffalo made the earth tremble. The settlers brought Durham cattle, Saxony sheep, and Kentucky horses; merchandise for the first store at Salem, Oregon, and several stocks of goods for Oregon City merchants. They brought peach pits, originating the Cox cling peach, first produced in Oregon, then in California; seed potatoes for the famous Dimick potato. Henderson Luelling brought 700 fruit tree sprouts planted in soil carried in the beds of his covered wagons. There was a bushel of apple-seed and a half-bushel of pear-seed. The wagon trains trampled the Cayuse grazing lands, burned the Indians' fuel, killed their game, and worst of all, brought epidemics of measles, dysentery, and fever. Yes, the Indians were disturbed and grew increasingly nervous.

There were many American hot-bloods who were unnecessarily cruel to natives. They failed to keep promises made to the Indians, engaged in unprovoked killings, and meted out self-determined punishments of various kinds. It was likewise true of the Indians that some of them—a few who were in authority but mostly young braves who wanted to make heroes of themselves—were ruthless in their treatment of immigrants and settlers. The blame for overt acts did not rest with one side alone. Of course, it was a fact that some Indians were thieves by nature. But there were also numerous exceptions among individuals, and an occasional tribe, such as the Flatheads or Nez Perces, were both honest and brave. Many chiefs wanted peace and fairness, as did most of the territorial leaders.

George Abernethy, Governor of the Provisional Territory, on December 10, 1846, sent a message to the legislative assembly, suggesting, among other things, that consideration be given to surveying the boundaries of Indian villages for the purpose of preventing white men from encroaching. He pointed out that "the Indians inhabited these villages previous to our arrival, and should be protected by us."

In its issue of March 4, 1847, the *Spectator* reported the killing of a Mr. Newton by Indians in the Umpqua country and several instances of horse stealing by the natives. On May 27, the same newspaper in an editorial by George L. Curry, then editor, blamed "ardent spirits" as the chief cause of some Indian disturbances "near the mouth of the Luckamute River" (the Luckiamute, north of Albany, Oregon). Curry said, "they have been destroying cattle on Tualatin Plains, they are in trouble with the settlers, and here in our midst we are uncommoded by them, indeed recently at the Clackamas a citizen was fired upon by one of these people." His editorial went on to blame liquor and called for the enforcement of the laws enacted to prevent the sale of intoxicants to Indians.

Also in the same issue, there was a significant announcement in the editorial columns which read, "EXPLORING COMPANY—We are requested to state that the company to explore the Clamet and Rogue River valleys will rendezvous at the Jefferson Institute, on the Rickreall, and positively start the 10th of June next, provided twenty men can be raised for the expedition. We are informed that General Gilliam, Colonel Ford, Major Thorpe, and W. G. T'Vault, Esq. are using their exertions to raise the company and will accompany it should it start."

On July 22, 1847, the *Spectator* published a letter from David Ingalls, dated June 18th, from Clatsop Plains, telling of the killing of one Ramsey by Indians and their threats to kill two or three others. According to the letter the cause of this crime was superinduced by liquor, sold to the Indians by George T. Greer, who was said to be buying quantities of salmon from the natives and furthering his success by plying his customers with liquor, and daring anyone to do anything about it. A sheriff's posse was formed to arrest Greer, which was only accomplished after pursuit in canoes and a tilt on the water during which Greer tried to dump his would-be captors into the water.

Editor Curry wrote an open letter to his paper, which was published in the edition of September 2nd. The missive told of a fight between immigrants and Shutes Indians. These were Wascopams, sometimes called DesChutes Indians. According to Curry, one white man was killed and one wounded, the Indians losing a chief killed and several warriors wounded, whereupon the whites ignominiously fled. Curry blamed the immigrants for starting the trouble.

The seeds of war were germinating.

Then occurred the Whitman Massacre at Waiilatpu Mission near modern Walla Walla, on November 29 and 30, 1847. It was the last straw, and precipitated immediate preparations for war.

Marcus Whitman had known of his danger but had relied upon the ultimate arrival of Federal troops.

Whitman, then 45 years of age, was not a minister of the gospel, though a deeply religious man. He was a doctor of medicine with several years of practice when his interest in the Oregon Country was first aroused. He was a rugged man. In later years he was characterized by Elizabeth Sager, who, with the other Sager children had been adopted by the Whitmans, in these words: "Father Whitman was a very determined man." It may be said without discredit to him that this trait of determination amounted to stubbornness.

He had first been excited by the account of the arrival in St. Louis of four Nez Perce Indians in search of the "white man's book of heaven." He pondered that news as he rode at night about the countryside in response to his medical calls. He was stirred by talk of the strange frontiers of the Far West and impelled by the good he might do.

Early in 1835 he joined with Reverend Samuel L. Parker, a missionary-money-raiser, in a journey to the Pacific Northwest. Whitman was gone for ten months, returning in December by way of St. Louis. Parker, who was aging, remained with the Nez Perces. With Whitman on his return journey were two sons of Nez Perce chiefs, given the paleface names of Richard and John.

Whitman always walked at an easy gait with his shoulders slumped, and ever gave the appearance of restlessness which was probably due to his boundless energy.

His wife, Narcissa Prentiss Whitman, six years younger than himself, had been a school teacher. She was tall and broad-shouldered. Her eyes were deep blue, her hair midway between blonde and brown, her mouth was wide and full.

The Whitmans, with Reverend Henry Harmon Spalding and his wife Eliza Hart Spalding, came to the Oregon Country late in 1836. Reverend Spalding was a rejected suitor of Narcissa Whitman. He was engaged to her just prior to his westward journey with Reverend Parker. Parker had been the emissary of Cupid in the romance. Their engagement was motivated by the refusal of the American Board of Missions to accredit an unmarried woman to the mission field in the Far West. That refusal resulted in her ready acceptance of Marcus, aided and abetted by Reverend Parker. While the mutual agreement to wed was prosaic, their companionship in marriage resulted in one of deepest love.

Both the Nez Perce and the Cayuse tribes wanted the Whitmans to settle among them. It had been planned originally that both the Whitmans and the Spaldings would establish the same mission but differences in temperament made that arrangement undesirable. So Whitman built the mission among the Cayuses, leaving the Nez Perces to Spalding. Spalding declared the solution to be eminently satisfactory. At the time, however, a Nez Perce chief told Whitman that the choice would turn out to be bad for the Whitmans.

At Waiilatpu the Whitmans began their work of medical service to the Indians and religious and academic instruction in their school. The mission soon became an important stopping point for the caravans of covered wagons headed for the Willamette Valley.

In March, 1837, a daughter, Alice Clarissa, was born to the Whitmans. The little girl was drowned in the Walla Walla River in June, 1839.

For several years the mission prospered. Crops were good and the mission work made a favorable impression on the Indians. The population at the mission gradually increased, among them seven orphaned Sager children ranging in age from fourteen down to five months. Their father had died from fever after the Green River crossing and their mother three weeks later. Other members of the caravan cared for the children until they reached Waiilatpu where the Whitmans adopted all seven.

However, the white man's caravans brought diseases strange to the red men. Measles was particularly bad, probably due to the Indian use of sweat houses. These mud and wattle huts were almost air-tight. An Indian would enter after filling the hut with steam manufactured by placing heated stones in water. Soon, dripping with perspiration, he would rush from the hut and jump into the river. The result of such drastic treatment was that the mortality from measles was very high.

In the fall of 1847 a caravan infested with measles stopped at the mission. Most of the immediate population contracted the disease, as did the Indians living nearby. Among the people was one Joe Lewis, a half-breed who had emigrated from Maine, and another half-breed, Jacques Finley. Lewis told the Cayuses that Dr. Whitman was shrewdly exterminating them by giving them poison in the guise of medicine. With as many as five deaths a day among the natives, added to the fact that many of the Indians were unfriendly to all whites, a plot for a massacre took shape.

Tiloukait (or Tiloukaike), war chief of the Cayuses, had always been able to hold his braves in check but he had once been offended by Narcissa Whitman. When Alice Clarissa was born the Chief brought two coyote paws as a present to the little girl, saying that the paws had been good medicine for him and would be for the baby because the child was a white papoose born in Indian country. Narcissa refused the gift and the Chief left in great anger.

His sons, called Clark and Edward, favored the Catholic missionaries on the Umatilla River. Five Crows, titular chief of the Cayuses, spent his winters at Lapwai attending Reverend Spalding's school, and wanted very much to be like the white men. However, he had a half-brother named Young Chief who was a Catholic. There is no evidence that this religious preference had any part in the events soon to follow. Clark, Edward, Young Chief, and two sub-chiefs, Tamayhas and Tamsucky, together with a dozen or so hot-blooded young braves, decided to rely upon Joe Lewis' accusations against Dr. Whitman and put an end to the mission.

Marcus had been warned of danger by Reverend Spalding who had heard rumors of Indian treachery from Indians whom he had befriended. Marcus had heard the same news from Indians friendly to him. Marcus told Narcissa and philosophized that if anyone was in peril it was he, alone. He promised, however, that if the feeling had not subsided by April, they would abandon the mission and move to the Willamette Valley.

On November 29, 1847, several of the Indians, including Tamayhas, went to the Whitman dwelling under pretext of asking for medicine, and started the attack. Tamayhas struck Dr. Whitman twice with a tomahawk and gunfire started. Narcissa dragged her husband into the dining room and placed a pillow under his head. She then asked if he knew her. He replied "Yes." Then she asked if there was anything she could do to stop the bleeding. He said "No." That was his last word.

Narcissa went to a window. A bullet struck her in the breast. She lived until the next day. Besides Narcissa and Marcus Whitman, eleven men were killed on November 29 and 30, and two little girls, afflicted with measles, died within a few days. Several of the residents managed to escape in the confusion, but five men, eight women, and thirty-four children were held as captives. Of course Joe Lewis was not molested. Neither was Jacques Finlay.

Lorinda Bewley, whose parents had yielded to her request and that of Narcissa Whitman to spend the winter at the mission, was taken to the lodge of Five Crows. This chieftain was deeply incensed at the massacre and also much enamoured of Miss Bewley. He treated her with utmost respect and offered every inducement and concession, even to living among the white people, if she would marry him. She refused and was among those ultimately rescued.

The tragic circumstances caused public indignation to run high. The massacre was the chief topic of conversation and provided a real opportunity for the settlers to review their isolation and the failure of the Federal Government to take notice of them. They recalled that, as yet, their national government had passed no laws protecting the residents of the Oregon Country; that not one gun nor one soldier had been furnished. They reminded themselves of the long, vain effort to secure recognition and aid. They told each other of the unending flow of petitions, resolutions, bills, and memorials submitted to Congress year after year. They hotly debated the rivalries between the missions — Methodist, Presbyterian, and Catholic. The settlers knew they would have to work out their own destiny in the crisis. The situation has never been better summarized than by Eva Emery Dye when she said, "The United States owes much to its pioneer Indian fighters. They held Oregon Territory in escrow for years."

On December 8, 1847, Governor George Abernethy told the Legislative Assembly of the imminence of Indian war. Decision to punish the Whitman murderers was quickly reached. Next day the first steps were taken to organize a regiment of volunteer riflemen to move against the Cayuse. It was also agreed to appoint commissioners to treat for peace, contingent upon the surrender of the Waiilatpu criminals.

Chief Fish Hawk of the Cayuse

Whitman Mission at Waiilatpu, 1843

"On December 8, 1847, Governor George Abernethy told the legislative assembly of the imminence of Indian war. Decision to punish the Whitman murderers was quickly reached. Next day the first steps were taken to organize a regiment of volunteer riflemen to move against the Cayuse." (page 11)

THE CAYUSE WAR

THE LEAVEN BEGINS TO WORK

THE first affirmative action was the formation of a company of about fifty officers and men under the captaincy of Henry A. G. Lee. It was to proceed at once to the mission station at The Dalles, to hold that place in case of trouble, and to await reinforcements. In less than twenty-four hours the company was enroute. On December 10 the *Spectator* at Oregon City reported editorially that publication of the issue had been delayed until the last possible moment in order that it might lay before its readers the most recent news about "the recent melancholy intelligence and the consequences thereof."

A news item in the same edition told of the formation of the rifle company under H. A. G. Lee and said that Editor George L. Curry had accompanied Lee so that the *Spectator* could be furnished with messenger service bringing news from the front. Thus Curry became the first war correspondent in the Pacific Northwest.

The same issue contained two letters to Governor Abernethy. One was from William McBean, the Hudson's Bay official at Fort Nez Perce; the other from James Douglas, one of the Chief Factors of Fort Vancouver: These letters acquainted the Provisional Legislature with the first details of the Whitman massacre. The paper also printed the resolution of J. W. Nesmith calling for military action.

Such was the condition of the territorial finances that the colony was in the paradoxical position of being willing to organize a punitive expedition but wholly without funds to finance it. Actually, the Territorial Government, under the several legislative bills pertinent to the situation, wanted nothing but to bring the murderers and their accomplices to justice.

Had their early capture or surrender occurred, there would have been no war as such.

Under one of the legislative bills, Commissioners were appointed to raise funds for financing the war and included an instruction that they try to borrow from the Hudson's Bay Company. The officials of that Company, anticipating such a request, were in a quandary. They sensed that if they assisted the Americans that the wrath of their British superiors might come down on their heads. Then, too, such assistance might wreck the Company's fur trade with the Indians generally, and the fur trade was the reason for the Company's presence in the Northwest. On the other hand, failure to assist would incur the ill-will of the Americans, who might be inspired thereby to make war on the British themselves. In that case opinion would favor the Americans, since the Hudson's Bay Company would be choosing between dollars and the lives of American settlers. The matter was resolved in two phases.

First, the Commissioners were denied supplies for the troops on the credit of the Territorial Government, but the personal credit of the Commissioners was good and it was pledged to the Hudson's Bay Company for necessities to supply Lee's rifle company.

The Commissioners also prepared a circular which was distributed to all merchants and many other citizens, asking for financial assistance toward the war, and they sent a letter in the same tenor to Reverend William Roberts, Superintendent of the Methodist Mission in Oregon.

On December 11th, Governor Abernethy issued an order to Lee including the statement that the Indians at The Dalles were friendly and that nothing was to be done which would disturb that friendship.

On December 14 the Commissioners made a progress report to the Legislative Assembly, announcing their personal pledge of $999 to the Hudson's Bay Company, the loan of $1600 from Oregon City merchants, and the probability of a loan of $1000 from Reverend Roberts. Feeling that their work had been accomplished, the Commissioners resigned. In a few days, December 20, 1847, a new Board of Commissioners was appointed which served until the end of the war. These men were A. L. Lovejoy, Hugh Burns, and W. H. Willson.

Here we have a lesson in financing which might well be used as an example to many governments of today. With about $4000, only a few dollars of which was in actual cash, a regiment of over 500 men was equipped and put into service. The period of enlistment was to be for ten months, unless the war ended sooner. The settlers pledged their wheat, which was the real currency of the territory, furnished provisions, arms, ammunition, clothing, horses—anything which the troops could use. Yet there was never enough. And all the time everyone was awaiting the arrival of

United States troops to take over the war—troops which had instead gone to Mexico.

While these matters were transpiring, Jesse Applegate had sent a communication to the Legislature urging that a messenger be sent to Washington, D. C. to acquaint the Federal Government with territorial conditions as they existed and to solicit aid. It then became known that Governor Abernethy had, in October, sent J. Quinn Thornton as a personal emissary to Washington in the interest of the Governor's party, styled the Missionary Party. Acting upon Applegate's suggestion, namely that any messenger sent to the national capital should be limited to the purpose of securing help and should not involve party politics, J. W. Nesmith presented a resolution to the Legislative Assembly and followed it with a bill providing for the messenger. The bill was passed December 15. A committee was appointed to write the message and Joseph L. Meek was agreed upon as the messenger.

Meek did not like some of the provisions of the bill because it required him to go east by way of California, and because it required him to borrow $500 on the credit of the Oregon Territorial Government for the purpose of financing the trip. Meek had seen how little that credit was worth in the effort to furnish Captain Lee's company with supplies. Meek had no better luck.

Governor Abernethy's reason for wanting the messenger routed through California was so that he might seek aid from Governor Mason there. Meek, for his part, wanted to accompany the rifle regiment as far as they were going and from that point to back-track the immigrant trail east. So he was delayed, and while cooling his heels other events of importance were happening.

On December 14 the Legislature had presented a resolution to the Governor asking that he "appoint three persons to proceed immediately to Walla Walla and hold a council with the chiefs and principal men of the various tribes on the Columbia to prevent, if possible, the coalition with the Cayuse tribe in the present difficulties," the selection of the men to be left to the Governor.

It is interesting here to record the unanimity of opinion regarding the proper course to be taken. In spite of the universal demand for punishment of the Whitman murderers, the settlers did not want a general Indian war and there were, of course, many good reasons for that attitude. Such a conflict would mean widespread killings and horrors, a halt to colonization, inability to fully harvest the next season's crops, a war debt with but little means for meeting it, and general economic disturbance. Bishop

Blanchet of the Catholic Mission had dispatched a letter to Governor Abernethy recommending the same course as that proposed by the Legislature, although the letter did not reach Oregon City until after the legislative resolution. Moreover, the Bishop's recommendation had been suggested to him by the Nez Perces.

The Governor appointed Joel Palmer, Robert Newell, and H. A. G. Lee as the three commissioners.

Governor Abernethy still believed that he could secure help from California and he was most critical of Meek for the latter's reluctance to go to Washington, D. C. by way of California. The Governor decided to send a message to Governor Mason and also a letter to the American consul at Honolulu, and the Legislature adopted resolutions to those ends.

Christmas Day, 1847, was a memorable one for the settlers. The Legislature held a secret session with the Governor on that day, the result being a proclamation appointing enlistment officers at various centers in the territory and designating the rendezvous for the troops. The *Spectator* in its issue of that day said editorially that there was nothing but conflicting rumors about the details of the Whitman Massacre and announced that it had decided to await more reliable information before publishing the conflicting reports, but expressed the opinion that the tribes on the upper Columbia had allied themselves to oppose the whites. The paper also reported that Lee and his company had safely made the portage at the Cascades but thought that Lee would find The Dalles abandoned by its settlers in view of the hostilities of the neighboring Indians.

There was another editorial alluding to a second proclamation by the Governor calling for an additional one hundred men for the Cayuse War. Still other space was devoted to the difficulties of the financial position and the suggestion that each county furnish and equip a company of at least sixty men and carry the expense. Recruiting and the accumulation of munitions and supplies started. All phases of preparation were under the direction of A. L. Lovejoy, as Adjutant-General, Joel Palmer as Commissary-General, and Colonel Cornelius Gilliam, Lieutenant-Colonel James Waters, and Major H. A. G. Lee; the latter three as the ranking officers of the rifle regiment.

On December 27 the Governor wrote a letter to Jesse Applegate asking him to head an overland mission to California in the interest of Oregon, and further suggesting that if Applegate himself could not go that he recommend someone else. Applegate was really the best qualified man in the territory for the task and accepted. He selected fifteen men to accompany him.

Consider that it was mid-winter and the doubtful prospect of any group being able to surmount the cold and the snows of the Siskiyous, and it is not surprising that the effort was destined to fail, in spite of valiant determination. They had to turn back and were fortunate to come through the experience without loss of life.

No American ship was due to be in the Columbia River until March, so an appeal to California could not go by sea. The letter to Honolulu did go because the British bark *Janet* stopped in the Columbia enroute to the Sandwich Islands.

So come what might, it was apparent that for the next few months at least, the colonists were to be left to rely on their own resources.

The Commissioners planned to assure the native tribes that the only purpose of military action was to punish the guilty among the Cayuses; to offset the story being circulated by the Cayuses that the settlers planned a war against all Indians; and to hold the situation in *status quo* until spring when the rifle regiment could arrive in the Cayuse country to begin operations. The Legislature passed a law (subsequently repealed in 1849) prohibiting the sale of arms and ammunition to Indians, a measure which was ill-received because even the friendly tribes needed powder and shot to supply themselves with food.

The second phase of the Hudson's Bay Company's dilemma in regard to their position with respect to the American military expedition resulted in an idea on the part of the Company's officials. They reasoned that Peter Skene Ogden was the man to ransom the captives held by the Cayuse after the Whitman Massacre. Ogden was then one of the Chief Factors, following long years as a Chief Trader for the Company and was respected by all Indians. Accordingly another Chief Factor, James Douglas, talked with the Commissioners Jesse Applegate, A. L. Lovejoy, and George L. Curry, all of whom understood what would next occur. In order to formalize the transaction, the Commissioners, on December 11, 1847, while in conference with Douglas, addressed their written request to him. Douglas replied in writing the same day, explaining the Company's position and announcing that Ogden was heading an expedition, fitted out at the Hudson's Bay Company's expense, for the purpose of rescuing the Whitman captives. It was at once a way to solve the Company's problem, and seemed to offer the best chance for effecting the rescue.

No one anywhere was as well qualified by experience and temperament as Ogden to fulfill the difficult task at hand. None had his rare insight into Indian character. He proceeded without delay and upon reaching the Cayuse country let the Indians know that he was displeased with them and that he was there for the purpose of ransoming all of the captives. He told the Indians the terms of his offer and the Cayuses accepted. Payment was made in trade goods and the prisoners were delivered to Ogden on January 2, 1848. They were taken to Fort Vancouver by boat. Some of the captives, particularly most of the young women, had been grossly mistreated, and all were in a state of terror and nervous collapse. In fact, the complete story of the massacre was never fully learned, because even some time later when their testimony was taken at Oregon City, they were in such a mental state that a coherent story could not be told.

The Protestants blamed the Catholics for encouraging the Cayuses' dislike for Whitman, but there has never been the least substantiation of such charges.

Reverend Spalding and his family had been spirited away from Lapwai and the Indians awaited the next move by the whites.

The New Year of 1848 had arrived, and with it the actual beginning of the war.

The following quotation is from page 262 of *The Peter Skene Ogden Journals* as edited by T. C. Elliott: "From 1845 to the time of his death Mr. Ogden made Fort Vancouver his headquarters, and with the retirement of Mr. McLoughlin became the ranking Chief Factor on the Columbia. He shared the management with James Douglas until 1849 when that gentleman removed to Victoria, after which he was the only Chief Factor on the Columbia until 1852 when Mr. Dougal MacTavish was transferred from the Islands to assist him."

THE FIGHTING STARTS

MAJOR H. A. G. LEE and his company had arrived at The Dalles on New Year's Day, 1848. To Lee, enroute, the Governor had written and had recommended the building of a blockhouse

Blue Mountains—Route of the Pioneers

"Major Lee . . . returned to camp on the 20th [Feb. 1848], reporting that he had followed the trail of a party of Indians headed toward the Blue Mountains but had failed to overtake them." (page 23)

Indian Sweat House

". . . the white man's caravans brought diseases strange to the red men. Measles was particularly bad, probably due to the Indian use of sweat houses." (page 9)

Willamette Mission, 1834

THE DALLES 1838
Methodist Mission

The Dalles Mission, 1838

". . . the settlers . . . hotly debated the rivalries between the missions—Methodist, Presbyterian, and Catholic." (page 11)

mounting one or two guns, at the Cascades. However, Joel Palmer, Commissary-General, had started a few men to the Cascades for that purpose. They built no blockhouse nor storehouse, but did erect a few cabins, and dignified the place by naming it Fort Gilliam.

At The Dalles Lee was having his moments trying to keep his men from returning home. There were shortages of everything—food, heavy clothing, ammunition. There wasn't even a spy-glass until sometime after January 5th when Abernethy wrote Lee: "Mr. McMillan has a spy-glass and is on his way with it."

The *Spectator* for January 6, 1848, printed copies of various legislative bills—those authorizing the rifle regiment; the appointment of Joseph L. Meek as messenger to Washington and empowering him to borrow $500; appointing commissioners to negotiate a loan; prohibiting the sale of arms and ammunition to the Indians; establishing at $1.50 per day the rate of pay for enlisted men in the Rifle Regiment. The same issue printed a letter from Major Lee in which he said that there was no news from Waiilatpu except Indian reports which, if true, were awful enough.

On January 8, Lee's men spotted some Cayuses rounding up livestock. These animals had been left in care of the settlers until they could be moved to the Willamette Valley in the spring. Lee ordered seventeen men to pursue the marauders. The Indians were well mounted, while some of the soldiers were afoot. The Cayuses drove off 300 head of cattle, taunting the soldiers about being unprepared to follow them and daring them to fight; Sergeant Berry was wounded and the Indians suffered three killed and one wounded.

Why that foray? Why such apparent boldness? Henry H. Spalding at Lapwai Mission had, on his initiative, given his word to the Cayuses that there would be no reprisals because of the Whitman incident. There had been a conference at the Catholic Mission at Walla Walla between the priests and the Cayuse chiefs, as a result of which Bishop Blanchet had written Governor Abernethy urging no reprisals. When the Cayuses became aware of the presence of the Rifle Company at The Dalles and had learned that an entire regiment was being recruited, they had decided that any promises made to either Reverend Spalding or the priests were null and void. In fact, a band of Cayuses had gone to Lapwai to capture Spalding, only to find that he had fled when the captives were rescued by Ogden.

Next day, January 9, Lee sent a detachment to see Siletza,

Chief of the DesChutes tribe, who had been robbed by the Cayuses for refusing to join against the whites. The soldiers captured sixty Cayuse horses, poor recompense indeed for 300 cattle.

The *Spectator* of January 20, 1848, contained lots of news. Its front page carried the story of the ransom and rescue of the captives and their safe return, and a letter from Reverend Spalding expressing fear for his life. There was a translation of a statement by four Cayuse chiefs, giving as their reason for the massacre at Waiilatpu, that Whitman had been poisoning Indians. The statement ended with a suggested basis for peace. Also printed was a list of the officers, commissioned and non-commissioned, of the 2nd, 3rd, and 5th companies of the regiment. Also a copy of a resolution passed at a public meeting at Tualatin Plains considering every man a member of the militia and calling for a survey of all men in the district, a sort of early ancestor to the modern armed services draft law. There was also a notice calling a meeting of the citizens of Champoeg County for the purpose of organizing an additional company of volunteers for the Cayuse War. Most important was the resolution passed at French Prairie to enlist a company for the Rifle Regiment, for there had been some doubt about the reaction of the French settlers living there, to an American war.

Colonel Gilliam had started for The Dalles with one contingent of his regiment. Several other companies were in various stages of preparation. At that time Cornelius Gilliam was forty-nine years of age. Born in North Carolina and raised in Missouri, he had served in both the Black Hawk and Seminole Indian wars, and became a captain under General Zachary Taylor. He was also a captain of State Militia in the effort to expel the Mormons from Missouri. He served in the Missouri Legislature and in 1844 led a large group of immigrants into Oregon. He had been ordained a minister of the Freewill Baptist denomination and settled in Polk County where he, as its minister, organized a church on the North Luckiamute River. Bigotry and narrow-mindedness in religious matters were to be found everywhere among the colonists and Gilliam was no exception. He was ready to believe that the Catholics incited the Indians; that the Hudson's Bay Company was doing likewise; that the Hudson's Bay Company was Catholic, when, as a matter of fact, Dr. John McLoughlin was the only Catholic among the Company's leadership in the territory. In fact, the Colonel declared he would "pull down Fort Vancouver about their ears," and the Hudson's Bay

Company thought he might try. There was a letter from Chief Factor Douglas to Governor Abernethy about Gilliam's threat and a conciliatory reply from the Governor.

Gilliam started out with 220 men, Joel Palmer accompanying him. They stopped at Fort Vancouver where, on their personal credit, they bought $800 worth of goods necessary for their immediate needs. The soldiers were mounted but had no pack-horses, hence their provisions were sent by boat, which necessarily slowed the troops.

At the Cascades they were met by a messenger from Major Lee telling of the first skirmish at The Dalles. At this news Gilliam decided that he would not wait for the peace commissioners to catch up with him and hastened toward The Dalles. Arriving there he found a number of military orders from Governor Abernethy, all cautioning non-offense to friendly tribes and impressing Gilliam with the single purpose of the expedition—to apprehend the murderers. The Governor enlarged upon that subject by saying hostilities would cease if the criminals were surrendered and restitution made for stolen property. There was also an official notice of the appointment of Palmer, Newell, and Lee as Peace Commissioners.

Late in January, 1848, Gilliam, with 130 mounted officers and men, went as far east as the Deschutes River for the purpose of punishing the Indians who had driven off the 300 head of cattle. Believing that he knew the approximate location of the Indians, Gilliam sent Major Lee, with a detachment, to investigate. Lee found the Indians but they had witnessed his approach and had started to move their families to the mountains. Lee attacked. In the skirmish one Indian was killed and two women and some horses were captured. The detachment decided to return to the main force but were attacked in a ravine. The Indians rolled boulders down on the soldiers but fortunately none of the latter was injured. After dark the return to Gilliam was accomplished and next day, January 30, the entire force started in pursuit. Overtaking the Indians, the troops charged and in the fray 20 or 30 Indians were killed, the exact number being seldom known in Indian warfare because of their practice of removing the dead from the field of action. The troops also recovered four head of cattle, 40 horses and several hundred dollars' worth of personal property. One soldier was wounded. The Indian village was destroyed but the old people, who had been left at home, were spared. Skirmishing continued for several days, usually under the personal leadership of Lee. During these days three soldiers were killed, one being accidentally shot by the guard, and two, Jackson and Packwood, having been decoyed from camp and killed. Two others were wounded by arrows.

When Palmer and Newell reached the Cascades they found cause for concern. Supplies there were being systematically robbed. Flour barrels had been opened, part of the contents stolen, and the barrels headed up again. But a cannon had arrived as had Captain Thomas McKay's company. The march toward The Dalles was resumed. The post at The Dalles had recently been named Fort Lee, officially, although it was most frequently referred to as Fort Wascopam. The two companies reached that fort on February 10 without any skirmishes enroute. Next day a conference was held between the officers and the commissioners for the purpose of agreeing upon a course of action. New companies were arriving and as each put in its appearance both parties fired salutes in spite of the shortage of ammunition. The regiment now numbered 537 officers and men.

On February 12 Colonel Gilliam notified the peace commissioners that he had issued orders to march on the 14th. The commissioners were disturbed because they were hoping for a council with the Nez Perces and feared that the movement of the troops would alarm the Indians and thus prevent a council. But discipline within the regiment was not good and Gilliam reasoned that the best cure was to get under way. Accordingly he left a corporal with 20 men to guard Fort Lee and removed Chief Siletza's band below The Dalles for their own protection as well as to remove temptation from them.

With The Dalles as a base of supplies, Gilliam pressed immigrants' wagons and ox-teams into service and marched. He crossed the Deschutes on February 16, taking a nine-pounder cannon which they mounted on two wagon wheels. Next day they camped on the east bank of the John Day River. The Commissioners had sent messengers ahead with a flag and presents of tobacco to the disaffected tribes along the Columbia River and had received information which caused them to conclude that all the tribes above The Dalles had united against the troops. From their camp on the John Day River the Commissioners sent a letter to the officers in charge at Fort Walla Walla and also a flag and presents with a letter from Reverend Spalding to the head men of the Nez Perces. The messenger was captured and the presents confiscated but the letters were forwarded to McBean at Fort Walla Walla. Fortunately, when William McBean received the letters, two Nez Perce chiefs, Timothy and Richard, were there and they were among the Nez Perces addressed in Spalding's letter. These chiefs hastened to their people with Spalding's request, supplemented by advice from McBean, and to this circumstance is due, in all probability, the neutrality of the Nez Perce tribe. McBean also sent a reply to the Commissioners but it fell into the hands of Chief Tauitowe, who had confiscated the presents. The chief destroyed the letter as well as one from Brouillet of the Catholic Mission. That was an unfortunate occurrence because the Commissioners did not know how to interpret the failure to receive replies and the circumstance caused many subsequent headaches.

While encamped, Major Lee was constantly on reconnaissance. He found the camp of a small party which had cached its property and retired to the hills. He was ordered to pursue them and did so on February 19, but returned to camp on the 20th, reporting that he had followed the trail of a party of Indians headed toward the Blue Mountains but had failed to overtake them.

On February 21 the army again took up its march and covered a difficult 20 miles, camping that night on Willow Creek. The wagons came up late. The men were tired, hungry, and ill-tempered. They were now 200 miles from the Willamette River and were poorly clad and only half-fed. They had come to fight and did not like the idea of escorting peace commissioners. They wanted to turn back. In fact, one company voted to return if all the flour on hand was not distributed immediately. Colonel Gilliam wisely decided to stay in camp on the 22nd. He held a regimental parade and made a speech which was well received by the men and they shot off some more of their precious ammunition to celebrate the Colonel's oratory.

A party of Deschutes Indians under Chief Beardy came into camp the morning of February 23. They brought the flag sent them from The Dalles and announced that they were present in answer to the summons. The army moved on but the Commissioners remained for a talk. The chief said that he would have arrived earlier except for the fact that the soldiers had shot at his people and caused them to run away. He further announced that he was willing to go to war against the Cayuses and that he wanted always to remain a friend to the Americans. To show that he meant what he said he accompanied the Commissioners to the camp of the army where a council was held. The chief was told to move to The Dalles and remain there until the Commissioners returned and that he could expect the arrival of other chiefs in the immediate future. Gilliam sent a note to the garrison at Fort Lee. Chief Beardy (sometimes known as Chief Sue) presented a fine horse to Captain Tom McKay as a gift from Welaptulet, head chief of the Deschutes. With the horse came word that the head chief would bring in all the property stolen from immigrants if that would secure the friendship of the Americans. Robert Newell subsequently reported that Colonel Gilliam would have preferred fighting the Deschutes because he could not excuse their previous conduct.

The regiment was about ready to start for the Umatilla Valley on February 24 when two Yakima Indians arrived bearing a letter from the Catholic missionaries saying that the Yakima tribe had listened to their advice and would not help the Cayuses and that the Yakimas had announced that they had no quarrel with the Americans.

Four days earlier word had been sent to the Umatilla Mission about the Commissioners' intentions but no reply had been received, so Gilliam decided to move on to Waiilatpu without regard for the Commissioners' plans and sent a messenger to Governor Abernethy with that information. The troops set out just before noon, the Commissioners riding in advance and carrying a white flag. They soon saw two Indians, evidently an outpost for they kept their distance. Then many Indians were seen in the hills, all of them making signs of hostility. The Commissioners fell back to the troops. Indians came from all directions, ranging themselves alongside the soldiers and the battle was on.

Numerically the two forces were about equal. The Indians had waited in a locale favorable to their type of warfare, but the troops knew something about fighting over uneven terrain, too. The soldiers deployed, extending their lines to protect the cattle and wagons. To the northeast, where the battle raged most violently, the soldiers suddenly advanced at double time. That took the Indians aback. The soldiers yelled louder than the Cayuses. This surprised the Indians even more. They stood long enough to fire one volley and then retreated to some rising ground. This sort of tactics continued—a volley from the Indians, an advance by the troops, and the Cayuses falling back to another hill. At last the Indians broke and fled, leaving their dead and wounded on the battlefield.*

* Some idea of the pressure by the troops is to be gained from that circumstance, because the Indians invariably tried to remove their dead and wounded.

The Indians lost eight killed and five wounded while the army's casualties were five wounded, one of whom was Lieutenant-Colonel Waters. The troops camped without water or wood. One incident in particular took some of the conceit out of the Indians. As the battle started, two chiefs, Gray Eagle and Five Crows, rode up near the wagons. Gray Eagle yelled that he and Five Crows were big medicine and that he could swallow bullets. Some accounts recite that he spotted Captain Tom McKay, whom he knew well, and shouted: "There's Tom McKay; I'll kill him." Other accounts say that McKay, hearing Gray Eagle's boast about being able to swallow bullets, said, "Then let him swallow this one," whereupon Captain McKay shot Gray Eagle through the head. At the same moment Lieutenant Charles McKay shot Five Crows, shattering his arm. This circumstance, plus the discovery that the Americans knew how to fight Indian fashion, disconcerted the Cayuses. In a letter to a friend under date of February 29, Lieutenant Charles McKay said that Five Crows got away only because the Lieutenant did not have a good horse.

But the Indians were not licked. They had boasted among themselves that when they met Gilliam's troops they would beat the soldiers to death with clubs and then go to the Willamette Valley to take the women and property of the Americans. They said that the Americans were women. There is some explanation of their point of view because American immigrants often took the safer way out of difficulties while traveling. Encumbered by families, goods, herds, and tired from weeks of travel, they would get to safety, if possible, instead of fighting, when harassed by Indians.

Soon after camp was made, the half-breed Nicholas Finlay, who was at the Whitman Mission at the time of the massacre, came into camp with two Indians who pretended to be brothers, but who were believed to be spies. Finlay's connection with the Indians is obscure. The fact is that he was living at Whitman's and was not molested. Robert Newell had no use for him and said that Finlay "told lies and showed much treachery." The troops had an uncomfortable night without firewood or water. They set out early on the morning of February 25th and traveled all day without water, surrounded by Indians. There was some evidence of dissension among the Cayuses. Some of them had not joined in the fighting the previous day and these sent messengers asking for a council; for that matter, even some of the murderers did. However, officers and commissioners alike declined to talk until they reached water, which did not occur until sundown at the Umatilla River. The troops were in bad humor. Not only had they been without water, but also without food while enroute.

That night the Americans camped on the west side of the river, the Indians on the east side four miles upstream. The Cayuses said that the troops would never cross the Umatilla but they did the next day and camped a mile closer to the Indians. Whenever the soldiers were on the move the Indians swarmed along the hills bordering the line of march. Most of the hostiles made war-like demonstrations. After the regiment encamped that night, Chief Sticcas and a considerable number of other Cayuses made overtures of peace and were told by the commissioners to meet them at Waiilatpu. These Indians told the commissioners that Five Crows had admonished his people to fight the Americans without interruption if he died, as he would do if he lived. One patent reason for the hesitation of the commissioners to parley was the failure to receive McBean's reply from Fort Walla Walla, which letter had been confiscated, as previously described.

It may be well to revert for a moment to the subject of the letters of McBean and Brouillet. As we have said, these letters were intercepted by the Indians, hence the commissioners did not known whether the Catholic Mission had been endangered or even whether their own letters had reached Fort Walla Walla. Subsequently, when the commissioners, with the army, reached Fort Walla Walla all the missing facts were supplied. Had the replies been received no doubt peace could have been made on the Governor's terms, namely, the surrender of the murderers and restitution of the property. But most of the guilty ones wanted to avoid surrender, and the commissioners coming with an army and refusing to hold council, because of the non-receipt of replies, caused the Indians generally to be confused. So they took the natural course—to fight.

On the morning of the 27th not an Indian was to be seen. Nothing had been stolen during the night, which was proof that the Indians had skipped. So the army continued its march toward Waiilatpu and on February 28 camped on the Walla Walla River. The Commissioners interviewed William McBean and the priests and learned that all were alarmed over the union of the Columbia River tribes with the Cayuses, but that Peu-peu-mox-mox, Chief of the Walla Wallas was in favor of peace. That was a good omen. Brouillet gave the Commissioners an account of the Whitman Massacre as he had learned of it.

On February 29 the troops moved six miles up the Walla Walla River and encamped. There they rested while Major Lee and a detachment went back to the fort for powder.

On March 1 Gilliam marched his regiment five miles to the camp of Chief Peu-peu-mox-mox who reiterated his friendship for the Americans and in proof of that contention sold several beef cattle to the commissary. From the Chief's camp the troops could see dust caused by Cayuses traveling toward Waiilatpu. On March 2 Gilliam camped near the despoiled mission.

Now the Americans could see for themselves. No whites had visited the site since the ransom of the captives. It was evident that care had been exercised in the original burials but that predatory animals had dug up the bodies. Robert Newell says in his journal that Dr. and Mrs. Whitman had been interred together with an ornamental picket fence around their grave and that all others had been placed under a common mound surrounded by a board fence. These attentions had probably been given by the captive men. However, the condition of the remains was such that they were hastily replaced in a common grave. Papers, letters, books were scattered about in mud and water. Wagon wheels and various odds and ends had been placed in the house before it was burned. The documents were quickly scrutinized and most of them destroyed. Had they been preserved it is probable that we might know more about the events which led up to the disaster. It was learned from them, however, that Dr. Whitman had been aware of his danger but stayed because he expected the arrival of United States troops.

The Commissioners reported that Colonel Gilliam was so incensed over the scene that they had no chance to hold a council with the Indians. Gilliam said that he had come to fight and that there was plenty of reason, so he would fight. He held a meeting with his officers and started building a fortification.

On March 4, 1848, three months late, Joseph L. Meek started for the national capital. A detachment of one hundred men accompanied him and his eight companions as far as the Blue Mountains. Meek's group wore the caps and cloaks of Hudson's Bay Company employees because it was safer to travel through Indian country as Britishers than as Americans.

On March 5 two men, William Craig and Joseph Gervais, went to meet a large party of Nez Perces who, it was reported, were coming to join the Cayuses who had journeyed to Waiilatpu for the conference with the commissioners. According to

Newell's journal, Colonel Gilliam did not like the approaching visit and threatened to do battle the next day. As it turned out no battle occurred because on the next day, March 6, Craig and Gervais returned saying that 250 friendly Nez Perces and Cayuses were near—in the afternoon these were brought into camp and received by salutes from the army. Next day a council was held at which several chiefs spoke. Old Joseph, Jacob, James, Red Wolf, Timothy, Richard, Kentuck, and Camaspelo, all professed friendship, or, at least, expressed a desire to avoid war. Then General Palmer and the other Commissioners spoke. Colonel Gilliam had been added to the staff of Commissioners and while, as military commander, did not like the proceedings, went along with the others in his role of Commissioner. The Nez Perce chiefs were asked to go to the Cayuse camp, then twenty-five miles away, to try to induce the Cayuse to surrender the murderers. The army was to wait one day, then follow to the Cayuse camp. That plan was followed and next day the army set out. After marching three miles they met the Cayuse Chief Sticcas (sometimes spelled Stikus or Stickus) with cattle, goods, and money taken from the mission and from murdered immigrants. This property had been given up by the Cayuses to create a favorable sentiment toward them. Sticcas wanted to parley. Gilliam did not but finally agreed and the troops camped.

In the course of the talk Sticcas said that the Cayuses would not give up Tamsucky or Tauitowe. The former was known to be guilty but Tauitowe had not been suspected. However, since Sticcas named them together it was reasonable to conclude that Tauitowe also was guilty. Gilliam offered to accept the half-breed Joe Lewis in place of five others but no agreement was reached. That did not mean that no progress had been made, for the Nez Perces remained neutral and the Cayuses were divided.

The army started out again on March 11 but without the commissioners. The latter, with Captain McKay and others who were ill, left for the Willamette Valley. The force which remained numbered 268 officers and men. When the returnees reached Fort Walla Walla they found Peu-peu-mox-mox there and still expressing friendship. He gave the Commissioners a wealth of information about the Whitman massacre.

McBean, of the Hudson's Bay Company, furnished an escort as far as The Dalles where the contingent arrived on March 17. There Palmer had a talk with Chief Beardy of the DesChutes tribe who promised to remain friendly, bring in stolen goods and stop stealing. On March 24 the group reached Oregon City.

The *Spectator* for March 23 was full of Indian news, aside from detailed reports of the Cayuse War. It reported that the dwelling and household goods of a Molalla chief had been burned by whites in retaliation for a small theft by a Klamath Indian. There was an editorial pointing out that Indian title to lands had not been extinguished and that settlers were having enough troubles without unwarranted wrongs against innocent natives. There was the account of a whipping administered to ten Calapooia Indians for cattle stealing and the report that Klickitats were committing depredations in the upper Valley. There had been two robberies by drunken Indians near Oregon City. The property had been recovered but who was responsible for selling the liquor? Three letters were published. One was from Colonel Gilliam to Governor Abernethy asking for more troops; one from Commissioners Palmer and Newell to McBean saying that prospects for adjusting the Cayuse difficulties looked good; and the third from Chief Factor James Douglas to Abernethy reporting on the favorable disposition of the Indians around Ft. Colville.

In the meantime Gilliam with his remaining troops had set out again, as previously stated. His plan called for a march to the Cayuse camp; they had not proceeded far when they were met by three Indians with a flag of truce and some stolen horses. The Indians reported that Chief Sticcas had decided to capture Joe Lewis as suggested by Gilliam; that he had done so and recovered some stolen property but that Lewis had been rescued by his friends and the property retaken. Gilliam did not know whether he could credit the report and thinking that Sticcas might be fooling him, hurried on his way. That night they camped on the Touchet River where they received a message from Tauitowe professing friendship and saying that he wished to disassociate himself from the Cayuses who were hostile. The information also recited that Tauitowe was camped on the Tucannon River; that Tamsucky had gone to join Chief Red Wolf on the Snake River; and that Tiloukaikt had gone down the Tucannon intending to cross the Snake River in the country of the Palouse tribe. Gilliam made a night march and before dawn arrived near the mouth of the Tucannon and the Cayuse camp. He waited for daylight and then moved within a few hundred yards of the Indian camp. An old Indian came out to talk to the Colonel and reported that this was the camp of Peu-

peu-mox-mox, Gilliam's friend, and not that of Tiloukaikt; that the latter had left, abandoned his livestock which could be seen grazing, and which the Colonel could take if he chose. The troops then went into the Indian camp where they found only a few braves. These were armed and dressed for war but seemed friendly. At the camp-site the Tucannon River ran through a canyon. After tiring work, the soldiers reached the far side where the cattle had been grazing, only to see the cattle swimming the Snake River and headed into the Palouse country. The army had been fooled. The soldiers rounded up the few cattle which remained and a large number of horses and headed back for their camp on the Touchet.

Then it happened. Four hundred Palouse, allies of the Cayuse, attacked. The Cayuse, including the murderers, had left their allies to fight the troops. It was really a vicious combat. The troops kept moving, fighting all the time, but their progress was slow. At night, still several miles from their camp, they stopped without fire or food. They had marched all through the previous night and were fagged out. They couldn't sleep because of constant harassing fire from the Indians. In the hope that firing would cease, they turned loose the captured stock but without any cessation in the firing. At daylight the troops set out again and the Palouse attacked at once. The troops went to the hills on the west side of the river to avoid ambush and as soon as all were in that general location gave an Indian war whoop of their own to let the Palouse know that they were ready for a fight. The Indians didn't hesitate. Again the running battle was on.

At this point an incident occurred which probably saved the troops. The companies from Yamhill and Washington counties were hardest pressed and called for reinforcements, which were furnished. Because the troops continued to move and also because the first attack had been repulsed, some of the soldiers thought that the Indians would not follow. The troops really wanted to continue the battle and sent an interpreter to a hilltop to yell a challenge, which stirred up the Indians again. As the regiment neared the Touchet, Captain William Shaw with 20 picked men was ordered to cut off the Indians who had been hanging onto the flanks all forenoon. The Indians sensed the plan and took a short-cut to beat the detachment to the river. But Shaw ran his horses for three-fourths of a mile and succeeded in beating the Indians to the vantage point, which was a life-saver for the army that day.

While the Yamhill and Washington counties' companies and their reinforcements were engaged, the rest of the troops were having a hot time in their own sector. The Indians had erected a crude fortification which the soldiers had to pass, resulting in several being wounded, one of whom died soon after the fight. The Indians lost four killed and 14 wounded. Then the squaws begged their warriors to stop fighting, which they did, and challenges could not get the braves to renew the battle. The Indians did not attempt to cross the river, so the victory was with the soldiers. The regiment was glad for a respite. They had been fighting without interruption for more than a day and the fact that the Palouse had enough was welcomed.

On March 16 the regiment arrived at Ft. Waters. There Colonel Gilliam held a council with his officers, all of whom understood the difficulties of their primary task. There were many unknown factors. It was probable that the Nez Perces would remain neutral and it was possible that the Yakimas and the Walla Wallas would not join the Cayuses. Of course the Palouses had firmly fixed their allegiance by their attack on the troops. The attitudes of several tribes farther north was unknown. Summarized, the whole situation simply meant that the pursuit of the murderers during the ensuing spring and summer might easily prove fruitless. Then there were always a few renegades from even the most friendly tribes and these few either actively joined the warriors or acted as informers. The council of officers could not agree upon a course of action. Some wanted to raise another regiment. Others wanted to keep only enough men in the field to hold the forts and let the rest go home. The condition of the commissary finally determined the decision. Provisions were running short in the field but were on hand at The Dalles. So it was agreed to keep half the force in the field, while the other half was to proceed to The Dalles to escort a supply train to Ft. Waters.

A CHANGE IN COMMANDERS

COLONEL GILLIAM decided to accompany the escort column, chiefly because he could take that opportunity for conferring with the Governor and of acquainting him with the situation, it being quite apparent that the peace commission had failed. Accordingly, Gilliam, with two companies and some casuals, left Waiilatpu on March 20. They camped that evening beyond the Umatilla River. There, when the Colonel was pulling a halter-rope from a wagon-bed, the rope caught on a gun trigger, resulting in the instant death of Gilliam. This left Captain H. J. G. Maxon as the ranking officer with the detachment.

The Colonel's remains were taken to the Willamette Valley for burial. Peter Skene Ogden wrote the obituary. Reports on the campaign were made to the authorities.

The death of Colonel Gilliam had, in itself, nothing to do with the further prosecution of the war nor the failure to apprehend the murderers. The Colonel had been a self-willed man, heading a volunteer army which did not conform very well to discipline. Gilliam and his paymaster had disagreed about the disposal of recovered property which had belonged to immigrants and which Gilliam ordered sold to apply to the maintenance of the regiment. He was accused by some of favoritism and of disregarding orders of the Governor. On the credit side he was clean, courageous, and energetic. But his death did provide cause for some further dissension. Lieutenant-Colonel Waters was now the ranking officer but Governor Abernethy appointed Major Lee to the vacancy. Some people approved, some criticised the appointment. The matter was settled by Major Lee himself, who of his own volition, retired from the command in favor of Waters, Lee retaining second in command.

The Governor had written Colonel Gilliam on March 17 saying that if more troops were to be raised that a special session of the Legislature would have to be called. A number of soldiers had been killed or wounded, others were ill, many wanted to get home to care for their crops. There were only about 150 men at Ft. Waters and they were still without adequate clothing, ammunition and flour. When Captain Maxon reported to the Governor and the Adjutant-General, he made an appeal to the public for support. His call was heeded and supplies began filtering into Ft. Waters. Enlistments were stimulated. About 250 newly enlisted men were added to the rosters. But all was not rosy. Wheat had to be floated down the Willamette to Oregon City where it was necessary to unload and reload it because of the falls. Then it had to be sold or exchanged for goods at Ft. Vancouver. Lead for bullets was purchased wherever it could be found, even a few pounds at a time. James Force, the Commissary at Salem, could purchase only six saddles. Pork and bacon was fairly plentiful. Credit was evaporating. Impressment of wheat was considered and that idea abandoned. Several officers resigned; some men deserted. Fraud was disclosed in the shipments of flour, many barrels containing flour on top and bottom, with shorts* filling the bulk.

Several of the Cayuse chiefs professed a change of heart. They had returned to the Umatilla and it was believed that the livestock of the murderers was mixed with other livestock there.

When Lee had been appointed colonel he was also made Indian Agent in place of Palmer who had resigned that position because of the press of his duties as Commissary-General. At the time that Lee had returned his commission as Colonel and accepted second place under Waters, he retained his place as Superintendent of Indian Affairs.

When news of Lee's position reached the Indians a large number of Nez Perces went to Waiilatpu to await Lee's return there and to request a council. That council was held and a satisfactory conclusion reached with the Nez Perces. Then another council was held with the Walla Wallas and such Cayuses as had returned to the Umatilla. Lee put the matter of the continuation of the war squarely up to them. He said that the soldiers would stay with the campaign until the murderers were punished and the property recovered or paid for, and asked the Indians what they were going to do about it. The answer was not an easy one; in fact nothing resulted except an expressed desire for peace and friendship.

Meanwhile the *Spectator* reported trouble from depredations by Klamath Indians near the Pudding River in the Willamette Valley, but warned the settlers to use forbearance instead of aggression. That paper copied Captain Maxon's letter to Adjutant-General Lovejoy telling of the death of Colonel Gilliam, appealing for more men and supplies, criticizing the lethargy at home and expressing the view that the Spokane and Pend Oreille Indians would join the whites. A later issue told of the death of Chief Ellis and sixty other Nez Perces from measles. Chief Ellis was a firm friend of the Americans and his death was a great loss to the cause of peace. Colonel Waters reported that the Walla Wallas now considered the Americans to be their enemies and expressed doubt about other tribes hitherto considered to be neutral.

---

* Shorts: The part of milled grain next finer than the bran, sometimes called "middlings."

Meanwhile, three new companies of volunteers had been formed, one jointly by Champoeg and Linn counties; Benton, Polk and Clackamas counties; and Yamhill and Tualatin counties. Fifteen young ladies of Oregon City announced that they would "refuse to condone any young man who would not enlist." There were shortages of both men and ammunition at the front. The *Spectator* of May 4 reported an enlistment meeting in Clackamas County and carried a rumor that United States troops destined for Oregon service had left Fort Leavenworth the preceding autumn. There was also news from Fort Hall and Fort Walla Walla that the murderers were in flight but that Indians in the vicinity of those two forts were desirous of peace. However, in the south a band of Klamath and Rogue River Indians, assisted by a few Molallas, had stolen sixty-five horses from a party coming up from California. Such was the ebb and flow of life in the Indian country.

In the meantime preparations for continuing the pursuit of the Cayuse criminals went ahead. On May 17, 1848, more than 400 soldiers set out on a march toward the Clearwater River. Next day Lee, now a Lieutenant-Colonel, with Captain Thompson and 121 men, was detached under orders to proceed to the camp of Chief Red Wolf at the Snake River crossing to try to cut off the fugitives from the mountains. The remainder of the force was to continue to the junction of the Palouse River with the Snake, thus cutting off the Indians from escaping down the Columbia. Some Palouse Indians had offered to help the troops but the Palouse were not at the crossing. Lee sent Major Magone and four men to find the Indians, which took an entire day. Then it took another day and a half to ferry the troops. On May 21 the command was again on the march.

A friendly Indian agreed to act as guide and to show them where Cayuse Chief Tiloukaikt was camped. Enroute they were met by a messenger from Cushing Eells, the missionary among the Spokanes at Chemekeane. His message indicated some division of opinion among the Spokanes but emphasized that these Indians in no wise condoned the murders. The messenger was accompanied by forty-three Spokanes who showed Lee where Tiloukaikt's cattle were grazing and offered to bring them in.

While this chore was under way two Nez Perces came up and reported that Tiloukaikt had fled to the mountains but that most of his livestock, herded by only a few men, could be found near the Snake River. Lee sent Major Magone with a detail to bring in the cattle and also instructed him to arrest any Indian who looked suspicious. Major Magone departed and on the trip one of his men killed an Indian in cold blood—one of those unwarranted acts which kept things stirred up. Magone saw no Cayuses and found only a few cattle. He did run across several Columbia River Indians under Chief Beardy, who told him how to reach the camp of the Nez Perce Chief Richard. Both Chief Beardy and Chief Richard told Major Magone that Tiloukaikt was a long distance away, probably near Ft. Hall. Chief Richard also told Magone that an express had gone from Lee at Lapwai to Colonel Waters. This information caused Magone to rejoin the main body of troops.

The purpose of Lee's express was a request for orders. He said in his dispatch that the Cayuses had fled, that the Nez Perces were friendly and had helped drive the captured Cayuse livestock to Waiilatpu. The messengers returned to Lee with an order to rejoin the main force, which was done on May 25. Lee left a long notice at Lapwai. It was in the nature of a promissory note payable in goods as a reward for the apprehension of the murderers.

The campaign had not resulted in the capture of the criminals and crops were maturing at home. Results to date were summarized. The Nez Perces were friendly and likely to remain so; the Palouses decided that it was expedient to suggest peace; Chief Tiloukaikt was finally convinced that the troops would continue to hunt him down and would never permit him to remain long in one place; the Walla Wallas, to show their changed attitude, caught and hanged one of the murderers and sent word that they were on the trail of another. True, some of these events were transpiring only because the army had made an impression. The tribes were gradually reaching the conclusion that they were no longer the real masters in their homelands.

Colonel Waters held a council of his officers wherein it was decided to abandon the campaign for that season. One contingent was sent to escort Indian Agent Craig and his family from such potential dangers as may have existed at Lapwai. Another detachment was sent to Ft. Colville to bring the missionaries Eells and Elkanah Walker and their families to The Dalles. At this latter place Colonel Waters found a suggestion from Governor Abernethy recommending that 70 men be left at Ft. Waters and 15 at Ft. Lee, both groups to remain until the expected arrival of United States regulars. Lee had anticipated the Governor's suggestion and had held a conference with his officers about garrisoning the two forts but the vote was 6 to 5 against the idea. Lee then called for volunteers and more men than necessary responded after Lee had agreed in writing that any of them who wished could colonize that district at once. He very much wanted the Governor's approval of this plan. The Governor approved but restricted colonization to occupation of the murderers' lands. Of course the subject of colonization was one of the causes of the trouble at Whitman's—the fear of white men settling in the Cayuse country. Lee also required of the Catholics that they establish no more missions in the troubled country until Federal troops could make it safe. The Catholics acquiesced but did not leave. Instead they farmed and mingled with the Indians so that their rights and properties would not be preempted. Captain William J. Martin remained to command at Ft. Waters and Lieutenant Alexander T. Rodgers at Ft. Lee; all others went home. Colonel Waters was ill and Lee had resigned his commission when the active campaign ended for the season. Captain S. B. Hall was in charge of the returnees.

It would be well to briefly appraise the top command following the death of Colonel Gilliam. Lee, as stated, had been placed in command by Governor Abernethy but, in the interest of harmony, deferred to Waters and accepted second place. That was a very generous act. Both Waters and Lee had their adherents and there seems to have been no doubt in Waters' mind that the command was his by right. Waters commanded capably but Lee did most of the important work with full loyalty to Waters. Upon return to Oregon City, Lee, on June 24, wrote a perfectly fair letter to the Governor explaining his deference to Waters. He said that he had done as he had to preserve good feeling in the regiment and to insure success to the campaign.

The *Spectator* of June 20 carried the news of the capture and hanging of one of the murderers, as previously recited. The article credited Chief Serpent Jaune (Yellow Serpent) of the Walla Wallas with the fact. It also stated that Yellow Serpent was in pursuit of Thomas, the Cayuse who had killed the miller at Whitman's mill. In the same issue were three notices. The first was signed by Felix Scott, who was Captain of the Independent Rifle Rangers, an organization enlisted for the purpose of escorting immigrants into the Willamette Valley. The notice ordered the rangers to rendezvous on July 8 "at the bridge over Salt Creek, South Yamhill." The second was from H. A. G. Lee, as Superintendent of Indian Affairs, telling all citizens who had suffered losses from Indians to submit their claims in legal form. The third was from Joel Palmer, Commissary-General, to all men returning from the Cayuse War to turn in their equipment to him at Oregon City.

Two weeks later the *Spectator* published Lee's proclamation opening the Cayuse lands to colonization and an editorial urging that colonization; a restatement of Lee's offer of reward for the capture of the Cayuse criminals; a copy of Lee's letter to Father Blanchet temporarily suspending any extension of Catholic missions east of the Cascades; a news item reporting an effort to raise a company of volunteers to protect the northern immigrant road; and the first authentic published news about United States troops having started for Oregon.

Also editorially, the *Spectator* of July 27 told of the arrival of a Hudson's Bay Company dispatch bearer who reported all quiet at Ft. Waters as he passed through there. The editorial also commented on the receipt of letters by several citizens from friends and relatives at Ft. Wascopam that all was quiet there and that the letters were full of rumors that the Snake River Indians were fighting the Cayuse in an effort to drive them out of the Snake country because they did not wish to harbor criminals. That issue also carried the first installment of the official report of the First Regiment, Oregon Riflemen. Aaron E. Wait was now editor of the *Spectator* and on August 10th editorially deplored the wanton burning of all Indian habitations at Linn City.

On August 14th, 1848, a bill was enacted in Congress creating Oregon Territory, but it was almost five months later before the official news reached Oregon City.

Things were returning to normal when once again the ugly spectre of intolerance in religious matters appeared. In the late summer of 1848 Lieutenant Rodgers, in command at Ft. Lee, seized a quantity of arms and ammunition being taken into the Indian country by the Jesuits. Immediately the cry arose that the Catholics were inflaming the natives. The priests were asked for an explanation which was promptly furnished. They reminded the Superintendent of Indian Affairs that they did not object to the seizure by Lieutenant Rodgers provided no confiscation ensued; that there was no law prohibiting transport through the Indian country at war; that the only law was a prohibition of distribution; that the material seized was the annual supply for four Catholic missions, namely, that to the Okanogans, Flatheads, Pend Oreilles, and Coeur d'Alenes; that the quantity was not large; that the priests, as well as the Indians, needed the supplies to subsist; and that the charge of inciting was untrue and unjust. Governor Abernethy published a statement in the Protestant press smoothing things over. Still, in the minds of many, the accusation was the same as proof. Without attempting to excuse the unwarranted accusation, it is well to point out that those were times of bitter religious oppositions. Religion was an important subject to the individual and almost every person possessed an unwavering devotion to the creed which he professed. The matter had reached such proportions that in December, 1848, the Legislature received a petition to expel the Catholics from the territory, which petition was rejected. However, the priests were not permitted to return to the Umatilla but retained all their other missions. Early in 1849 the seized arms and ammunition were delivered to Ft. Vancouver for the credit of the Catholic missions.

Meanwhile the citizen soldiers at Forts Lee and Waters carried on. The Cayuses had been discredited and they steered shy of the soldiers and did not bother the immigrants. Still the murderers had not been captured and their ultimate voluntary surrender will be told in its proper place.

EVENTS BETWEEN WARS

WHILE the Cayuse War was in progress some tribes nearer the Willamette Valley took advantage of the absence of the many men at the front. Both the Klamaths and Molallas conducted raids. There was an attack in Lane County; cattle were stolen in Benton County; a farmhouse was attacked in Champoeg County. This latter instance is to be noted chiefly because a man today known only as Knox, but who was the first United States mail carrier in that part of the country, saw a man running from Indians and trying to gain refuge at the farmhouse. The mail messenger spread the alarm and about 150 men assembled and organized under elected officials.. In the meantime the Indians had left the vicinity of the farm but when departing threatened all sorts of future depredations. The Indians camped on a creek several miles distant. The volunteers pursued, those on horses going up one side of the creek, those on foot taking the other side. The Indians spied the mounted men and thinking that they were being trailed by no others ran into an ambush by the foot soldiers. Two Indians were killed but no whites were hurt. Night came and with the dawn the pursuit was resumed. That day seven Indians were killed and two wounded while the volunteers suffered only one man wounded. The prompt action of these citizen soldiers definitely stopped those tribesmen for some time to come.

The Calapooias and the Tillamooks also went on a rampage. They murdered an old man and stole cattle. Again settlers volunteered and promptly took care of the situation by killing two Indians and flogging ten more. That stopped those tribes from committing further depredations.

Superintendent of Indian Affairs Lee had appointed Felix Scott as an Indian Sub-agent on April 10th, 1848. Scott was instructed to raise a company for the defense of the southern end of the valley where horses and cattle were being stolen, but the Indians had become wary and had skipped to the mountains.

Scott was elected captain of the company on May 11 and on July 7 he took his small command to Southern Oregon to escort immigrants coming into the territory by the southern route, a task which he performed without interference from Indians.

So isolated was Oregon at that time that even the Governor did not know that the United States had taken over California, just as Oregon had not known for a long time that the United States and Mexico had gone to war. Consequently the Governor had written W. Bradford Shubrick, commander of the United States squadron in the Pacific, urging that a warship be anchored in the Columbia River as notice to the Indians of the interest of the United States in Oregon. The same letter asked that the navy furnish a supply of ammunition to the Oregon volunteers. But the message did not get through overland, and on March 11 the Governor wrote again, sending the request by the brig *Henry* which left the Columbia River in mid-March, enroute with supplies for the army in Mexico by way of San Francisco. The second letter contained the same requests as the first.

Strange to relate, and without knowledge of the situation in Oregon, the United States transport *Anita* arrived in the Columbia River on March 16 for the purpose of enlisting men for the Mexican War, unaware that a treaty concluding that war had been signed on February 2nd. That ship brought a letter from R. B. Mason, Governor of California, in support of Mexican War enlistments. Of course Abernethy had a war of his own and wrote Governor Mason about Oregon's inability to furnish men and again stressed the need for artillery, ammunition and other munitions of war. Major James A. Hardie was the recruiting officer aboard the transport and he reported that there were no military supplies aboard the ship. The Hudson's Bay Company was worried about the purpose of the *Anita* in the Columbia River and Peter Skene Ogden wrote Abernethy inquiring into the matter. There was a considerable exchange of correspondence between Ogden and Abernethy concerning the failure of the United States to protect Oregon. The Governor continued to bombard Congress, even writing direct to President Polk, pleading for relief.

President Polk had, a year previously, appointed Charles E. Pickett as Indian Agent for Oregon. Pickett had first come to Oregon in 1843 and was County Judge of Clackamas County in 1845. He was not generally acceptable to the settlers. He preferred to sojourn in the Sandwich Islands from where he moved to California. There he advised Californians traveling to Oregon to kill Indians wherever and whenever found. Even if this had been justified by the character of the Indians it was poor policy because every Indian killed called for reprisals. Pickett never actively served as Indian Agent. Governor Abernethy wrote Pickett in California insisting that he try to secure the agreement of the United States Naval Commander to send a warship. T. A. C. Jones had relieved Commodore Shubrick and Jones said that he had only three ships to hold all the Mexican ports but that others were due and that if he could possibly spare one he would do so.

Then occurred another of those circumstances which served to confuse the public mind. The United States Commissioner in the Sandwich Islands was A. TenEyck. On June 5, 1848, he also wrote Jones, who had received a letter from some Oregon Anglophobes saying that Abernethy and James Douglas were engaged in a round of bitter correspondence; that volunteers had threatened Fort Vancouver; and that Douglas had requested that a British warship be sent to the Columbia River. Because of this latter missive, which TenEyck knew about, he urged that the United States Navy send help to Oregon. Of course the facts were different. Abernethy and Douglas had not been engaged in bitter correspondence. The volunteers had not threatened Fort Vancouver. It was true that before Colonel Gilliam had started for The Dalles the previous winter, he, believing that the Hudson's Bay Company was hindering our war efforts, did say that he would pull down the fort about the ears of the Company's men, but no semblance of such a move ever occurred. As to Douglas' request for a warship, that might have been true. After all, the Hudson's Bay Company knew that Abernethy was repeatedly requesting a United States warship. Ogden had been concerned about the arrival of the United States transport and the Company would have been within its rights to have requested a British warship.

Meanwhile Abernethy received a copy of TenEyck's letter to Commodore Jones and hastened to deny the rumors. All this mess finally brought arms and ammunition to Oregon though not until the immediate need had passed. But it was now on hand for future emergencies, having arrived on August 9, 1848.

Still the United States regulars did not come. The season's immigrants arrived in the fall with the news that while a regiment had been recruited for Oregon service, it had been sent to the Mexican War instead.

Then, to divert the minds of Oregon settlers, gold was discovered in California. This was welcome diversion, indeed. Many Oregonians went to the California goldfields and many of them found gold.

The *Spectator* of October 12 reported that the last of the riflemen who had stayed at Forts Lee and Waters had come home and had been discharged and that the Indians in those two districts were quiet. The issue of October 26, 1848, carried two items of interest, namely, that Joseph Meek had arrived in Washington, D. C. with the Oregon memorial, and that the sloop-of-war *Eveline,* Captain Goodwin commanding, had been ordered to the Columbia River. Another interesting item appeared in the December 14 issue. That article told of an exploration party finding at The Dalles, the Indian who had killed the volunteer riflemen Jackson and Packwood during the Cayuse War. The entire party of explorers formed itself into a jury, tried the Indian, convicted him, sentenced him to hang, and promptly carried out the sentence.

The Oregon Legislature, which sat in the winter of 1848-1849 passed a coinage act under which $5.00 and $10.00 gold pieces were to be minted. The Territory itself never minted the coins, because the Act of August 14, 1848, creating Oregon Territory resulted in the appointment of Joseph Lane* as Governor and he arrived on March 2, 1849, before coinage was started. On the day of his arrival Governor Lane issued a proclamation declaring Oregon to be a Territory of the United States and since Zachary Taylor was inaugurated as President on March 3rd, 1849, it left the first day of the life of the new territory under the regime of President James K. Polk. Governor Lane promptly declared the coinage act to be unconstitutional and a private company, known as the Oregon Exchange Company, actually minted the coins. Later they were reduced to U. S. coinage at the San Francisco mint at a handsome profit to the Exchange Company because of the pure gold content of the coins.

At the same time that Lane was appointed Governor, Joseph L. Meek was named United States Marshal for Oregon. Governor Lane had also been appointed Superintendent of Indian Affairs and at once began to compose differences between various tribes and to conclude treaties. He had just made peace between the Klickitats and the Walla Wallas and settled some minor disturbances south of the Columbia River when word

* See the *Spectator* of January 25, 1849, for first news of Lane's appointment.

reached him of a plot by Chief Patkanin, of the Snoqualmish tribe in the Puget Sound area, to capture Ft. Nisqually, a Hudson's Bay Company post, and to drive out or kill all Americans in the upper Puget Sound district. In fact Patkanin apparently tried his coup, in the course of which two Americans were killed and one wounded, but the garrison was alert and the attempt failed. Nisqually was in charge of Dr. W. T. Tolmie, who understood Indians but the Snoqualmies even threatened him. After these Indians went back to the hills they sent word to the American settlers that they would permit the settlers to leave the country. The Americans sent back notice that they had come to stay and to prove that point immediately began the construction of two block-houses.

Lane heard about these things and decided to go to the Puget Sound country. A lieutenant and five soldiers were all that remained of the Governor's escort across the plains so he took them with him and carried a supply of arms and ammunition to the settlers. When he arrived at Tumwater, where one of the block-houses was being erected, he was overtaken by a messenger saying that the U. S. S. *Massachusetts* was in the Columbia River with two artillery companies aboard and that Major Hathaway, their commander, said he was willing to send part of his force to Puget Sound. So Lane went back to the Columbia River but notified Dr. Tolmie that the new Territorial Government was ready to protect Fort Nisqually and was prepared to punish the Indians. Lane requested Dr. Tolmie to see that the Indians were made acquainted with that announcement.

J. Q. Thornton was assistant to Lane as Superintendent of Indian Affairs. Thornton quickly got into difficulties. First, he took a month to accumulate information which he could have obtained from Dr. Tolmie in a matter of hours. Next, he bungled the transfer of troops to the Puget Sound country. Following Major Hathaway's permission, one artillery company was sent to Puget Sound, under orders to establish a military post near Fort Nisqually and then to demand the surrender of the hostiles who had killed the two Americans. The ship transporting the artillery company was British. Thornton arrested the captain of the ship because the captain gave the customary dram of liquor to the Indians and the half-breeds who helped unload the ship. Then Thornton offered a reward to the Snoqualmish for the surrender of the murderers of the Americans at Fort Nisqually. Lane was displeased and Thornton resigned. The artillery company was under the command of Captain B.

H. Hill and established itself at Fort Steilacoom. Hill was given charge of Indian Affairs in the Puget Sound district. In September, 1849, the Indians accused of killing the two white men at Fort Nisqually were surrendered and two of them were executed. They were Quallawort, a brother of Chief Patkanin, and another named Kassas.

When Lane came to the Oregon Territory the Federal Government had appointed three assistants to him as Superintendent of Indian Affairs. They were Robert Newell, J. Q. Thornton, and George C. Preston. The latter never qualified because he never came to Oregon, so Newell was assigned the territory south of the Columbia River and Thornton that north of the Columbia.

The Indians quieted down except for killing a lone artilleryman soon after the executions, but the murder was committed so surreptitiously that no one could be charged with the crime.

Once again the anti-British got busy with their tongue-wagging and letter writing, attempting to show that Dr. Tolmie was trying to incite the natives against the Americans, but the truth was that the quiescence of the Indians was largely due to their masterly handling by Dr. Tolmie.

A piece of unfinished business remained. The Whitman murderers were still at large and nothing could be done in that direction until the arrival of the long-delayed regular troops. So after years of effort a regiment consisting of 631 officers and men was recruited for Oregon service and started its trek from Fort Leavenworth on May 10, 1849. Accompanying were a few wives and children and the usual contingent of civilian employees, such as guides and teamsters. There was a large herd of livestock and the customary collection of movable property. The commander was Brevet-Colonel W. W. Loring. Enroute they established two army posts, one at Fort Laramie and the other at Fort Hall, leaving two companies at each.

That summer was marked by a deadly cholera epidemic among the immigrants and the troops likewise lost a number of men from that disease. To add to the spectre of disease a herd of beef cattle which was to have been delivered to the troops at Fort Hall failed to arrive, thus reducing the rations. There were some desertions. Finally, the regiment, reduced by deaths, desertions, and the garrisons left at the two military posts, reached The Dalles. The regiment had lost 70 men; property losses included 45 freight wagons, an ambulance, and over 300 horses and mules. Part of those arriving at The Dalles went by river to Oregon City. Several soldiers were drowned and many supplies lost. The other contingent went inland around the Mt. Hood road, and while they finally got through they lost most of their horses. Reaching Oregon City they found that no preparations had been made for barracks so some buildings were rented for that purpose. This latter circumstance was typical of many which caused people to wonder how anything was ever accomplished in any endeavor. On every hand and for many years there had been many evidences of lack of good planning. Also, there were the ever-present jealousies between the Americans and the British, mostly on the part of Americans.

While the border question had been settled in 1846, it was recognized that the British had been in the Territory a long time and had built forts and habitations. The fact that the boundary had been fixed at the 49th parallel of latitude did not mean that the British were dispossessed. In truth, so firm was the conviction that the British had property rights, and so uncertain was any American's title to the land he occupied, that the barracks, when finally built, were erected on land at Vancouver purchased from the Hudson's Bay Company. Similarly, Fort Steilacoom was erected on land leased from the Puget Sound Agricultural Company.

To show further the lack of co-ordination in the affairs of the Territory, we relate another circumstance. At about the time that Hathaway, now a Brevet-Major, and his artillerymen arrived in the Columbia River, another newcomer showed up. He was Captain Rufus Ingalls, of the U. S. Army Quartermaster's Department, who had been ordered to Oregon to establish Quartermaster Departments. He came on the ship *Anita* which tied up at Vancouver, but his supplies, supposedly sufficient to supply the troops for two years, came on another ship, the *Walpole,* which had cleared for Astoria instead of for Vancouver. Moreover, no material was aboard with which to construct barracks, nor had any carpenters or millwrights been provided to do the work. But everything aboard was unloaded at Astoria, from where it was laboriously hauled by small boats to Vancouver.

Now that the United States Government had at long last started to garrison the Territory, other arrivals made their appearance. In September, 1849, General Persifer F. Smith, commanding the Pacific Division, arrived with H. D. Vinton, Chief Quartermaster. Their job was to select locations for military posts. They approved those already located but vetoed the proposal to locate a fort on the road to California, giving as their reason that in view of the gold rush to California that any soldiers stationed on the road would desert for the gold fields.

It was finally agreed that the artillery would permanently station at Astoria by the spring of 1850 and that the infantry would station at Vancouver Barracks. General Smith had reasoned well, proved by the fact that 120 men did desert and head for California and its gold. They travelled in a group, behaved well, told the settlers as they journeyed southward that they were a government expedition, and secured their supplies on credit. Governor Lane and Colonel Loring took out after them and overtook 70 of them on the Umpqua River. Lane brought them back to Oregon City. Meanwhile Loring went on after the rest and found seven trying to get through the snow in the Siskiyous. He brought them back. The rest were never heard from and were presumed to have perished or to have concealed their identity afterwards.

In May, 1850, Major S. S. Tucker was ordered to The Dalles with two companies of riflemen to establish a supply post. He decreed an area ten miles square to be the military reservation. The reservation at Vancouver had been established as four square miles and the one at Astoria embraced properties already settled upon and improved. All this caused dissatisfaction. In fact these decrees were the beginning of the antagonisms between the settlers and the regular army which were to pyramid and continue for years. But the real impetus to the ill feeling came with another attempt to set aside lands for the military. Henderson Luelling had brought several hundred fruit tree cuttings across the plains and had planted them in the now historic orchard at Milwaukie, Oregon. Colonel Loring attempted to set aside this Luelling orchard and some adjacent land belonging to Luelling's son-in-law, William Meek, for arsenal lands. The settlers arose en masse and sent word to Congress that they could take care of themselves. They asked that the regular troops be sent home, saying that the settlers would fight the Indians as they had done before. Feeling ran high. There was mutual contempt between army and settlers. These antipathies were to increase until after Steptoe's defeat several years later. Again it was a wonder that anything was ever accomplished.

The *Spectator* of October 18, 1849, recounts the trial of six Indians at Ft. Steilacoom. These six were charged with the murder of Leander C. Wallace and the trial under the direction of Judge Bryant resulted in the conviction, sentence, and ultimate execution of two of the defendants.

The same journal in its December 27 issue carried a news item of the court martial of three deserting soldiers. They were convicted, given 30 lashes each in front of the regiment, and sentenced to wear ball and chain for the rest of their enlistment period.

Again, on February 21, 1850, the *Spectator* told of the desertion of about 100 soldiers; announced that Colonel Loring had established his headquarters at Vancouver Barracks; and copied the proclamation of Governor Lane offering a reward for the apprehension of deserters and calling on all good citizens to help on such arrests. Life, civil and military, in the Pacific Northwest really had its complications.

Once more, but this time finally, reference must be made to the ubiquitous subject of the Whitman murderers. Ever since Governor Lane had arrived he had been trying to gain custody of the criminals without having to go out and get them. To the surprise of most people, when Lane brought the 70 deserters back to Oregon City from Southern Oregon he learned that five Cayuses had surrendered themselves. Lane, with a small military escort, went to The Dalles to receive the prisoners. They were Tiloukaikt, Tamahas, Klakamas, Isaiachalkis, and Kiamasumpkin. Most of their relatives and many friends were with them. Why they had surrendered no one really knows. Father Blanchet, in his *Authentic Account*, says that they only consented to come in to confer with Government representatives. In this case Blanchet was probably mistaken since these Indians did offer to pay in horses for a defense, hence they must have expected to be tried. It is probable that the Cayuses were tired of fleeing and hiding out. They must have seen the increasing number of immigrants. The Indians could not procure ammunition. They may have had a series of tribal councils wherein it was finally determined that they would eventually be caught and that perhaps it would be better to surrender voluntarily. The real facts are unknown so we may only conjecture.

Lane brought them to Oregon City and established them on an island at the Falls of the Willamette, the island being connected to the shore by a wooden bridge under constant guard by soldiers. Every care was taken to assure a fair trial. A jury panel of 38 citizens was called and immediately those who were old settlers and those with a background of personal experiences which had embittered them, were excused as jurors. United States District Attorney Amory Holbrook was prosecutor and three defense attorneys were appointed. They were Kintzing Pritchette, who was Territorial Secretary, Captain Thomas Claiborne, Jr., of the rifle regiment, and R. B. Reynolds, paymaster. The defense based its case on the theory that at the time of the massacre United States laws had not yet been extended to Oregon. However, Judge O. C. Pratt overruled that position as well as a motion for change of venue. The trial proceeded and it is to the credit of defense counsel that they tried every legitimate argument to acquit their clients—but there was plenty of direct testimony against all but Kiamasumpkin, witnesses having testified to having seen the other four actually kill. Since Kiamasumpkin had voluntarily and without prior notice given himself up, that act was assumed to mean admission of participation.

The trial opened May 22, 1850. On June 3 a verdict of guilty as charged was returned and execution ordered. Then Pritchette made an unusually surprising and clever move. Governor Lane was absent somewhere to the south. Pritchette declared that Lane's absence made the Territorial Secretary, who was himself, the acting Governor, and that as such he would reprieve the defendants until the United States Supreme Court could review the case. The United States Marshal did not know what to do until Judge Pratt told him that since there was no certainty that Governor Lane was outside the boundaries of Oregon Territory that any act of Pritchette's as acting Governor would be an unauthorized act. When Pritchette learned of that interpretation he desisted and the five were hanged. A Catholic priest, Father Veynet, accompanied the convicted men to the scaffold. Thus, finally and in fact, ended the Cayuse War, or rather, in that manner the principal cause was cleared. There only remained the necessary legislative and congressional documents and approvals to pay the costs of the war.

Governor Lane's absence from Oregon City at the time of the trial was because he was going about his duties in Southern Oregon as Superintendent of Indian Affairs. Depredations there were continuing and the Rogues had attacked a group of whites at Rock Point, robbing them of all of their possessions, the white men saving their lives by fleeing to the forest. This incident was only the most recent of a long series and Lane had decided to go down to the area to see if he could do something to make travel safe. He had 15 white men and 15 Klickitats under Chief Quatley with him.

Enroute Lane overtook a party driving cattle and accompanied them to the south side of the Rouge River where he went into camp and sent word to the Indians thereabout that he was there to make a treaty and invited them to a council, requesting that they come unarmed. Two chiefs and 75 warriors came. Lane greeted them affably and invited the chiefs to sit with him. At that moment another party of Indians appeared fully armed. Lane, through Chief Quatley as interpreter, asked the newcomers to lay down their arms and join the circle, and then opened the council. He told them who he was and why he was there; that the purpose of the council was to make a treaty of friendship, but that in order to do so the Rogues would have to stop robbing and killing white travelers. He promised that if the Indians would agree that he would see that they were paid for any lands settled by whites and would send an agent to live among them to protect their interests. Their principal chief arose and addressed his people briefly, whereupon all jumped up and flourished weapons. But Jo Lane knew Indians and anticipating such a move had, at the beginning of the council, ordered Quatley and a few of his Klickitats to stand near the chiefs and if things looked like trouble to seize the chiefs. Quatley did his duty. He and his Klickitats seized the principal chief, Quatley holding his knife at the chief's throat. Lane then walked among the warriors, knocking their weapons aside and ordering them to ground their arms. The Chief, finding himself in a helpless position, seconded Lane's order. Lane then told them to leave and return in two days but that in the meantime he would hold the Chief as hostage. The Indians didn't like the idea but had no choice. Lane was a different type of white man than they were used to meeting. He improved his time during the next two days to make a favorable impression on the Chief. Finally the latter spoke in Chinook jargon, the made-to-order universal language for traders, elementary and easy to pronounce. He asked, "Are you Jo Lane?" "Yes," replied Lane in the same jargon. Whereupon the Chief asked Lane to give his name to the Chief. Lane compromised by giving his first name to the Chief, who was ever after known as Chief Jo. The result was that Lane so favorably impressed the Rogues that they agreed to his treaty terms. While there Lane learned that he was to be displaced by a Whig Governor, and instead of returning to Oregon City went south to the Shasta district gold mines accompanied by a Modoc slave boy presented to him by Chief Jo of the Rogues.

In 1850 Congress passed an act extinguishing Indian title to land west of the Cascades. Anson Dart had immediately been appointed Superintendent of Indian Affairs and with his secretary, P. C. Dart, arrived in Oregon in October, 1850. Joseph Lane had been succeeded as Governor by John P. Gaines who, with Alonzo A. Skinner and Beverly S. Allen, were appointed Commissioners to make Indian treaties west of the Cascades. Also three sub-agents were appointed under Dart, namely, A. G. Henry, Elias Wampole, and H. H. Spalding. The latter was an old-timer in Oregon. Wampole came out in 1851 but Henry never arrived.

Twenty thousand dollars had been alotted to the Superintendent of Indian Affairs to build living quarters for himself and his assistants and to buy presents for the Indians. The treaty commission had also received an appropriation of $20,000.00 with which to buy goods to pay Indians for title to lands and for expenses. It was not until April, 1851, that the commissioners started to work. They quickly made six treaties with Willamette Valley tribes and had spent all but $300 of the appropriation before receiving word that Congress had discontinued all Indian treaty commissions, leaving that business to the Superintendent of Indian Affairs.

Superintendent Dart was also short of funds. He had assigned H. H. Spalding to the Umpquas but Spalding seldom went to their country. Dart asked for his removal and E. A. Sterling was appointed to succeed Spalding. Then Sterling was ordered to Astoria. Dart, himself, went east of the Cascades in June, 1851. There he found the Cayuses to be a mere skeleton of that once powerful tribe. There were only 36 Cayuse warriors left.

Dart also visited the sites of the missions of Waiilatpu and Lapwai. He decided to place an agency on the Umatilla and in so doing used the last of his funds. In spite of all his handicaps Dart did a good job. He had a vast territory and little competent assistance and very little money. He appraised the situation as being favorable to the whites, except in regard to the Snakes and the Rogues and recommended that troops be stationed among the Snakes to protect the immigrant route. He learned that the Nez Perces were preparing to war on the Snakes and discouraged that enterprise by persuading the Nez Perces to wait until the next year (1852) when, if United States troops were not quartered in the Snake country, he would interpose no objection to their war. It turned out that the decision was not a good one because later in 1851 the Snakes went berserk, making life miserable for immigrants, killing 34 of them, wounding

Kettle Falls on the Columbia near Fort Colville

"Another detachment was sent to Ft. Colville to bring the missionaries Eells and Elkanah Walker and their families to The Dalles." (page 35)

Fort Walla Walla, Noted Hudson's Bay Post

"The messenger was captured and the presents confiscated but the letters were forwarded to McBean at Fort Walla Walla." (page 22)

The Dalles, with Mt. Hood in the Background

"With The Dalles as a base of supplies, Gilliam pressed immigrants' wagons and ox-teams into service and marched." (page 22)

Vancouver Barracks

". . . better times were coming, not without Indian wars, but the beginning of the end of such wars, for in September, 1852, the remnant of the 4th United States Infantry reached Vancouver Barracks. There were 268 men under Lieutenant-Colonel Benjamin L. E. Bonneville. They were the survivors of the crossing of the Isthmus of Panama, but they were too sick and the season was too late for any affirmative action that winter." (page 70)

Lt.-Col. Benjamin L. E. Bonneville

and outraging many, and stealing $18,000 worth of immigrants' property.

Wampole did not last long. He started trading on the side instead of attending to his duties as sub-agent and after three months was ousted.

Sub-agents came and went, most of them inefficient, but one, J. L. Parrish, attached to Methodist Mission projects, was outstandingly successful.

Governor John P. Gaines

"Gaines, using the women and children as an inducement, prevailed upon some of the Rogues to agree to a treaty. . . . Thus ended what we may designate as the First Rogue River War." (page 56)

Chief John of the Rogues

"As the new day dawned, Chief John came in, the last of his band. Twice he raised his rifle as if to fire and twice decided not to pull the trigger, and with reluctance joined the rest of the prisoners." (page 107)

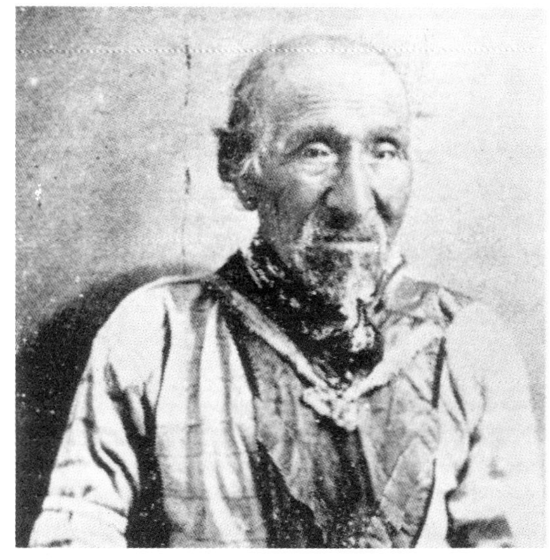

ROGUE RIVER WARS

VIOLENT BATTLES

THINGS were happening which couldn't be fathomed. Beginning in 1850 tribes which had previously caused little or no concern became restless. People talked about it, editors wrote about it, army officers tried to analyze it. No doubt the sight of increasing numbers of settlers revealed to the Indians the end of their free control of the wide-open spaces. Then, too, there was the temptation to steal and rob when immigrant trains, particularly scattered wagons, offered ready opportunity. Sometimes retribution came in the form of bullets from the covered wagons,and when an Indian was killed there was sure to be a balancing of the account. Also there were those who blamed the Mormons for inciting the Snakes. The Hudson's Bay Company, still operating but now subject to American law which prohibited the sale of ammunition to Indians, observed that law. But in its very observance the Company's prestige suffered in the Indian mind. The great Hudson's Bay Company no longer ruled the land and the Indians knew it. No more did they stand in awe of the British. It was probable that the Cayuses in their enforced wanderings had inoculated the Snakes with hatred toward the "Bostons," as they called the Americans. At any rate depredations increased. In all sectors there was a pyramiding of "Indian troubles." In the south the Shastas, Rogues, and their allies made the road to and from California increasingly hazardous.

Then in May, 1851, David Dilley was shot in cold blood by two Rogues. The other white men who were with him escaped over the mountains to California with the news. A company of volunteers was quickly formed, crossed the Siskiyous, killed two Indians, and captured a number whom they held as hostages pending the surrender of the two killers. The head chief refused to deliver the murderers.

On June 1st, farther down the river, a party was attacked by hostiles and one Indian was killed. Next day, at the same crossing, three different parties were attacked, one of them losing four men. On June 3rd a group of 32 headed by Dr. James McBride, returning from the gold mines, were attacked in their camp south of the Rogue River. The Indians outnumbered the whites 6 to 1 but after several hours of battle their chief was killed and the Indians retired. The whites suffered no serious casualties but the Indians carried away a considerable quantity of movable property. There were certainly other Indians killed or wounded, but that could not be proved because of the Indian habit of carrying away their casualties. These events properly translated meant nothing less than that another Indian War was in preparation.

The mounted rifle regiment assigned to Oregon was in the process of returning to Jefferson Barracks, Missouri, via California. The first detachment had left in March and the rest, under Major Kearney, was traveling slowly trying to seek out a route which would avoid the Umpqua River canyon. Kearney received word that the Rogues were warring on the whites and that the Indians were assembling at Table Rock, which was about 20 miles east of the usual crossing of the Rogue River. Kearney hurried forward with a detail of 28 men but high water delayed them until, on June 17, he reached a point five miles below Table Rock. The Indians were expecting an attack and were not disappointed. Eleven Indians were killed and a number wounded. Three soldiers were wounded, two only slightly, but Captain James Stuart died in a few hours. The creek on whose bank he was buried was named for him.

Table Rock was a mesa projecting over the Rogue River and from its top a wide view was commanded. Kearney knew that he could not storm the place with his small force so encamped for several days awaiting the main body of his troops. Meanwhile volunteer units of riflemen were being formed at the mines, for news of the outbreak had traveled fast. Governor Gaines could do little as under the territorial plan there was no provision for militia. He did write to the President for troops although Samuel R. Thurston, Territorial Delegate in Congress, had said none were needed. In fact, Thurston's statement was the reason for Kearney's departure.

Having written President Fillmore, Governor Gaines set out for the Rogue country. He had no escort and arrived in the Umpqua Valley to find that his effort to raise a company of volunteers was doomed to failure because most of those who had been available had already gone to the scene of the fighting. Lacking an escort he stayed in the Umpqua Valley till the end of June. Meanwhile Jesse Applegate was busy recruiting as was Jo Lane, who, by the way, had just been elected Territorial Delegate to Congress. At the ferry on the Rogue River Applegate met a group of miners on their way to Yreka. He suggested their enlistment and 30 of the miners did so and went at once to Willow Springs, a strategic point where they could join the regulars when the latter came through, or, if the Indians fled in that direction, they could intercept the hostiles.

Lane had been on his way to inspect his mining property in the Shasta district before proceeding to his official duties in Washington, D. C. when he heard of the battle of June 17 in which Captain Stuart had lost his life. He had about 40 men with him and hurried toward the locale of hostilities. On the night of June 22 he had reached the mountains in the Rogue River country when he was met by a messenger from Kearney who said the latter would march that night in order to attack the Indians at daylight on the 23rd. So Lane hastened to catch up with Kearney but missed him and went back to Stuart's Creek to await news. There W. G. T'Vault and Levi Scott with a detail, came for supplies for Kearney's force, so Lane went with them and was royally welcomed by both regulars and volunteers. Lane was popular, and T'Vault was to become one of the most important men of early Oregon.

There were two fights on June 23 at Table Rock. The morning encounter was brief but the afternoon battle lasted until nightfall. The Indians suffered heavily but characteristically carried away their casualties. Several whites were wounded but none killed. Chief Jo, the namesake of Lane who had made the treaty the previous year, challenged Kearney to more fighting when the major proposed a new treaty.

Actually, Kearney wanted a little time to figure things out, intending to attack at daybreak on June 25, but the Indians hitailed it down the river. Kearney pursued. The Indians' trail crossed the river seven miles below Table Rock, then it went up Sardine Creek, which empties into the Rogue River just west of Gold Hill, at which point the troops caught up with the Indians. The warriors fled to the forest leaving their women and children to be captured. Kearney tried for two days to engage the warriors, after which he returned to the camp on Stuart's Creek taking with him 30 prisoners.

Lane was recognized by the Rogues, who called across the river that they had been harassed by whites who were overrunning their country. Lane told them that they were the ones who had broken the treaty, whereupon the Indians said that they were tired of war and wanted peace. But Lane was no longer Superintendent of Indian Affairs and Kearney, who had been delayed in his trip to Jefferson Barracks by way of Benicia, California, had said that he would have to be on his way. So Kearney set out, planning to take the prisoners with him since there did not seem to be anything else to do with them. They were actually in his custody when he started. He had not gone far when Lane sent word offering to deliver them to Oregon City. So Lane acquired the prisoners and set out for Oregon City. However, on July 7 he met Governor Gaines at a point where the Governor had understood he would find the troops - only to discover that he had been too late. Gaines, using the women and children as an inducement, prevailed upon some of the Rogues to agree to a treaty. This was the same faction within the Rogue River tribe which always professed willingness for peace whenever their warriors had taken a beating. They agreed to accept United States jurisdiction and protection and to return stolen property.

When Governor Gaines returned to Oregon City he recommended that an agent with a military guard be sent to the Rogues.

Thus ended what we may designate as the First Rogue River War.

INCIDENTS – COINCIDENTAL AND FOLLOWING

WHILE Kearney and Lane were busy with the foregoing, other Indian troubles were in progress. In May, 1851, Captain William Tichenor, who was operating the steamer *Seagull* between Portland and San Francisco, announced that he intended to found a town on the Southern Oregon coast and build a road into the Southern Oregon gold district. He expected to set up a store for miners' supplies and said that he had chosen a site. It turned out to be the place where present-day Port Orford stands. He gathered a group of nine men led by J. M. Kirkpatrick to initiate the undertaking. Tichenor insisted that the local Indians were friendly but the men refused to go unless supplied with firearms. The Captain provided them with a nondescript assortment of weapons among which was a little old cannon with three or four shells, each holding two pounds of powder. Tichenor told the two men that he would reinforce them on his return trip in about two weeks, when he would also bring supplies.

As soon as the ship had sailed from the townsite the Indians started to menace the small colony, which promptly set up log defenses on a prominent rock, since known as Battle Rock and now preserved as a state park. The colonists loaded their cannon and awaited developments. On the morning of June 10 the Indians gathered in large numbers, held a war dance and were harangued by a tall fellow wearing a red shirt. Then the Indians advanced to storm the barricade. They had no knowledge of cannon and crowded together. The first shot from the cannon killed seventeen of them, one being the red-shirted orator. He proved to be a white man, a Russian, and had probably been a deserter from some Russian ship, or may have been marooned by his captain. Thus it seems that we had a Russian agent provocateur even in that early day. Then another leader exhorted the natives and again they attacked. That leader also was killed. The type of energetic reception accorded them caused the Indians to pause. A long-range conversation ensued in which the white men told the Indians that the ship would return in 14 days when they would leave on it. The natives decided to wait. On the 15th day, the ship having failed to appear, about 400 Indians congregated on the beach. The white men decided that their only chance for survival lay in escape. They had a limited supply of ammunition and knew that it would be only a question of time until the natives, through overwhelming numbers, would be victorious. The white men slipped away. Traveling by night and hiding by day, staying near the coast, finally, hungry and exhausted, they reached the settlements near the mouth of the Umpqua River. Meanwhile Captain Tichenor had returned, found the site abandoned and evidence of the battle. Among other things he found a diary containing an incomplete account of the battle. He concluded that all the white men had been killed and thus reported his conclusion. The newspapers on the coast published accounts of the supposed massacre.

But the effort to colonize Port Orford continued. In August, 1851, the settlers there numbered about 70 and felt sufficiently powerful to hold their own against the Indians and to explore a right-of-way for a road to the gold diggings. Twenty-three men under the leadership of W. G. T'Vault set out on the exploring trip. By August 22nd most of the group were ready to give up the enterprise as a bad job and 13 of them returned. T'Vault and nine others plodded on. September 1st they, too, decided to abandon their trip. The horses couldn't negotiate the tangle of underbrush and they decided to employ local Indians to take them down stream in canoes. The river was the Coquille and the Indians were of the tribe of the same name. On the 14th the Indians suddenly beached their canoes at their village where word of the expedition had evidently preceded them. The Indians immediately surrounded the whites and attempted to gain possession of their firearms. The fighting was terrific. The Indians were armed with bows and arrows, war clubs and knives. Their knives had been fashioned from iron salvaged from the wreck of the pilot boat *Hagstaff* which had been lost at the mouth of the Rogue River. Patrick Murphy, A. S. Dougherty, John P. Holland, Jeremiah Ryland, and J. P. Pepper were massacred. T'Vault, Gilbert Brush, L. L. Williams, T. J. Davenport, and Cyrus Hedden escaped, though Brush was severely injured, in addition to his other injuries being partly scalped.

Appeal for a garrison was made to the army at Astoria. The post commander had received a report from Kearney telling of the battles with the Rogue River Indians, which with the added intelligence about the Coquille massacre caused Lieutenant A. V. Kautz and 20 soldiers to be sent to Port Orford, supposedly the best station from which to hold the Indians in check. The post commander had been told that Port Orford was only 35 miles from Camp Stuart on Stuart's Creek, whereas it was three times that distance, all of it through very rugged country. So the stationing of Lieutenant Kautz' small group was of no value as an aid to the miners and the force was too small to go into the mountains to fight Indians.

On September 12th, 1851, Anson Dart, Superintendent of Indian Affairs, with two agents, J. L. Parrish and H. H. Spalding, sailed from Portland on the steamer *Seagull* for Port Orford. The purpose of their trip was to make treaties with the Coast tribes. They arrived on the 14th, the very day of the massacre on the Coquille and two days later heard that news from T'Vault and Brush, who credited the care given them by the Cape Blanco Indians with their survival. Dart was on a spot. He had come to conclude treaties. To do so now would make it appear to the Indians that the whites were backing down. He had Lieutenant Kautz and only 20 soldiers so he couldn't lead a punitive expedition. However Dart had Parrish who knew Indians. Parrish persuaded the Cape Blanco natives to find out who had survived at the Coquille River besides T'Vault and Brush. So two Cape Blanco women went to the Coquille village and while there buried the five victims, but did not know how to identify them. The Indian women returned reporting that some had escaped but just who they didn't know. After several days of discussion Parrish decided to go to the Coquilles for a talk and took no escort. Instead he had with him one Indian from a Columbia River tribe who had stolen from the Coquilles as a boy. Parrish took presents by means of which three principal chiefs were induced to come to his camp but the council came to nothing as the Coquilles refused to place themselves under the supervision of the white people.

Dart knew that the Rogues had not kept the treaty made with Governor Gaines and that numerous robberies and murders had occurred, so he sent word to the Rogues to meet him at Port Orford. That was an error because it was customary that one tribe would not cross the territory of an unallied tribe unless to fight them and Dart should have had knowledge of that fundamental. Hence his order was rebuffed and the Rogues got tougher. In fact that summer (1851) the Rogues committed 38 known murders and many thefts and robberies.

Upon hearing of the Coquille River massacre, General E. A. Hitchcock ordered Companies A, C, and E of the First Dragoons to Port Orford. Company C was mounted, the other two dismounted. Lieutenant-Colonel Silas Casey of the Second Infantry was assigned to command. Companies A and E arrived at Port Orford on October 22, 1851, and Company C on October 27th. On October 31st they started out to punish the Coquilles. It took them until November 3rd to reach the mouth of the Coquille River because of the difficulties of the trail. Their guide was Gilbert Brush, one of the survivors. On November 5th the Indians assembled on the north side of the river and challenged the troops. The Indians felt their oats because they had supplemented their bows and arrows with the firearms and ammunition captured at the time of the massacre. The Indians and the troops fired at each other across the river without damage to either side.

The soldiers built a raft and on November 7th the dismounted men crossed, the mounted men with Lieutenant-Colonel Casey remaining on the south side. Then both detachments started upstream. That march continued for several days — struggling through underbrush and swamps, up, down and across canyons. It was raining and the men slept in wet clothes and wet blankets and didn't see an Indian. They did run across several abandoned villages which they burned. Casey changed his plan and ordered a return to the mouth of the river. There he acquired three small boats, packed 60 men into them, and rowed up stream for four days to the junction of the North and South Forks. The weather continued bad and the stream was swifter by reason of continued rainfall.

On November 21st Lieutenant Thomas Wright with 14 men in one boat went up the South Fork while Lieutenant George Stoneman with 14 men in another boat went up the North Fork. After proceeding seven miles Stoneman saw the Indians in force on both sides of the stream; he fired a few shots and then returned to the junction. Wright also returned, having gone farther but having seen no Indians. Next day all started up the north branch. Fifty of the men were on the south bank, while the other ten men in two boats went ahead. When within a half mile of the camp one company crossed to the north side, all advancing silently. Of course the Indians saw the boats and assembled to prevent their landing. Casey had hoped for that very thing because it gave the troops on one shore a chance to rush in from two sides of the Indian camp, while those on the opposite bank picked off any Indians who straggled close enough. In a few minutes 15 Indians were killed and many wounded. The surviving hostiles fled to the forest. Casey figured they had had their lesson and returned to the mouth of the river where they erected a log barracks. In December the three companies were sent to San Francisco and thus ended another Rogue River campaign.

In January, 1852, the schooner *Captain Lincoln* was chartered to carry a garrison to Port Orford, which was ordered to be designated thereafter as Fort Orford. Lieutenant Stanton, who had been with Lieutenant-Colonel Casey in the Coquille River campaign, was in command. The vessel went aground on a sand spit two miles north of Coos Bay. All personnel, together with the stores, were safely landed and habitations were devised from the ship's sails and spars. They were there four months with nothing to do except to keep thieving Indians from stealing the stores. The men named the place Camp Castaway. Twelve dragoons were detailed to mark a trail to Fort Orford so that a relief train could get through. The dragoons also carried messages for forwarding to the military authorities in San Francisco and were ordered to stay at Fort Orford until replies came from San Francisco. However, the mail steamer with the answers, and with a Quartermaster named Miller aboard, scheduled to stop at Fort Orford, made a mistake by concluding that the entrance to the Rogue River was Port Orford, and when the error was discovered became panicky and hit out for the Columbia River so that the quartermaster did not get to Fort Orford until April 12th. From there he headed a pack train for Camp Castaway. It took four days to go 50 miles so Miller went up to the mouth of the Umpqua where he found the schooner *Nassau,* which he chartered and brought to Coos Bay, the first vessel to enter there. The brig *Fawn* soon arrived at the mouth of the Umpqua, loaded with quartermaster's wagons. Mules were sent there to haul the wagons to Camp Castaway. There was no road but the job was done. They hauled the supplies from the wreck across sand dunes to Coos Bay where they were loaded on the *Nassau,* for Fort Orford, arriving there May 20th. This merely indicated some of the difficulties attendant upon fighting Indians.

Fort Orford was by that time garrisoned by twelve dragoons under Lieutenant Stanton and 20 artillerymen under Lieutenant Wyman. At that time no road had been opened into the interior, in fact it was not until that year that the first road was made available. Since horses could not get through the underbrush and the canyons the garrison wasn't of much use for trailing Indians, nor could they hurry here and there through the interior as emergency calls came, so they remained at Fort Orford as an evidence of moral suasion. After all, there were 32 of them, well armed so they could shoot, which demanded some respect from the natives.

As pointed out elsewhere in this book, there was a wide variation in the intelligence quotient of the many different tribesmen. The Rogues and Shastas, who were of the same nation, were far down the scale from the Cayuses, who, in turn, were surpassed by the Nez Perces. The Rogues and Shastas were most primitive in their habits, passions, and morals. With them it was survival of the fittest by whatever means necessary. They had no property except the barest necesssities, but were always willing and anxious to acquire that of others. The Rogues were never quiet for long.

In the spring of 1852 a series of outrages occurred in Southwestern Oregon which was to eventuate another Rogue River war. A settler who lived on Grave Creek, which empties into Wolf Creek, a tributary of the Rogue River, was robbed. Then in April five prospectors were attacked in their camp on Josephine Creek in the Illinois River country. One of them slipped out and made his way to Jacksonville for aid. The other four built a barricade and held off the Rogues for two days when relief came in the form of 35 miners.

The prospectors had found the remains of men recently murdered. Calvin Woodman was murdered by the Shastas under Chief Scarface on April 8th at a creek running into the Klamath River. Scarface was chief of the tribe in Shasta Valley; John was chief of those in Scott Valley. The miners and settlers of both valleys combined and arrested Chief John, who was considered by some to be the Head Chief, but only because his father had been the principal chief. Demand was made of Chief John to surrender Chief Scarface as the murderer and also Chief Bill, as an accessory. Chief John refused the surrender and somehow escaped. So the miners set out to punish the Indians. In the fight which followed, the sheriff was wounded and several horses belonging to the posse were killed. The Indians began moving their families out of the neighborhood in preparation for hostilities.

Another phase of the attempt to arrest Chief Scarface came in an incident sparked by Elisha Steele. He was a man who always held the confidence of Indians.

While traveling north from Yreka and arriving at Johnson's ranch in Scott Valley, he met a company of the miners who had been vainly trying to apprehend the murderers of Calvin Woodman. Fearing for the safety of the Johnson family in case of war, Steele decided to hold a council and succeeded in persuading several important Indian leaders to meet with him. These Indians were Chief Tolo, head of the tribe in the country around Yreka; Philip, who was Tolo's son; Chief John of the Scott Valley tribe with his brother Jim and two less important brothers. All these Indians assured Steele that they wanted only peace and offered to go on a search for the murderers with Steele. So Steele organized a group which went to Yreka and secured the necessary warrants for the arrest of Chief Scarface and Chief Bill.

Setting out they found that the two criminals had gone to the district which was under the rule of Chief Sam of the Rogue River Indians. Chief Sam had already declared war on the whites, his alleged reason being that he accused Dr. G. H. Ambrose, a settler, of appropriating land which traditionally had been used as winter quarters by the tribe and, further, that the doctor had refused to betroth his infant daughter to the Chief's infant son. Which of these excuses was most impelling we do not know but when Chief Tolo, his son Philip, and Jim, who was Chief John's brother, learned of them, they declined to accompany Steele any further but did assign two young braves as their substitutes and pledged that the braves would find the criminals or stand trial before the law in their stead.

We must now consider another of those trying sets of circumstances which caused people to wonder how affirmative results were ever accomplished. It will be remembered that Alonzo A. Skinner was Indian agent in the Rogue country. As such it was his prime duty to avoid war and to conclude peace treaties and, also, to see that the rights of the Indians were protected, and that the natives were compensated for lands occupied by settlers. After the withdrawal of Chief Tolo and the others from Steele's party, part of Steele's group with himself at its head, went to the Rogue River. The other detachment under Benjamin Wright went to the gold mines on the Klamath River. While these two parties were traveling, news of Chief Sam's war declaration reached the mining community at Jacksonville. There a company of almost a hundred men under John K. Lamerick, as captain, was organized. When agent Skinner heard about it he obtained a promise from the volunteers that he would be given time to council with the Indians before the volunteers attacked.

Skinner and a committee of four found Chief Sam who agreed to talk. He said that he was in favor of peace but that he preferred to wait until the next day in order to give time for Chief Jo to join the council. Skinner agreed to wait. While these events were transpiring, Steele had arrived at Jacksonville to demand the surrender of Scarface and Bill. Skinner agreed that their surrender be made a condition of the council's results. So all of them went to the council – Skinner, Steele, Lamerick and his company. The Indians were waiting on the far side of the river. A messenger was sent across to ask Chief Sam to come over with Chief Jo and a small bodyguard. Sam agreed but seeing the volunteers armed and in formation thought it was a trap and hesitated, whereupon Skinner ordered the volunteers to stack their arms, which was done.

Steele was there to arrest two Indians and Skinner was present to negotiate a peace. The messenger reported that the murderers were in Chief Sam's camp. Sam refused to council until Steele freed two Rogues whom he had captured enroute. Skinner spoke to the prisoners saying that he, as their white chief, freed them. Steele, in turn, told them that if they tried to leave they would be shot and stationed men for that purpose. Under these poor circumstances the council got under way and while in progress about 100 Indians crossed the river from Sam's camp and mingled with the crowd. This made the volunteers nervous so they took up their stacked arms. This council occurred July 19, 1852, and under the circumstances was a failure. Even under the best conditions it would have failed because Sam never intended to to enter into a binding treaty. Finally Sam said that he would not surrender the criminals, at least until he had gone back across the river to discuss the matter with some of his people. So he went across and yelled back that he was not returning and defied the volunteers to come over, promising them a hot reception.

Of course the challenge could not go unanswered. After all the volunteers had come for the purpose of fighting Indians but Skinner and Steele, with a considerable number of Indians, were still on the council ground. So half of the volunteers went to a ford above Sam's camp and the others down stream below a sandbar beyond Sam's camp, prepared to cross and attack if Skinner and Steele were threatened. Skinner, ever an individualist as far as his own decisions went, and anxious to avoid hostilities but judging that a battle was likely to occur, crossed the river. About half of the Indians did likewise. Steele was alarmed at Skinner's action and placed a guard to prevent the rest of the Indians from crossing. Steele also sent a Shasta Indian over to warn Skinner of his peril. That Indian knew the murderers, and Skinner could have asked him to point them out but did not, fearing bloodshed.

Just then it was reported that Scarface and two others were seen sneaking off in the direction of the Klamath River. This news caused a commotion among the volunteers which alarmed the Indians, who hastened into a nearby grove. The volunteers thought that the Indians had gone there to prepare for an attack. Steele's party then got into position to intercept them. It surely looked as if a fight was only a matter of minutes. At that moment Martin Angell, a settler who had formerly lived in the Willamette Valley where he had the respect of the Indians, came up and suggested to the Indians in the grove that they lay down their arms and agree to remain as hostages until the murderers were surrendered. The Indians agreed and were told to occupy a log building in the vicinity. As they walked past Steele's party, ostensibly to go to their assigned quarters, they suddenly made a run for the woods. From the woods the Indians would have had the advantage in firing, so Steele ordered his men to attack. Both sides were well armed and both ready to fight. Recall that part of Captain Lamerick's volunteers were at the ford above camp. Hearing the firing, Lamerick left some men to guard the place and then set off up the valley to warn the settlers, the first of whom was Dr. Ambrose, previously mentioned.

The battle didn't last long. Sam's warriors made a noisy charge for the purpose of liberating the two prisoners held by Steele. The prisoners started to run towards the river. One was shot before he got that far; the other after he reached the opposite shore. Sam then sent some braves to cut off Steele but they were observed by one of the volunteers and several of them killed. The only white casualty was one man wounded. Skinner, who had taken no part in the fighting, went to his home, which he started putting into a state of defense.

That evening news was received that some of Sam's warriors had, during the council, gone down stream to a bar where a small company of miners were washing gold and killed the miners. Lamerick at once crossed the river and placed his force in the pass between Table Rock and the river. Steele and his party went farther up stream so he could intercept the Indians and turn them back towards Lamerick's position the following morning. The Indians were out-generalled. Finding themselves trapped, they asked for peace and agreed to settle on the terms offered the previous day, which terms included the surrender of the killers. Word was sent to Skinner who called a council for the the next day, July 21, 1852, which was duly held. There it was learned that Scarface had not been with Sam. Instead it was one from Chief Tipso's band from north of the Siskiyous. The Indian's name was Sullix, a man who resembled Scarface and who also had his face scarred, to which more scars were added by wounds received in the fight. Scarface was said to be hiding in the Salmon River Mountains.

Scarface had probably been on the Salmon, for, after Steele's failure to arrest the Woodman killers an expedition under Ben Wright set out to find them. With Wright were several Indians including Scarface in spite of the fact that he was very much suspected by the whites. Proceeding towards the Klamath River the party divided. Scarface, alone, ventured too near Yreka and was seen by several white men who decided to add him to their long list of Indians whom they had killed for the Woodman murder and who had probably never heard of Woodman. Afoot, Scarface led his mounted pursuers a race for 18 miles before he was caught. They hanged him to a tree in what is still known as Scarface Gulch. Wright returned with two Indians suspected of killing Woodman. A trial, witnessed by immense crowds, was held at Lone Star Ranch. One of the Indians was convicted and hanged, the other released.

In the treaty which Skinner made with Chief Sam the latter was required to hold no communication with the Shastas. Since the Rogues and the Shastas belonged to the same family such a requirement would seem to have been futile. But as bad as things were in the Rogue River country, they were better than they had been in 1851 when measured by the number of murders, since only 18 killings were perpetrated by the Rogue River Indians in 1852 as compared with 36 proved the previous year.

In the treaty councils Indians were told that the Federal Government would pay them for lands in money or in other things of value. Shortly after the treaty with Chief Sam the Superintendent of Indian Affairs was notified that all treaties which had been made in Oregon Territory had been ordered laid on the table in the United States Senate and Dart was instructed to make no more except where absolutely necessary to maintain peace. The reason given was that the Federal Government wanted time in which to define its Indian policy. Dart thereupon, in December, 1852, tendered his resignation to become effective in June, 1853.

It must be recalled that Joseph Lane was Territorial Delegate in Congress in 1852. There he was trying to obtain military protection for the northern immigrant route. He was reminded that his predecessor Samuel R. Thurston had said that the mounted rifle regiment was unnecessary and in fact Kearney was withdrawing the last remnants of it when he intervened in the Rogue River War of 1852. Lane stressed his point, indicating the large number of murders and robberies in 1851.

However, the 1852 immigration, which was the largest of all, was so well equipped as well as so numerous that the Indians were not very bold although some stealing occurred. The southern route had another story to tell and a sad one. That route roughly paralleled the southern boundary of present-day Oregon with slight serrations due to the topography of the country. There Fremont had been attacked in 1843. There Captain W. H. Warner was murdered in 1849 while surveying for a railroad. The route had always been subjected to attacks. Tule Lake, now mostly farm land but then a large body of water, was a favorite spot for the Modoc Indians to waylay immigrant trains. There was a particular spot which was worse, that being on the north side of the lake at what was named Bloody Point, a place where the wagon trail ran between the lake and an overhanging cliff. Many immigrants were attacked there in 1851 but 1852 had to roll around to mark the high spot in troubles at that location. That year almost a hundred men, women and children were murdered, wagons burned, and large quantities of goods stolen.

We have previously stated that Benjamin Wright had left Steele near Jacksonville to go to the mines on the Klamath River. Near Yreka he met a party of 60 male immigrants, the advance group of a larger number coming by the southern route, who said they had come through without Indian molestation, but they also reported that there were many parties on the road, some with their families, and that Indian signal fires were burning in the mountains. Upon learning of the signal fires it was decided to raise a company of volunteers in Yreka to escort immigrants through Modoc land. A company of about 40 men under Captain Charles McDermit was organized and set out for Tule Lake. Arriving there they met another group of men bound for Yreka. McDermit assigned two of his men to act as guides and the rest of his company remained in the lake country. As it turned out the two guides were wounded in an Indian attack but they and the party they were escorting escaped when a lucky shot removed the top of an Indian's head and temporarily demoralized the Indians.

At Goose Lake the volunteers met a small party of ten wagons headed for Western Oregon. There were only 20 men, five of them with families. McDermit warned them of the dangers near Tule Lake and detached two more men to serve as their guides. On August 19th they neared the southeast part of Tule Lake with no Indians in sight. The guides explained that it was a bad indication when Indians were not visible so the train cut northwest across the flats. As a combination safety measure and ruse, the women and children were placed inside the wagons and the canvas fastened down. When almost at a safe location the Indians rushed toward them but seeing the men all armed with rifles and fearing that other men might be concealed in the wagons, retreated to some rocks where they were out of range. The wagons were formed in a circle and the Indians were challenged in Chinook jargon by one of the guides. It was finally agreed that the Chief and the guide would meet unarmed and parley. That was done but J. C. Tolman, who was in charge of the train, noticed something going on which aroused his suspicion. It was that Indians, apparently unarmed, gradually strolled near the parley and Tolman noticed that they had tied their bows to their toes with thongs, the bows dragging some distance behind. He warned the guide who ordered the chief to send his warriors away. The Chief, seeing that he had been out-guessed, did so and agreed to let the party proceed without harm. The train started and soon discovered some mounted Indians who had concealed themselves, who upon becoming aware of their discovery went away.

On August 23rd Tolman's party was traveling west and was met by an exhausted man on an exhausted horse. The man was so weak that he had to be lifted from his horse and fed before he could talk. He at length was able to say that he was the only survivor of a party of eight who had been overpowered by the Modocs and that he had ridden for three days without dismounting and without food. Tolman's party took the man with them to Yreka but by the time they arrived the man was completely demented. The citizens of Yreka, hearing the reports of the guides, the story about the demented man, and a recital of Tolman's experiences, organized a second company of volunteers. It didn't take long to recruit a company because Tolman's party was the first that year to come through with women and children and the miners got to thinking about their own families and what might have happened had McDermit's company not been on duty. Benjamin Wright was chosen Captain.

In six days they were at Tule Lake, three of the days having been devoted to equipping the company. They arrived at the lake in the nick of time, for a battle was in progress between a surrounded wagon train and the Modocs and two whites had already been wounded. When the Indians saw the relief forces they scattered, some hiding in the tules around the lake shore and others going to an island not far away. Wright's company escorted the wagon train beyond danger and then returned. First they discovered the bodies of the men reported as slain in the recital of the demented man. Then they found the bodies of three of McDermit's men who had been detached to act as guides for immigrant trains. It was plain to Wright and his company that the Indians were attacking every train, and, enraged at the sight of the dead men, the company determined to hunt down the Indians.

They went back to the lake at a point near the island and went into the tules after the Indians. There was a fierce fight in which more than 30 Modocs were killed. After the battle Wright went eastward and at Clear Lake met a large immigrant train. A ruse was decided upon. Several wagons were unloaded and filled with armed men. Some, dressed in women's clothes, walked along with the drivers as they proceeded in the customary leisurely manner along the trail. But the Indians did not fall for the trick. Either their spies had witnessed the preparations or the recent battle had temporarily taken the fight out of them. Wright went to Yreka to order some boats so he could get his men to the island. Meanwhile his men continued to patrol the road through Modoc land.

The news of these Modoc attacks reached Jacksonville where another company under John E. Ross was organized and went immediately to the Modoc country. When Ross' company arrived Wright went back to Yreka for the boats but they were of no use to him for the Indians had left the island and gone to the lava beds between Tule Lake and Clear Lake. But Wright's men did find plenty of evidence in the former camp of the Indians—women's dresses, babies' stockings, many other things until the men actually wept in their anger. Whether to try to form an army and hunt down the Modocs to the last man or whether to effect a treaty was the question. Finally it was decided to try for the latter. Wright and his company stayed and Wright started plans to bring about a council. From two Indians whom they had captured it was learned that two white women were captives. Wright thought that a treaty might save the lives of the women. Wright had a cross-breed Indian—part Modoc—as a personal servant, and sent him to the Modoc chiefs to arrange a parley. Four chiefs agreed to talk. Wright proposed to them that they return the two women and stolen property, whereupon he would take his company back to Yreka unless the Indians preferred that he stay for a while to trade with them. The chiefs agreed and one went back to get the women while Wright retained the other three as hostages.

Wright's company had, by that time, been reduced to 18 men. The fourth Chief returned without the women but with 45 warriors. Wright denounced the chief for breaking his promise. The Chief said that since Wright had held the other chiefs as hostages that now Wright and his men would be held as hostages by the Modocs to insure good conduct on the part of all white people. It was a bad situation. Outnumbered 5 to 2 he succeeded in putting off the Indians until the next day, for his decision. That night Wright moved fast. They were camped at a ford on Lost River. Six of his men sneaked across and got back of the Indians' camp. At daybreak Wright fired a gun which was the prearranged signal to attack and the six men on one side of the Indian camp and Wright and his 12 men on the other charged. In a few minutes 40 Modocs were dead and four of Wright's men wounded. Stretchers were made of rifles and the four men were carried 15 miles and a messenger sent back to Yreka for help. Upon their return to Yreka, Wright and his company were feted and praised. The two white women were sacrificed—how we do not know, but probably with all the cruelty peculiar to savages, of whom the Modocs were worst.

It is not difficult to assert that had McDermit and Wright, their companies and their sponsors not aided the immigrants the progress of settlement would have been delayed. But better times were coming, not without Indian wars, but the beginning of the end of such wars, for in September, 1852, the remnant of the 4th United States Infantry reached Vancouver Barracks. There were 268 men under Lieutenant-Colonel Benjamin L. E. Bonneville. They were the survivors of the crossing of the Isthmus of Panama, but they were too sick and the season was too late for any affirmative action that winter.

We now return to the handicap placed upon the Superintendent of Indian Affairs and his agents. Skinner could not make good on his promises to Chief Sam because of the government order previously mentioned. Chief Sam didn't want a treaty anyway. Still, through fear or some better quality, although Sam did not possess many, Sam, himself, kept faith with the treaty for almost a year. But one of his lesser chiefs, known as Taylor, did not. Grave Creek, a tributary of Wolf Creek, was the scene of the murder of seven men by Taylor and his braves. A cloudburst had occurred and during the downpour the murders were committed. Taylor reported finding the seven men drowned. Other overt acts were blamed on Taylor and rumor also had it that Rogues were holding white women captive at Table Rock. All these stories were not true but enough of them were to inflame the settlers, particularly with the addition of the proved and known murders and robberies in Modoc land. Desire to retaliate was rampant. In June, 1852, Taylor and three of his warriors were captured by a posse from Jacksonville and the four were hanged. The posse then went to Table Rock to rescue the white women. Not finding any they killed six Indians. Things were in a mess. Both whites and Indians committed unwarranted acts against each other. There was no military authority in the Rogue River Valley and no Indian agent. This latter need was because there had been another change in the Superintendency of Indian Affairs. Joel Palmer had replaced Dart. Skinner had resigned as Indian Agent and Palmer had not yet filled the vacancy. The nearest Federal troops were at Ft. Orford on the coast and Ft. Jones in Scott Valley. Joseph Lane had returned from

Washington, D. C. with a commission as Governor of Oregon Territory, but upon his return he had been re-elected Territorial Representative in Congress. Lane preferred the latter position which left the Territorial Secretary George L. Curry as Acting Governor. Lane was residing at Roseburg.

Suddenly the whites in the Rogue River Valley were attacked. On August 4th Richard Edwards was killed at his home on Stuart's Creek. On the 5th Thomas J. Wills and Rhodes Noland were killed and two others wounded. Volunteer companies were quickly recruited, the settlers were warned, and the women and children were gathered at centralized locations where the houses were fortified. A guard detail was left to protect them and the rest of the volunteers went to punish the Indians. On August 7th two Shastas were captured, both of them in war paint. They were guilty of two of the murders and were hanged at Jacksonville. Then the whites hung an innocent young Indian. If any white man felt like objecting he kept silent, such was the emotional state of the majority. Feeling was running high and if an innocent Indian, more or less, was to be hanged, why protest? Acts like that had their repercussions. Many settlers' homes were burned. A party headed by Isaac Hill attacked a nomad band near Ashland and killed six. Within two weeks the Indians evened the score by attacking an immigrant camp at Ashland killing two whites and wounding four. Four days later the Indians ambushed a volunteer patrol killing Dr. William R. Rose and wounding John R. Hardin so badly that he died. Then it was open season on Indians.

A petition was sent to Captain Alden, commanding at Ft. Jones, asking for arms and ammunition for the settlers. He came at once with 12 men to fulfill the request. Then a request was sent to Governor Curry asking him to requisition arms and ammunition from Colonel Bonneville at Vancouver Barracks and to include a howitzer in the requisition. Governor Curry acceded to the request and Bonneville honored the requisition. The munitions were forwarded in charge of Lieutenant A. V. Kautz and six soldiers plus 40 volunteers under Captain J. W. Nesmith. At the same time recruiting was under way in the Rogue River Valley. In a short time 200 had enlisted, who were formed into three companies under Captains John F. Miller, John L. Lamerick, and T. T. Tierney. Simultaneously 80 were recruited at Yreka and were divided into two companies under Captains James P. Goodall and Jacob Rhodes. All companies reported to Captain Alden, who was in over-all command.

They learned that the Indians were congregating at Table Rock and decided to attack on the night of August 11th. But news came that the Indians were killing and burning in the Valley, so many of the volunteers rushed away, without permission, to go to the aid of their families. For several days they patrolled the valley but finally assembled again. During their absence Alden, with a small force, was challenged to battle by Chief Sam but Alden didn't have enough men left to risk an encounter. On August 15th, most of his men having returned, Alden moved against the Indians who were supposed to be in a canyon five miles north of Table Rock. The Indians had fled, first setting the forest afire.

On August 17, Lieutenant Ely of Yreka, with 25 men, found the Indians encamped on Evans Creek, 15 miles north of Table Rock. Ely knew that the main force had gone to Camp Stuart for supplies, so he retired to an open piece of ground between two creeks whose banks were lined with willows. From there he sent a messenger for reinforcements. Ely's maneuver was not lost on Chief Sam who had his warriors wade across under cover of the willows and attack. Two of Ely's men were killed at the first volley. Ely then retreated to a wooded ridge about 500 yards away but the Indians quickly surrounded them. The ensuing fight lasted three or four hours during which four more of Ely's men were killed and four wounded, Ely among the latter. Then Captain Goodall and the rest of the Yreka volunteers arrived and the Indians fled.

Joseph Lane was at Roseburg when news of this newest outbreak reached him. Lane and 13 men, one of them Pleasant Armstrong of Yamhill County, left at once for the scene of action and upon arrival Captain Alden offered Lane the command, which Lane accepted on August 1st. The decision was to wage war aggressively. The troops, both regular and volunteer, were divided into two battalions. The plan called for Lane, with Alden and the companies of Goodall and Rhodes to proceed up-stream to the place where Ely had been defeated. The other battalion under John E. Ross was to go to the mouth of Evans Creek, thence up-stream to a junction with Lane, this joint maneuver to prevent the Indians again returning to harass the settlements.

The first day was difficult because of the smoke from the burning fires but they did find the enemy's trail. The second day was about as bad. On August 24th they were barely under way when Lane, who was out in front, heard the crack of a rifle and voices. He directed Alden to take Goodall and his company and to proceed on foot quietly so that they would be able to attack from the front. He then sent ten picked men from Rhodes' company under Lieutenant Blair to work its way to a ridge on the left to turn the Indians if they were driven back. Lane himself was to stay where he was until the rest of the troops came up, when he would lead them into the fight. Alden succeeded in getting within shooting distance of the Indians before they were aware of his presence. The Indians were stationed behind log fortifications and had plenty of arms and ammunition. Their camp was surrounded by dense thickets, thus making a charge by troops both difficult and dangerous. Blair and his men were also handicapped by the thickets and the terrain so that he was not able to go to the left as planned but did get around to the right where he engaged the enemy. The troops took cover behind trees in true Indian fashion and the battle raged.

When Lane came up with his troops he found Alden seriously wounded, in fact so badly that he never recovered, though it was two years before he died as a result of his wounds. Lane looked the situation over and in spite of the fact that he found the Indians in strong position on Evans Creek he ordered a a charge which he led. A rifle bullet struck him in the arm near the shoulder. He ordered his men to take individual cover, so from behind trees and boulders they fought for several hours. Lane had to retire to have his wound dressed and at about that time the Indians learned that Lane was in command. As usual that knowledge brought results, for the Indians had a hearty respect for Lane. They called out to the volunteers that they were tired of war and said they wanted to talk with Jo Lane.

When Lane returned to the battle he learned of the expressed wish of the Indians and held a council with his officers. As always happened there were two opinions. Some thought that the hostiles wanted to quit; others considered it a move to gain time or some other advantage. It was decided to take a vote, all volunteers being declared eligible, but less than half actually voted. The decision was to send two men to talk to the Indians. Robert B. Metcalf and James Bruce went inside the Indian lines and returned with the word that the Indians still insisted that they wanted to talk to Jo Lane. So Lane went, concealing his injured arm beneath his cloak. He met his namesake Chief Jo, who with his brothers Chiefs Sam and Jim, told Lane that they were sick of war. Lane outlined treaty terms which included going into reservation and the Chiefs agreed. A date in early September was fixed for the treaty council and Lane returned to his lines. The wounded were being treated and the dead were being buried. Three white men had been killed, one of them being Pleasant Armstrong, previously mentioned and for whom a small valley was named. Three whites were wounded, one, Charles C. Abbott dying within a few days. The Indians lost eight killed and 20 wounded. Ross' battalion arrived too late for the battle and they were prevented from renewing the battle by Lane. He decided to remain where he was for two days and camped within 400 yards of the Indians. So great was their personal regard for Lane that the Indian women carried water to the wounded whites and brought them on litters into the troops' camp. Thus was Indian nature, from one extreme to the other.

On the 29th both forces moved down the valley, each watchful of the other. It had been agreed that the council would be held on the south side of the Rogue River near Table Rock. Both forces went into camp, Lane's men at the spot where Ft. Lane was established soon after the council was held.

Since the treaty council had to await the arrival of Joel Palmer, Superintendent of Indian Affairs, an interim armistice was agreed upon. Meanwhile the peaceful *status quo* which should have ensued was interrupted. Four days after the Evans Creek battle a detachment under Lieutenant Thomas Frazell encountered a group of Rogue River Indians at Long's Ferry. A fight occurred at once and Lieutenant Frazell and an enlisted man, James Mago, were killed. Lieutenant Frazell had been attached to Captain Owens' company, and soon after Frazell's death Owens induced a group of Indians to come into his camp on Grave Creek where the Indians were immediately shot. According to Government documents Robert L. Williams, a captain of volunteers, also killed 12 Indians in a one-sided fight, the volunteers losing one man. Martin Angell, a settler, shot an Indian in cold blood for which he was ambushed and killed by Indians a long time afterward.

While waiting for Palmer there were other arrivals on the scene. Captain A. J. Smith came from Ft. Orford with his dragoons. J. W. Nesmith brought his company of volunteers and Lieutenant Kautz, of the artillery, arrived with the howitzer. The Indians stood in abject terror of the big gun and begged that it not be fired.

On September 4th a preliminary council was held in which

Lane required that a hostage be furnished and a son of Chief Jo was delivered for that purpose. It turned out to be a wise precaution. The various principals met within the Indian lines about a mile from Lane's camp. In addition to Lane there were Colonel Ross, interpreter Robert B. Metcalf, and the commanding officers of the several volunteer companies. The Indians were represented by Chiefs Jo, Sam, and Jim of the Rogue River Indians and Chiefs Limpy and George of the tribes on the Applegate River. The white men were unarmed except for a pistol which Captain John F. Miller had secreted. The councillors sat within a circle of armed warriors. The situation didn't look good but all the chiefs except Limpy made speeches in favor of peace. When Limpy's turn came he made a bitter speech in which he said that he would never agree to the occupation of his country by the whites. The fact that Chief Jo's son was a hostage was probably the only reason that the white men left the meeting alive. As it was, Lane required other hostages to be furnished before the real council meeting—which was set for September 8th—and also the presence of armed guards near the unarmed councillors when the meeting took place.

The treaty was concluded. The Indians accepted $60,000 for their lands in the Rogue River Valley, less some damages to settlers for losses. Payment was in agricultural implements and other goods. One hundred square miles near Table Rock was set aside as a temporary home for the Indians until a permanent reservation could be selected; and the laws of the United States were to prevail. Another treaty was made with the Umpquas of the Cow Creek band by which they sold 800 square miles for $12,000 plus some presents for their chiefs.

After the conclusion of these treaties Samuel H. Culver was made Resident Indian Agent among the Rogues and Ft. Lane was built near Table Rock. Gradually normal life seemed to be returning to the valley. All volunteer companies except that under Captain John F. Miller were disbanded. Miller's outfit was sent to the Modoc country for patrol duty, keeping the road safe for immigrants. They discovered Modoc families hiding out on the islands in Tule Lake and found the Indian children wearing the blood-stained garments of murdered immigrant children. The volunteers took the law unto themselves and wiped out these Modocs in retribution for the murders which they had committed.

In October, 1853, the miners in the valley of the Illinois River asked that troops be sent to punish Indians from the coast tribes who had been driven inland by the miners working on the beaches. Lieutenant R. C. W. Radford at Ft. Lane was ordered to take a small detachment and stop the Indians' forays. He found the Indians too numerous for his small detail to handle and sent for reinforcements. They arrived under the leadership of Lieutenant Caster and on October 22nd started to round up the Indians. After three days the soldiers caught up with the hostiles. A fight followed in which ten or twelve Indians were killed. The troopers lost two killed and four wounded. Some stolen property was recovered and a treaty was made. This treaty was observed until January, 1854, when a party of miners who were attempting to track down some robbers who were unidentified, attacked the Indians who had made the treaty, with some losses to both sides. The attack was a blunder by the miners and should not have occurred. The incident was not closed until the Indian Agent arrived and succeeded in convincing the Indians that the whole affair had been a mistake.

The number of killings by Indians in Southern Oregon in 1853 was about 100, while the Indians lost many more. Technically the boundary between Oregon and California was at the 42nd parallel but the natural geography of the country lent itself to considering the dividing line as indefinite. Hence, in the progress of Southern Oregon Indian troubles the troops and the Indians both criss-crossed the actual boundary and it was not always easy to determine in which territory a killing or a fight had happened. That year the financial loss to the settlers was heavy and due to governmental red-tape many legitimate claims resulting from these losses to Indians and damage by them were not settled for 30 years.

Peace did not last a great while after the treaty of September, 1853 and the erection of Ft. Lane. The Indians were displeased with the treaty they had accepted and became troublesome. On October 5th Thomas Wills, a merchant of Jacksonville, was murdered by Indians. Next day his partner, James C. Kyle, was killed within a short distance of Ft. Lane. There were other killings down the river. The murderers of Wills and Kyle were Indian Tom and Indian George. They were caught in January, 1854, and fairly tried in court, convicted and executed. Their execution was set for February 19th but owing to the uneasiness pervading the district, the sentence was carried out within a few days after the conclusion of the trial. The execution did not help the general situation.

About January 18, 1854, Chief Bill led a group of Rogues, Shastas, and Modocs in the theft of the horses which belonged to the miners who were working Cottonwood Creek. A volunteer company was organized at once and started in pursuit to recover the horses. The volunteers were ambushed and four of them, Hiram Hulan, John Clark, John Oldfield, and Wesley Mayden were killed. Help was asked from Ft. Jones and Captain Judah and 20 men responded. The soldiers trailed the Indians to a cave in the canyon walls of the Klamath River and finding the cave impregnable without artillery sent to Ft. Lane for a howitzer. On January 26th Captain A. J. Smith and Lieutenant Ogle and 15 dragoons arrived with the howitzer. The volunteer company under Captain Greiger had joined with the regulars and Captain Judah falling ill, the command passed to Greiger, who attacked on the 27th. The cave was in an inaccessible place and the howitzer shells served no purpose except to frighten the Indians. Captain Greiger was killed by a shot from the cave and then the Indians indicated a willingness to talk.

The following day Captain Smith and a citizen held a parley with the Shastas. Captain Smith accepted the Indians' story that the miners had mistreated the Indian women as the reason for their acts, and further accepted their apologies for the thefts and murders. The volunteers considered it useless, in the face of Captain Smith's gullibility to attempt to further punish the Indians and returned home in disgust.

Other trouble broke out the same month between the Coquille Indians and the miners at Coos Bay and Port Orford. A meeting of citizens was held and a punitive expedition organized under George H. Abbott, Captain; A. F. Soap, 1st Lieutenant, and William H. Packwood, 2nd Lieutenant. The objective was the same village where the Coquille River massacre had occurred. It was located about a mile and a half up stream and occupied space on both sides of the river. Captain Abbott divided his volunteers into three detachments. Lieutenant Soap's group was to take a position on rising ground commanding that portion of the village on the north shore. Lieutenant Packwood was to take a roundabout way to his position near the upper part of the village on the south shore, while Captain Abbott would cover the lower portion of the south shore village. At a signal gun all attacked just before daybreak, the Indians being completely surprised. They lost 16 killed and four wounded, the surviving warriors fleeing to the woods. They abandoned their families, of whom 20 members were captured, as well as all the native stores of food. When the warriors fled, many of them left their arms and ammunition in their habitations, which were burned. The white men suffered no casualties. Abbott sent three of the captive women to ask the Chief what he wanted to do. They returned with the reply that the Chief wanted to make a treaty, which was done.

We have previously mentioned the mutual antipathies existing between the regular army and the volunteers. Perhaps the man who was most responsible for that situation was General John Ellis Wool, for some time in command of the Pacific Division. It is true that the year 1854 carried a small number of murders by Indians compared with the several years immediately preceding, but still there were murders. Edward Phillips was murdered in his house on Applegate River on April 15th; Daniel Gage was killed in the Siskiyous June 15th; a man was killed on the Klamath River on June 24th and Thomas O'Neal in the same district at about the same time. Four men were murdered by either the Modocs or the Pit River Indians in June and in September another man was killed by the same Indians. None of the murderers was punished. The reason for non-punishment undoubtedly lay in General Wool's attitude of special dislike for volunteers, in fact for all civilians, and the desire of his subordinate officers to temper their action and reports to find favor in the General's opinion. The General did send a mounted force to Klamath Lake and back, reporting no danger from Indians. Wool even went so far in requesting additional troops that he said he needed an increased force to protect the Indians against the white men. His request for reinforcements was not honored. He later reported that, in his opinion, the increasing immigration into Oregon would render military occupation almost unnecessary and that, if left to his discretion, he would abolish most of the army posts in the Territory. So the settlers were again forced to rely chiefly on themselves for protective volunteer units. Governor Curry approved a volunteer force under the command of Jesse Walker to protect the southern route. They did no fighting and the expedition was criticised for its expense, but its presence was probably responsible for the prevention of untoward acts by the tribes.

At the close of 1854 there were 335 regular soldiers of all departments stationed in Oregon Territory. Congress invoked a law of 1808 for providing arms for militia, and that constituted the Federal protection for the Territory when the year 1855 began. Indian trouble elsewhere in the Territory was occupying official attention, which, of course, included the Governor and the Superintendent of Indian Affairs. We will, in a later chapter, take up those events, but now confine ourselves to the continuance and the conclusion of the Rogue River wars.

BLOODY 1855

In October, 1854, Joel Palmer, Superintendent of Indian Affairs, notified the tribes with whom he had treaties, that Congress had approved them. However, there were some amendments to the Congressional legislation, among which was a measure consolidating all Rogue River tribes into one, a provision which was traditionally unacceptable to the Indians. Another amendment provided that one tribe could be placed upon a reservation set aside for another. The Indians didn't like that either. In the early part of 1855, while Palmer was busily engaged with treaty matters in the northern and eastern sections of the territory, new troubles were brewing in southern and southwestern Oregon. About June 1, 1855, Jerome Dyar and Daniel McKaw were murdered on the road between Jacksonville and the Illinois River Valley. In the same month the Indians raided a mining camp, killing miners, and made off with a large quantity of personal property.

John E. Ross was Colonel of Militia in Oregon Territory and as such recognized a newly organized company of volunteers, the Independent Rangers, formed at Wait's Mill on the Rogue River under the captaincy of H. B. Hayes. When the Indian Agent heard of the formation of this new company of volunteers he notified Captain Smith, in command at Ft. Lane. Smith set out with his soldiers to round up stray Indians and get them back on their reservation adjacent to Table Rock where the volunteers would pursue them. Smith was only partly successful, some of the stray Indians deciding to go to the mountains, where Smith pursued. Several skirmishes occurred in which one white man and one Indian were killed.

In August an unidentified white man sold some whiskey to a group of Indians who were off reservation. They attacked a mining camp on the Klamath River killing ten miners, the Indians themselves having several of their number killed. That resulted in the immediate formation of another company of volunteers from south of the Siskiyous with William Martin in command. They marched to the Rogue River reservation and demanded the surrender of the killers. Captain Smith, of Ft. Lane, refused the demand saying that there was no authority for delivering suspects to volunteer organizations. Later that year some arrests were made upon presentation of proper legal documents from Siskiyou County. Also in August, near the mouth of the Rogue River, an Indian wounded James Buford. The Indian was captured and turned over to Benjamin Wright, the Indian Agent, who delivered the prisoner to the Sheriff of Coos County. There was no jail in which to hold the Indian so the Sheriff turned him over to a detail of soldiers who were to take him to Ft. Orford and keep him in the guardhouse until time for trial. Buford didn't like the way the Indian was being shunted about. The soldiers were transporting their prisoner and another Indian by canoe. Buford, enlisting the aid of two other white men, followed. They fired on the canoe killing both Indians. The soldiers returned the fire killing two of the white men instantly, and wounding the other so badly that he died. That affair caused a bitter upsurge of public opinion against the military. Technically the soldiers were within their rights in attempting to protect a prisoner in their custody, but many settlers showed a tendency to fight the soldiers as well as the Indians. The whole situation widened the breach between the regulars and the settlers.

On September 2nd several white men entered the reservation to recover stolen horses. One white man, Grenville M. Keene, was killed and two others wounded. September 24th Calvin Fields and John Cunningham were killed and two other white men wounded while crossing the Siskiyous with their ox teams. The Indians also slaughtered the oxen. Next day Samuel Warner was killed in the same locality. Captain Smith sent out a detachment to apprehend the guilty but no arrests were made.

In early October a group of reservation Indians were encamped near the point where Butte Creek empties into the Rogue River. That was off-reservation and the settlers suspected that among the group were some of the Indians who had committed several of the recent murders. A company of militia, commanded by Major J. A. Lupton, decided to attack the Indian camp and did so, surprising the Indians just before daylight on October 8th. There was a very bloody fight in which the Indians lost 23 killed and many wounded. Major Lupton was killed and eleven of his men wounded. Then it was discovered that most of the Indians who had been killed were old men, women and children. The surviving natives took refuge at Ft. Lane. On that same day, and too soon for the Indians to have organized because of the slaughter on Butte Creek, Indians killed two white men and wounded another, who were in charge of a pack train. That incident occurred at Jewett's Ferry. The Indians also shot into Jewett's house but injured no one there. A large number of Indians were congregated at that point and they were well armed and well supplied with ammunition. Under reservation regulations Indians who were off-reservation and who were armed were considered to be suspects and the group at the ferry must have had their plans laid for a long time.

Next morning, October 9th, the Indians moved down stream to Evans' ferry where they intercepted Isaac Shelton, who was traveling to Yreka, fatally wounding him. Still farther down river lived J. K. Jones and his wife. They killed Jones and mortally wounded his wife, robbed the house and burned it. A short distance farther was the home of John Wagoner. The Indians headed for the Wagoner home but paused on the way to kill four men they met. Wagoner was away from home that day, which left his wife and four-year-old daughter, Mary, alone. What happened to them is not actually known. The Indians burned the house and its contents. There are various stories. Some Indians said later that Mrs. Wagoner barricaded the house and, with the child, perished in the flames. Other Indians said that she and her daughter were captured and that the child was killed because it cried too much and that Mrs. Wagoner refused to eat, dying of grief and starvation. But Captain John M. Warren said, after the battle with the Indians on Cow Creek in 1856, that among the scalps recovered were those positively identified as those of Mrs. Wagoner and her child.

From the Wagoner place the Indians went to the farm of George W. Harris who saw them coming and suspecting their intentions ran to the house, grabbing his gun, killed one Indian, wounded another, and was then himself killed. Mrs. Harris dragged her husband's body indoors, barricaded the house, and kept the Indians at bay all day by firing at them through crevices in the walls until night came and the Indians retired. As a rule Indians did not fight at night. After dark Mrs. Harris and her young daughter stealthily left the house and hid under a pile of brush not far away, where they were found by Major Fitzgerald and his regular troops from Ft. Lane. The slaughter continued on this, the bloodiest day that Rogue River settlers would ever experience. One woman, two children, and at least nine men were the next victims. They were killed between Evans Ferry and Grave Creek. Two young women were killed between Indian Creek and Crescent City; and three men were slain on Grave Creek.

When news of the massacre reached Jacksonville a group of 20 vounteers were quickly assembled and started out to punish the killers. Major Fitzgerald with 55 mounted men from the garrison at Ft. Lane overtook the volunteers and the two forces joined. When they reached the site of the Wagoner place they found about 30 Indians there, searching the ruins and the outbuildings. The Indians at first showed fight because the volunteers put in their appearance first, but when the troopers came up the Indians fled to the mountains. The white men followed but their horses were so tired from the forced march that the Indians outdistanced the troops. So the regulars returned to Ft. Lane and the volunteers to their homes, all to prepare for a conclusive campaign.

A messenger had, in the meantime, been sent to carry word to the Governor, the Superintendent of Indian Affairs, and the military authorities at Vancouver Barracks. Coincidentally a messenger was on his way from Vancouver Barracks to Ft. Lane to ask help for the war developing to the north.

On October 10th, without any knowledge of the previous day's events, Lieutenant Kautz, of Ft. Orford, had set out with a few soldiers and some civilians to investigate a proposed road to Jacksonville. On the second day they learned something of the massacre from the settlers in the lower part of the valley where they feared a continuation of the Indian attacks. Kautz turned back to Ft. Orford to more adequately equip his force and then started back to the hostile country. He was attacked and in the fight lost five men killed, while there was no certainty about any Indian casualties. By rare good fortune he was able to retreat and save the rest of his command.

Let us now examine the situation as it existed. All the tribes in southwestern and south central Oregon and in northwestern and north central California, except Chief Sam's band, were hostile. The settlers knew from the appeal for help from the north

Battle Rock at Port Orford

". . . the Indians started to menace the small colony, which promptly set up log defenses on a prominent rock, since known as Battle Rock and now preserved as a state park." (page 57)

Empire City

"The settlers . . . at the mouth of the Coquille River moved their families to the settlements at Empire City, which had been fortified . . . and a house at the mouth of the Rogue River was fortified as a haven in case of Indian outbreaks near there." (page 91)

Governor Joseph Lane

"So great was their personal regard for Lane that the Indian women carried water to the wounded whites and brought them on litters into the troops' camp." (page 74)

Governor Isaac I. Stevens

"On June 16th [1855] Governor Stevens departed to treat with the Colvilles, Coeur d'Alenes, Spokanes, and other Northeastern Washington tribes." (page 111)

that they could expect no assistance from that quarter, so it would be necessary for them to meet their own problems. A calculation revealed that there were probably about 400 Indians available as warriors, and that it would take 1200 whites to subdue them. That was because the hostiles knew every square foot of the country, could move about with facility, and could wear out any force which was only equal to their own. Also, the Indians were well supplied with arms and ammunition and knew how to use them. On the other hand there were plenty of white men available but they were short of both arms and ammunition. Not a settlement was safe from attack; every pack train ran the risk of capture, no traveler's life was safe.

A regiment of volunteers was authorized under John E. Ross, as Colonel. By October 20th, fifteen companies had been recruited. The organization was designated as the 9th Regiment of Oregon Militia. However, through October 11th only 150 had been mustered because no more could be properly armed by that time. Therefore nothing could be done for the next few days except to protect the settlements which seemed to be most endangered and to keep the north and south roads open.

One of the first companies in the field was that of Captain J. S. Rinearson. His organization was divided into several small detachments which were sent to a number of exposed or strategic points. On October 12th Colonel Ross recapitulated his prospect of the maximum number of troops he might expect for use in a major campaign. There had been two troops of dragoons at Ft. Lane under Major Fitzgerald and Captain Smith but Fitzgerald and one troop had just been ordered north thus leaving Captain Smith and one troop. There were 64 infantrymen in the Umpqua Valley under Lieutenant H. S. Gibson. They had been acting as an escort for Lieutenant Williamson who was surveying a railroad route and as soon as they learned of the massacre of the 9th of October they started for Ft. Lane. Then there was the very small garrison at Ft. Orford which had all it could do to take care of itself. So much for the regulars. As for the volunteers, three companies were already in the field with others mustered and ready to move as soon as they could be properly armed. Other companies were rapidly whipping into shape. Thus it looked like there would be enough men. As rapidly as companies could be equipped they went into active service. Some detachments guarded the more exposed districts; others escorted pack trains; still others searched for the hostiles. It was quickly apparent that the pack trains needed major protection because the Indians would have to rely on what supplies they could capture for their subsistence.

The first clash occurred on October 17th at a place called Skull Bar in the Rogue River. Company "E" was camped just below the mouth of Galice Creek, Skull Bar being just a short distance below their camp. All the miners in the neighborhood had been brought into the camp for protection. The bar was near the south side of the river and was backed by a high bluff heavily forested with underbrush and young trees. The troops, helped by the idle miners, cut away much of the brush within rifle range so that the hostiles could not use it as cover. On the day mentioned a large number of Indians were observed in the wooded section of the bluff adjacent to the cut-over section. Six men under J. W. Pickett were sent to dislodge the Indians but were met by a withering fire. Pickett was killed and his men were forced back. Then Lieutenant Williamson led a detachment to a position from which he fought for four hours. He and several of his men were wounded and they, too, had to retreat. Then Captain W. B. Lewis was wounded severely. At that time the Indians attacked the left side of the camp, losing their leader. Finding themselves unable to rout the volunteers by gunfire the hostiles shot flaming arrows into the camp which kept the soldiers and miners busy preventing a major conflagration. Meanwhile a group of the Indians burned the mining village of Galice almost completely. By nightfall one-third of Company "E" was either dead or wounded. The campsite surely proved to be a poor one from the standpoint of defense. The wounded Captain Lewis, in his report to Colonel Ross, said that the Indians had fired 2500 rounds of rifle ammunition at the troops that day.

The Indians kept the troops guessing. Wherever the soldiers went in the expectation of finding the hostiles, disappointment resulted. For example, Colonel Ross was sure that the Indians could be located below Galice Creek at a place called The Meadows, but instead the Indians had gone to the valley of Cow Creek, some distance to the north. There, on October 23rd, they killed Holland Bailey and wounded four other white men at a ford. That same day they burned several settlers' houses in Cow Creek Valley. For the most part the houses had been temporarily abandoned, the settlers having congregated in a few strategically located homes which were fortified and guarded. There were just not enough troops to protect all properties, particularly since the

Indians kept the soldiers jumping here and there in a futile effort to bring about a decisive engagement.

However, on October 28 an Indian camp was discovered on Grave Creek by Major Fitzgerald and his company. They were on their way to Vancouver Barracks in response to the recent order transferring them north. Fitzgerald sent a request for help. Five companies were immediately ordered to Fitzgerald's location, two other companies adding to the reinforcement a few hours later, which made a total of about 250 men concentrated in the locality by October 30th. Colonel Ross arrived that evening and placed Captain Smith of the Ft. Lane dragoons in over-all command. They marched at 11 P. M., being joined by two more companies from a battalion called out by Governor Curry and which had just arrived at the scene. The plan for the attack had been well laid but the rugged terrain and the underbrush defeated their primary purpose.

The next day was three-fourths spent in a futile search for the hostiles when contact was suddenly made about mid-afternoon. Captain Smith made an assault with part of his dragoons. They were driven back losing several men, killed and wounded. Night came and the exhausted men hit their blankets without supper. At daybreak the Indians attacked. The fight raged for several hours, ending in the repulse of the hostiles. The volunteers then went back to a camp on Grave Creek having lost 26 men killed, wounded, or missing. The regulars lost four killed and seven wounded. As usual the losses of the Indians were concealed but since they had the advantage of position it is probable that their losses were less than those of the troops.

During this episode Joel Palmer issued an order to all Indians, Indian Agents, and citizens defining and creating regulations for the conduct, supervision, discipline and care of Indians. Governor Curry made a proclamation on October 15th calling for the formation of two battalions of volunteers for service in the Rogue country. Each battalion was to consist of five companies of 60 men and eleven officers, commissioned and non-commissioned. One of the battalions was to be known as the Southern Battalion and was to be recruited in Jackson County. The other was to be known as the Northern Battalion, to be recruited from Lane, Linn, Douglas, and Umpqua counties. The Southern Battalion was to congregate at Jacksonville, the northern at Roseburg. It will be observed that the term "northern" was used in its relation to the Rogue River Valley and was not applicable to the geographical limits of Oregon Territory.

Five days later Governor Curry disbanded Colonel Ross' regiment. The Governor had learned of the attack of October 8th on the Indian camp by Major Lupton's company. Whether his information was inaccurate, causing him to think that Lupton's force was a part of Colonel Ross' regiment, or, whether he had reached the conclusion that all organized troops in the Rogue River Valley were oppressors of the natives is not known, but the 9th Regiment of Oregon Militia was ordered disbanded. Equally inexplicable was the invitation extended to the members of the 9th Regiment to join the two newly created battalions. There was a bad odor to the whole circumstance since, by the disbanding order and the invitation to the men to join the new outfits, the leading officers of the 9th were left to bear what ever criticism existed. Those officers, for the most part, belonged to the political party opposing Curry and there were some people who felt that it was a method of administering a political spanking to the Governor's opponents. At any rate, the order put a stop to enlistments for three weeks. Then, on November 7th, Colonel Ross mustered his regiment at a place called Ft. Vannoy on the Illinois River to give the men an opportunity to re-enlist in the new battalions, each of which was to be commanded by an elected major. James Bruce, who had been a captain in the 9th was elected major of the Southern Battalion. He seems to have acquired quickly the viewpoint of the Governor, for Bruce, on November 11, issued an order which recited that his battalion would enforce the disbanding of all military units not affiliated with the two battalions authorized by the Governor's proclamation.

In spite of the invitation to the old 9th only four companies were recruited for the Southern Battalion, so the Governor and Adjutant-General E. M. Barnum decided to inspect the new force in the south. The result of that inspection was to consolidate the two battalions into a regiment to be known as the 2nd Regiment of Oregon Mounted Volunteers. Then, to confuse matters, Captain Robert L. Williams of the Northern Battalion was elected Colonel and Major William J. Martin, who had been in command of the Northern Battalion, was elected Lieutenant-Colonel.

It will be remembered that with the departure of Major Fitzgerald, only one troop under Captain Smith was left at Ft. Lane. Smith agreed with officers of the volunteers to meet them at the fortified house on Grave Creek which had been dubbed Ft. Bailey, where, about November 9, they would join in running down the hostiles. But again the facility of Indian movements was demonstrated by the return of the hostiles to the reservation long enough to burn all the properties there, including that of Chief Sam, and to kill all the cattle on the reservation.

The Indians departed, burning a number of houses on a nearby creek. The troops, with a few regulars newly arrived from Ft. Jones, took the field and caught up with some of the Indians, of whom they killed eight.

Then a concentrated effort was made to find and engage the main body of hostiles. The Indians, in strength, were discovered on a river bar. On November 26 a company of regulars under Captain H. M. Judah marched to a point opposite the Indian camp where it was planned that they would be joined by Major Bruce and about 300 volunteers. The plan also provided that the volunteers would cross the river on a raft and when in position would give a signal whereupon the regulars would open fire on the camp with a howitzer. But the Indians were alert and at the moment when the raft was first placed in the water the Indians opened fire and Bruce had to retire. That night a conference of officers was held which decided to send for additional supplies and some reinforcements, after the arrival of which a real effort was to be made to dislodge the Indians.

On December 1, 1855, Captain Smith sent a messenger to Captain Judah saying that he was twelve miles down-stream from Ft. Bailey and could get no farther because of rain and snow. Major Bruce returned to Ft. Vannoy headquarters and on December 7 the several companies were ordered to various points in the valley for two reasons, first, to afford protection to the settlers, and, second, to provide adequate grass for the horses.

That arrangement did not remain stable for long. Early in December roving Indians destroyed 15 houses on the west side of the South Fork of the Umpqua. The owners of the houses were absent, having fled to the protection of the forts and other fortified places. On December 25th Captain Miles T. Alcorn and his company, which was a part of the Southern Battalion, as originally constructed, discovered an Indian camp on the North Branch of Little Butte Creek. He attacked, killing eight Indians and capturing some horses. At the same time Captain E. A. Rice and his company, also of the same battalion as Alcorn, discovered an Indian camp on the north side of the Rogue River. Rice's company numbered only 30 men at the time but he attacked and after several hours of fighting had killed all the warriors and captured the women and children, who were sent to Ft. Lane. It was winter weather and some of the captives suffered frozen feet. This caused General Wool to voice his anti-volunteer sentiments again in an official report in which he expressed pity for the captives and characterized much of the recent military action as murder.

Late in December Major Bruce received word that a band of Indians had occupied some deserted cabins on the Applegate River and had fortified them. Bruce ordered Captains Alcorn and Rice to get ready for a winter campaign while Bruce, himself, went to Ft. Lane to ask Captain Smith to provide a howitzer. Captain Smith agreed. Bruce then, with Captain Rice and his company, started for the Applegate on January 1, 1856. Continuing his march on January 2nd he met a company of Independent Volunteers who had surrounded the cabins. There the combined force waited for the howitzer to arrive. The weather was severe, the snow a foot deep. There was sporadic shooting in the course of which the Indians lost three killed and several wounded, while Captain Rice lost one man killed and the volunteer company had three men wounded. Late on January 4th Lieutenant Underwood with 40 men and the howitzer arrived from Ft. Lane. The first howitzer shot hit one of the cabins, wounding one warrior and two Indian children. The occupants fled to another cabin and a few more shells were fired without appreciable effect before dark. The several companies took up positions intended to halt any effort by the Indians to escape. Nevertheless about 11 P. M. the Indians tried to get away. They crept close to the sentry lines, then with a yell and many gun-shots some of the hostiles managed to dash through the troops. After the first effect of surprise passed, the regulars drove part of the Indians back towards the creek where the densely wooded banks made it possible for more hostiles to escape.

As it turned out only the warriors had tried to get away. They had left their women and children. It was very cold and the men relaxed their vigilance to come into camp to get warm, when the Indian women and children also made good their escape to the hills. The troops then searched the cabins and found that the Indians had, according to their custom, burned their dead, and had left a wounded Indian boy behind. He said that his band belonged to that headed by Chief Jo. These Indians had done a job of fortifying worthy of the best military science. They had evidently spent a lot of time in the preparation of their stronghold, for a tunnel led from the cabins to an outlet some distance away. Deep pits had been dug in each corner of every cabin. The pits were so deep that loop-holes were provided under the bottom logs through which rifle fire could be directed without much danger to the Indians.

The trail was easily followed because of blood on the snow and Major Bruce wanted to take up the pursuit, but Lieutenant Underwood and the volunteers were not prepared for the rigorous service demanded by the winter weather, so the regulars went back to Ft. Lane and the volunteers to their homes. Major Bruce and his men made camp on the lower Applegate. Both the men and the horses needed rest so they remained in camp until January 18th when they were joined by Captain Alcorn with part of his company and Captain O'Neal, who had succeeded to the command of Captain, now Colonel Williams' company, with part of his men. In grand total there were now available 73 officers and men.

A pursuit plan was laid. Captain Alcorn with 38 men went up the Applegate. Major Bruce, with Captain O'Neal and the rest of the men, went up Williams Creek. Nothing happened for five days at the end of which Bruce ran across two Indians who fled and were chased for 12 miles to their camp. Bruce and O'Neal had separated for their scouting activities and as soon as the Indian camp was located Bruce sent a messenger to O'Neal to come up as quickly as possible because it was apparent that there were five or six dozen warriors. Firing started at once, in the course of which one of Bruce's men was killed and another severely wounded. Though greatly outnumbered Bruce succeeded in driving the Indians out of their position and improving his own. Night came and with it Captain O'Neal, who said that he had sent Lieutenant Armstrong with 28 men to attack the Indians on their right. Bruce and O'Neal then withdrew for the night making camp about five miles away but Armstrong did not join them. Instead he stayed in position, next morning attacking the hostiles who retreated. They had, as usual, burned their dead so their casualties were not known. That day, January 24th, Colonel R. L. Williams arrived and assumed command.

While the companies of the former Southern Battalion were thus engaged, those of the former Northern Battalion, under Lieutenant-Colonel W. J. Martin, were busy scouting, guarding settlers, escorting pack trains and casual travelers. Stations were manned at Camas Valley, southwest of Roseburg; at the headwaters of the Coquille River; at Ft. Smith, which was the fortified house of William H. Smith on Cow Creek; Camp Eliff, at the south end of the Umpqua canyon; Ft. Bailey, five miles south of the ford on Cow Creek; Camp Gordon, eight miles above the mouth of Cow Creek; at the reservation limits near the mouth of the Umpqua; and on Ten-Mile Prairie.

Lieutenant-Colonel Martin had issued orders to take no prisoners but many Indian women and children were captured. About the first of the year, 1856, Martin ordered these captives taken to the Grand Ronde reservation in Yamhill County but the Indian Agent, Robert B. Metcalf, refused permission because of relationships among the captives and the Indians already on the reservation.

The type of duty which the 2nd Regiment of Oregon Mounted Volunteers was called upon to fulfill was, except in the actual fighting, unspectacular and irksome. The weather was miserable, accommodations in camp were seldom comfortable, and the problem of supplies was always present. Pay, if any, was little and delayed. Many of the men of the regiment applied for discharge in January, 1856. They pointed out that their term of enlistment had expired when their service with the northern and southern battalions was considered and, besides, their horses were jaded. So the Adjutant-General authorized their discharge and issued an order for replacement recruiting. As recruits replaced those eligible for discharge, the latter left for their homes but the work of escorting and guarding was uninterrupted because the Indian chiefs steadfastly refused to listen to peace on any terms.

THE LAST MONTHS OF CONFLICT

WHILE the latter events of the foregoing chapter were transpiring, there was much elsewhere to disturb the security of the settlers. The Yakima War had started in the north and the tribes on the southwest coast were committing atrocities. It is of events in this latter district that we next tell, leaving the Yakima conflict for the succeeding chapter.

Benjamin Wright was still the Indian Agent for several tribes below Coos Bay. He acquainted those Indians with Superintendent Palmer's recent order restricting them to their reservations unless furnished with written permission to go elsewhere. He also warned those who had wandered into his district from interior reservations that they must return immediately or submit to arrest. These stragglers obeyed but with obvious reluctance. When Wright reached the settlement at the mouth of the Coquille he found the settlers there greatly concerned over the attitude of the Coquilles. Wright conferred with those Indians, who assured him of their peaceful and friendly intentions. The Indians told him that they themselves were worried about two fears, first, because there was a camp of Rogues nearby and the authorities might consider that the Rogues were there with the acquiescence of the Coquilles; and, second, that they were worried because they feared that the troops who were operating in the Rogue and Umpqua River Valleys would swoop down and exterminate them, because rumor indicated that to be the intention. Wright apparently allayed their fears, appointed David Hall as local sub-agent for the Coquilles, and returned to Ft. Orford.

The settlers were not satisfied that the Indians planned no trouble. Those at the mouth of the Coquille River moved their families to the settlements at Empire City, which had been fortified. The miners from the Randolph district moved to Ft. Orford for protection, and a house at the mouth of the Rogue River was fortified as a haven in case of Indian outbreaks near there.

Wright himself was not sure about the situation and to play safe asked Major R. B. Reynolds, commander at Fort Orford, to keep his force intact, to which request Major Reynolds agreed.

It will be remembered that the Governor had outlawed independent companies of volunteers. Nevertheless, a small company of 19 men from the Coos Bay area, in order to circumvent Governor Curry's proclamation, petitioned Agent Hall to enroll them as assistants, which Hall did on November 6, 1855. Also on that day it was decided to erect a fortification on the Coquille River, which was built within a few days and named Fort Kitchen. Then a small detachment from the little company under Captain Packwood made a quick scouting trip up the South Fork of the Coquille. They found that a house had been robbed and upon returning Packwood notified Wright of the robbery and the fact that some of the Indians were off reservation, and asked Wright to come for the purpose of discussing matters. Meanwhile the male settlers who had gone with their families to coast points for protection returned to the Coquille River Valley but left their families on the coast. These men fortified the Roland residence, naming it Fort Relief. Captain Packwood remained there to await Wright's appearance and while there ordered the off-reservation Indians to return to their reservations or be arrested. He did arrest Long John and Elk. Long John escaped within a few days and subsequently Packwood released Elk.

On November 22nd sixteen men from Coos Bay joined those guarding Fort Kitchen and Agent Hall was replaced by William Chance, who accepted the 16 men under the same conditions as those under which Hall had agreed to use Packwood's company. Packwood had been instructed, after Long John's escape, to treat all Indians who were off reservation without written consent, as enemies, because a band headed by Chief Washington had already gone on the war-path. They had burned one house, robbed two others, cut the Coquille ferry-boat adrift, and otherwise made themselves obnoxious. On November 23rd Agent Chance with some guards under Captain Packwood went upstream to attempt to persuade Chief Washington to return to his reservation. Instead, they found the chief installed behind a barricade commanding the river and threatening Chance and his party with a rifle. Chance returned to Ft. Kitchen while Packwood's group met two off-reservation Indians, one of whom menaced the guards. The guards opened fire, killing one of the Indians and wounding the second, who succeeded in escaping. Later, on the same trip, they wounded another Indian and returned to Ft. Kitchen.

Meanwhile there had been no news from Wright and on December 11th the 16 men from Coos Bay returned there having become alarmed for the safety of their families at home. Thus Fort Kitchen was again guarded by its original small force. Two of these Ft. Kitchen guards went to the beach to secure some reserve provisions which they had left in a cabin there. Upon arrival they found Long John preparing a meal in the cabin with several Indians watching him. John gave a war-whoop, apparently to summon aid, whereupon the guards shot him.

Wright arrived at Ft. Kitchen on December 24 and held a three-day conference with the Indians who blamed all recent disturbances on the white men. Wright accepted their promise to remain quiet and obey his instructions and then notified Captain Packwood that the Governor would have to approve the volunteer organization which Packwood had formed before any compensation could be paid, so Packwood discharged his company.

Later, under a new order of the Governor, Packwood reorganized his company as Coquille Minute Men. Meanwhile Packwood made a written report to Governor Curry explaining his view of the situation and justifying the acts of his men. The report indicated clearly the apparent indifference of the regular army to the incipient dangers from Indians on the Southwest Oregon Coast.

During this period local Indian Agent E. P. Drew became concerned that the Coos Bay Indians were plotting with the Coquilles. An attack was made on the Indians at Drolley's farm on the lower fork of the Coquille River, four Indians being killed and four captured and hanged. Such chastisement kept the remainder of that band quiet for the rest of the winter.

Also in November, 1855, a company of volunteers was raised among the miners at Gold Beach and other points on the Southern Oregon coast, with John Poland as captain. While this company was not authorized by the Governor, neither did it violate his proclamation because that section of the territory was not included in the Governor's edict. Poland's company established its camp at the Big Bend of the Rogue River where they stayed until February, 1856. They then moved down stream to a place within a few miles of the mouth of the river to build up the company by recruiting. To all appearances the Coast tribes had quieted down. On the night of February 22nd a Washington's Anniversary Ball was given at Gold Beach. Captain Poland and most of his men attended, leaving ten men as a nominal guard at their camp. At daybreak, and before the return of the revellers, a large force of Indians furiously attacked the camp. Eight of the ten guards were killed. One of the two who escaped was Charles Foster. He concealed himself in the woods, witnessed the massacre, and using extreme caution succeeded in carrying news of the disaster to Ft. Orford.

At the time of this slaughter Benjamin Wright was at the McGuire home which was located between Captain Poland's camp and Gold Beach. Captain Poland was on his way back to camp, unaware of any tragedy, and stopped to see Wright. While there some Indians from the tribe living across the river from McGuire's place called on Agent Wright saying that Enos, a half-breed who had spent the winter with the Rogues, was in their camp and that they wanted him arrested. Without any thought of treachery, Wright, accompanied by Captain Poland, went to the Indian village to arrest Enos. Both Wright and Poland were murdered immediately and their bodies horribly mutilated. The Indians even cut out Wright's heart, cooked it and ate it, believing that in so doing they would acquire some of Wright's well-known courage.

Enos was to avoid arrest until 1857 when he was captured and hanged. The murders of Wright and Poland were just incidents in a carefully planned day of blood. Sixty houses from the Big Bend almost to the Coast were burned that day on the Rogue River. Twenty-six citizens were killed in the first attacks and five more later in the day. One woman and her two daughters were taken captive. Seven different settlements were attacked in twelve hours.

When the news of these outrages reached Gold Beach some of the men of Captain Poland's company, including 1st Lieutenant Relf Bledsoe, were still there. Lieutenant Bledsoe was elected Captain. A fortification known as Miners' Fort was in process of construction and Captain Bledsoe ordered its immediate completion. He concentrated 130 men, women and children there and stocked the fort with all the available provisions. They prepared as best they could to withstand a siege, for there was no other military force, regular or volunteer, in the southwestern Oregon coast section to rescue them.

When Charles Foster reached Ft. Orford he reported his intelligence to Major Reynolds. As often stated, the garrison there was small and Major Reynolds could not divide it, nor would any few soldiers have been able to resolve the situation with the hostiles could they have been spared. Besides there were only about fifty residents of Port Orford and they begged Reynolds not to reduce his garrison. However, the residents did send a whaleboat down the coast to carry word of the critical situation. But an unkind fate decreed that disaster was a continuing process. The boat overturned in the surf and the crew of six citizens were drowned. Indians, who had been watching the boat, cut the dead bodies to pieces — drowning was probably an easier death than would have been their lot had they landed.

When the whaleboat did not return, Captain William Tichenor, who had founded Port Orford, sent his schooner the *Nelly* to rescue the people at Miners' Fort. But adverse winds prevented the *Nelly* from approaching the shore near enough to bring off the besieged in small boats. Some days later the schooner *Gold Beach* arrived off-shore from Crescent City with a company of volunteers sent to fight the Indians but it, too, failed to effect a landing. These several efforts were all visible to the besieged who must have felt that all nature was in league against them. Moreover, they were not well supplied with arms and ammunition because the Indians had captured all those necessities belonging to Captain Poland's company at the time of the massacre. The occupants of the fort were, however, successful in keeping the hostiles at a distance by sniping at any Indian who came within range. On February 25th the Indians did try to reach the fort but were repulsed and seemed to have made a decision to bide their time until the citizens were weakened by starvation. Occasionally a cow would graze near enough to the fort for some one to go outside and obtain milk for the children. The citizens tried to dig potatoes from the fields one night but were discovered by the alert enemy and one white man was killed and four wounded before the foraging party reached the safety of the fort.

Thus the siege continued for 30 days. It need not be pointed out again that information traveled slowly in that part of the world in 1856. News of the massacre and siege had reached no place but Port Orford. Ships made infrequent trips along the coast. It took time for word to reach Governor Curry in Oregon City and the military authorities in San Francisco. The Indians had chosen their time well. They knew of the mustering out of the battalions and the slow progress being made in recruiting for the 2nd Regiment. When Governor Curry did hear of the disaster he authorized the organization of companies of minute men in localities which were remote and endangered and approved those volunteer groups which had sprung up in violation of his proclamation and from real necessity.

The Governor sent George H. Abbott to Ft. Johnson on the Chetco River to recruit volunteers to go to the relief of Miners' Fort. Abbott learned about the arrival of the Federal troops under Lieutenant-Colonel Buchanan at Crescent City and that they were marching up the coast to take charge of the Indian war. Abbott had recruited only 34 men when he obtained the foregoing information and decided to await Buchanan's arrival before venturing toward Gold Beach. The volunteers made their camp north of the Chetco River until March 16th when Buchanan and his regulars were within five miles. Then the volunteer company started for the Pistol River which empties into the Pacific Ocean about midway between the Chetco River and Gold Beach. Abbott and his men reached the Pistol River in the early morning of March 17th and prepared to attack the Indian village located there. But the Indians had fled and the village was burned. Then a few Indians were observed herding horses in the foothills and Abbott took a detail of 13 men to capture the horses. Approaching the herd many Indians were seen with more arriving every minute so Abbott wisely decided to retreat to the shore to join the rest of his men. The Indians pursued and a running fight developed with the Indians finally being repulsed. Abbott sent a messenger to Buchanan and then the hostiles encircled the volunteers. The Indians were kept at a distance by rifle fire while a barricade was erected. The soldiers placed their supplies and water inside the enclosure, the horses were picketed just outside and Abbott and his men awaited the arrival of Buchanan's troops.

Late in the afternoon of the 17th the Indians were reinforced by a large number of Rogues. That evening the Indians departed from an almost universal practice of not fighting at night. Just about dark they started slowly but methodically for the barracks. The approach was from three directions, some of the hostiles rolling logs in front of themselves for protection. Abbott considered his situation and pronouncing it critical made his decision on the principle that the best defense is an offense. He sent one detachment to the cover of a sand dune to the south, led another party to a pile of drift logs on the beach, leaving the rest of his men in the barricade. Both sides fought desperately. Abbott's men first used their rifles. Greatly outnumbering the volunteers, the Indians kept moving forward. Then the soldiers used their pistols. When it was too dark to see clearly they changed to shot-guns. The Indians' loss was heavy compared with that of the volunteers, the latter losing one man fatally injured and one slightly wounded. The Indians captured ten horses and 20 mules and then withdrew. Next day the fighting was intermittent but continued throughout the day and until 2 P. M. on the 19th when Buchanan's regulars arrived. Buchanan had taken three days to make a march which could have been accomplished easily in one day. He merely commented that he did not wish to engage the Indians at the Pistol River. As nearly as could be determined the Indians had lost 12 killed and at least that many wounded.

Lieutenant-Colonel Buchanan was apparently an officer of the General Wool school. The latter had instructed his regulars not to recognize volunteers in the field. Buchanan, on his part, criticized the citizen soldiers for meddling with things which he said they did not understand. He had been sent to show men untrained in military science how to conduct an Indian war. Meanwhile, General Wool had received a petition from the citizens of Jackson County. They pointed out to the General that business was suffering because residents were moving to the Willamette

Valley due to the insecurity of living in Jackson County and asked that a large enough force of Federal troops be sent to Southern Oregon to end the war, or if not that, to assure protection to the people.

It must be pointed out that General Wool's attitude toward civilians, and volunteer soldiers in particular, was always one of superiority, impatience and contempt. The Governors of all the States and Territories which came within the department of the Pacific disliked him. Complaints were made to the Secretary of War who criticized and reproved the General. The reproval did not set well with a man of Wool's temperament but the General was a trained soldier and as distasteful as the order was he did obey the Secretary of War when instructed to give his personal attention to Oregon and Washington Territories. He therefore went to Vancouver Barracks in November, 1855. That official visit was brief; he did not confer with Governor Curry, and soon returned to San Francisco. Shortly thereafter he re-visited Vancouver Barracks for the purpose of investigating some of his officers who had so far forgotten his injunction that they had recognized volunteer organizations in the field and on one or two occasions had asked the citizen soldiery for aid. "Such acts by his subordinates might need a reprimand," mused the General.

In March, 1856 he again went to Vancouver. This time he brought troops to accomplish two objectives — to placate the petitioning Jackson County residents and to whip the Indians. It was on this trip that he left Lieutenant - Colonel Buchanan and 96 officers and men at Crescent City on March 8th. When General Wool reached Vancouver he sent Captain Augur of the 4th Infantry with a detachment to reinforce Major Reynolds at Ft. Orford. He also sent Captain Floyd Jones of the 4th Infantry with his men to Crescent City. Both these officers were directed to protect friendly Indians and guard government stores. Next he ordered Captain Smith of Ft. Lane to go to Ft. Orford with 80 of his dragoons to meet Buchanan, when their combined force would go to the Illinois River Valley where the Superintendent of Indian Affairs would hold council with the tribes, after the hostiles had been subdued by the regulars. Buchanan and Smith were also to make it their duty to prevent the volunteers from bothering the Indians.

Of course Governor Curry and the settlers learned of General Wool's orders and knowing more about Indians and Indian warfare than he, proceeded to take additional measures for their protection. The Territorial Legislature in Oregon elected J. K.

Lamerick as Brigadier General of Militia. Lamerick was from Southern Oregon so his election stimulated recruiting in that section of the Territory. R. L. Williams was displaced as Colonel of the 2nd Oregon Mounted Volunteers by John Kelsey; Lieutenant-Colonel William J. Martin resigned and Captain W. W. Chapman was elected to succeed him; Major James Bruce retained his command in the south; and William H. Latshaw was elected Major in the north. It should be understood that while these changes in ranking officers were being made there was no interruption in the activities of the volunteers. There was Indian trouble in almost every important district and it may be well to relate a few examples of the types of military activity being conducted by the volunteers while the regulars were, in more leisurely fashion, carrying out the orders of General Wool.

In February, 1856, while the tragic events at Ft. Kitchen and Miners' Fort were happening, the Indians of the Illinois River Valley began killing. They murdered two settlers and wounded three more in their first foray. Then they shot Settler Guess while he was plowing. He was alone at his farm, having sent his family to one of the fortified places for their safety. Captain O'Neal, with his company, was scouting nearby and upon hearing of this latest murder immediately went to the scene. O'Neal and his men made the trip at night and encountered an Indian camp. There was some firing by both sides but O'Neal recovered the settler's body and took it to the bereaved family, and then those troops spent the rest of the month escorting pack-trains, scouting and recruiting.

Captain Bushey's company was organized on February 19th and devoted the rest of the month to scouting. In March he found a large Indian camp on Wolf Creek and sent to Major Bruce for reinforcements, which were furnished, but by the time they arrived the Indians had moved. Bushey then escorted government stores. Captain Tobey Buoy and his company exercised similar functions, as did Captain Abel George.

On March 23rd a messenger arrived reporting two men killed on Slate Creek and that a large force of Indians was on its way to the Hayes farm. Lieutenant Armstrong with 50 men was detached and sent at once to intercept the hostiles. When within sight of the Hayes house the Indians opened a heavy fire on the volunteers from all directions. Armstrong estimated that there were 200 warriors but issued the command to reach the house. His men succeeded, finding the Hayes family safe inside but the volunteers lost two men killed and one wounded in the process. The fight continued all day, then the Indians burned their dead and left. A courier was sent to Major Bruce asking that he send reinforcements and that the settlers in the valley of the Illinois River be notified of the uprising. Major Bruce arrived the next day with all his available men and preparations were made to pursue the Indians.

While these plans were formulating a messenger arrived saying that a pack-train had been robbed on Deer Creek, one of the tributaries of the Illinois River. Accordingly, the troops set out for Deer Creek and, encountering the enemy, began another battle. At the first volley from the Indians two men from Captain George's company were killed and two from Captain O'Neal's company were wounded. Three Indians were known to have been killed. Outnumbered, Major Bruce with part of his force, went to the main valley of the Illinois River to assemble the settlers for protection, while the other detachment from Bruce's force went back to the Hayes place and camped there.

On March 24th there was a battle on Cow Creek, which is about 50 miles north of the Illinois River. John M. Wallen had succeeded to the command of William H. Latshaw's company when the latter became a major. Wallen's company and 20 men from Captain Sheffield's company, the latter under Lieutenant Capron, were in the Cow Creek neighborhood, and it was this force which engaged in that battle. One volunteer was killed and one wounded. The Indians fled with the soldiers in pursuit. The volunteers followed the Indians for six days without developing another battle, though there was sporadic firing and one Indian was killed.

Captain Laban Buoy resigned in March and was replaced by P. C. Noland, who had barely assumed his command at Ten-Mile Prairie when he received word that the Indians were loose in Camas Valley on the Coquille River. Nolan took his company there at once, finding several houses burning and others already destroyed, but the Indians had fled to the mountains. Noland pursued, located the hostiles, killed two of them and wounded several, but had a number of horses stolen by the Indians.

After the Governor's proclamation of March 11th authorizing companies of Minute Men, John Creighton organized a company at Port Orford. On March 27th his force moved to the Coquille River. He attacked an Indian camp on the 30th, killing 15. He also captured all their provisions, arms and canoes and took 32 women and children captive. Creighton sent the prisoners to Ft. Orford and went on upstream to the Forks of the Coquille where he forced another engagement in which three Indians were killed and several women and children taken prisoner. Next he went to the Umpqua Valley where he captured five Umpquas, 20 Coquilles of Chief Washington's tribe, and 23 other Coquilles from the North Fork of the Umpqua.

W. H. Harris, of Coos Bay, raised a company of Minute Men there. They spent March and April scouting and rounding up Indians for placement on reservations. He succeeded in persuading a number of the Coquilles to enter reservation life but was unsuccessful with the Indians from Cow Creek and the Umpqua. Harris then sent Lieutenant Foley with 12 men to round up a number of Coquilles who had left the reservation near Port Orford. Foley captured the entire group consisting of eight men, six women, and three children who were taken to Port Orford. Harris' company also escorted pack-trains between the Umpqua and Coos Bay and between Eugene and Port Orford.

Captain W. A. Wilkinson's company devoted their attention during April and part of May to escort duty between Ft. Vannoy and Ft. Leland, Camp Hayes and Camp Wagoner, and also between Crescent City and Camp Vannoy. Captain James Barnes' company engaged in dangerous spy duty all during the campaign.

On April 11, Colonel Kelsey combined a detachment from Captain Robertson's company, Captain Barnes' spy company, and part of Captain Wallen's company, and set out, going down Grave Creek from Ft. Leland in search of the hostiles. They encountered a blizzard and had to abandon the effort.

Thus it will be observed that the volunteers were busy and the regulars inactive (for the earlier part of the period), which caused Brigadier General Lamerick to write the Governor that he was convinced that General Wool had issued orders to the regular troops prohibiting them from cooperating with the volunteers. That may have been true but Lamerick also reported that the regular officers at Ft. Lane told him that they would cooperate at all times.

At any rate the volunteers were working valiantly at the difficult job of protecting settlers and punishing hostile natives. The weather had been miserable, in fact as late as mid-April, 1856, it was still cold with chilling rains and plenty of snow in the higher elevations. General Lamerick and Colonel Kelsey had agreed to keep at their task. They also agreed upon a plan for bringing the entire regiment together near Big Meadows, which was the main camp of the dissident Indians, and cleaning up the war in one major battle. The idea seemed worthy of success, for some Indian bands, hungry and cold and disillusioned, had given themselves up and had been taken to Ft. Lane where they were assured of food, shelter and protection.

On April 16 Lieutenant-Colonel Chapman and Major Bruce, with the entire southern battalion, moved down the south side of the Rogue River towards Big Meadows. The northern battalion, except for Captain Thomas W. Prather's spy company, went down the north side. The troops took provisions for thirty days and General Lamerick told the Governor that he intended to pursue and fight the hostiles until they were whipped. The first contact occurred April 21st while the regiment was camped at Little Meadows. There a sentry was fired upon and 40 men were sent to engage the Indians but the hostiles fled. Captain Barnes then went out with 25 men from his spy company and located the Indians on a sand-bar on the south side of the Rogue between Little and Big Meadows.

The northern battalion numbered 210 men. Colonel Kelsey, with 50 men, went out on the morning of April 22nd to determine what he could learn about the Indian camp. He was discovered and fired upon and deployed his men for battle, but again the Indians retired. Next day, April 23rd, the southern battalion, mustering 335 men, arrived. This made a total of 545 volunteers on the scene. On the 24th Colonel Kelsey and Major Latshaw led 150 men of the northern battalion in the direction of the enemy. One-third of this force was sent in advance, the plan being to decoy the hostiles into a battle when confronted by an apparently small force. Simultaneously Major Bruce with 150 men from the southern battalion, went to Big Meadows expecting to find large numbers of Indians there. To his surprise the Indians had departed, nor could either group find the hostiles that day.

Next day, April 25th, a detachment of 25 men from the northern battalion went to a position on an elevation of their camp to see whether the Indians were moving into the mountains to the west. A similar group from the southern battalion went to high ground southeast of camp to see what they could discover. All were aware that the Indians had their families with them and that their grand total numbered several hundreds.

The regiment had a number of beef cattle along for its commissary and late in the day on the 26th some of the cattle had strayed some distance from camp. The Indians started shooting some of the cattle so Colonel Kelsey with 100 men went after the hostiles. But again the Indians fled. It surely seemed that the Indians were evading battle.

On April 27 Colonel Kelsey and Major Latshaw again set out, this time with 200 officers and men. They left before dawn so that they could be sure to occupy a canyon one mile west of the Indian camp. At the same time Major Bruce with 150 men went forward to a position opposite that of Colonel Kelsey. The plan called for Colonel Kelsey's troops to force a battle and, if the Indians retreated, to run them into Major Bruce's force. A heavy fog blanketed the river, which enabled Kelsey to get into position undiscovered. Suddenly the fog lifted and there was not an Indian in the canyon. This was a surprise, for the spy company had reported it to be well guarded. So Kelsey's force advanced through the thick forest for another mile and a half to a point opposite the camp on the sand-bar. This movement was executed so quietly that the volunteers were within 300 yards of the camp before they were discovered. Instead of rushing to battle the Indians were in a panic. Squaws and children were running about in confusion. The volunteers opened up a heavy rifle fire. Gradually the warriors took protective shelter behind trees and rocks and returned the fire. The majority of the hostiles took positions out of range to watch the battle and were so intent that they were not aware of the approach of Major Bruce's contingent until his soldiers opened fire. The battle continued all day. The Indians suffered heavily while the volunteers had only one man wounded. The fighting ended at nightfall and the troops camped at Big Meadows.

On the morning of the 28th Colonel Kelsey and Major Latshaw with 150 men went downstream to a point two miles below the scene of the previous day's battle. They carried two canvas boats and the purpose of the trip was to discover a place where the troops could cross the river and come down on the Indian camp from the mountains behind the sand-bar. Lieutenant- Colonel Chapman with 150 men took the position occupied by the volunteers the previous day so that they could cut off the Indians, should a retreat be attempted, and also to divert the Indians' attention from Colonel Kelsey's investigation down river. But the Colonel didn't get to start his investigation. The Indians were alert and were in position in thick timber when Kelsey and his force approached. Firing started at once but because of the long range was largely ineffective. After three hours of shooting, the volunteers returned to their camp having one man wounded, while the Indian loss, beyond two warriors known to have been killed, could not be determined.

That night the Indians pulled out, going down river. When, on April 29, the volunteers' spies notified the officers of the absence of the Indians, the regiment crossed the river to the abandoned hostile camp. They counted 75 camp fires which was indicative of the large number of Indians. Evidences of stolen property were found everywhere – empty ammunition cases, broken food containers, and innumerable bones of cattle. The Indians hadn't been short of supplies. Indeed, this was the place to which the off-reservation Indians and those who raided pack-trains and committed other robberies, went for refuge all winter long. The troops were running short of provisions, their clothing was wearing thin, and the weather continued miserable. Colonel Kelsey reported these conditions and was ordered to return to Ft. Leland. It was also agreed that a fort be built at Big Meadows. So, on May 1st, 1856, four companies under Major Bruce were detailed to erect the fort, to be called Ft. Lamerick. Two companies were sent to Roseburg, while five companies accompanied the Colonel to Ft. Leland.

While the month of April, 1856, was keeping the volunteers busy as detailed, it also ushered in activity on the part of the regulars. It will be recalled that Captain Smith of Ft. Lane was to join Lieutenant-Colonel Buchanan and the joint force was then to meet Superintendent Palmer at the Illinois River. Joel Palmer had been Superintendent of Indian Affairs for Oregon Territory for a long time and was well qualified for the task. He did, however, at the moment have a large percentage of the tribes under his jurisdiction either in a state of actual war or on the verge of outbreak. He was anxious to do something affirmative to bring peace and quiet to the Territory. Also he had come to accept the view that the settlers were in large measure to blame for the unsettled conditions. He did not believe that the Indians would accept peace unless on their own terms. His conclusions were not completely those of the regular army but he leaned much farther in that direction than to the viewpoint of the settlers and their volunteers. But the fighting was continuing. The volunteers insisted that their theory of preventing robberies and murders was a better one than that of the regular army which chastised the Indians after misdeeds were committed. So now Palmer was to accompany the regulars who were to try to demonstrate that their system of Indian control was the better.

Captain Smith and his 80 dragoons left Ft. Lane April 13,

1856. As they crossed the Rogue River they attacked and destroyed an Indian camp there. He had a difficult march across the mountains to Ft. Orford and while Smith knew more about the tribulations of winter campaigns in Oregon than did Buchanan, still he acquired an idea of what the volunteers had contended with for months. Buchanan's force also had a lesson. When they arrived at the mouth of the Rogue River the troops dashed into the forest in pursuit of fleeing Indians. They quickly experienced the difficulties of mountain warfare in bad weather. This thing of climbing steep slopes, scrambling through tangled underbrush, getting soaked to the skin in the cold rains, wet feet and consequent bad colds, with Indian arrows coming their way from unseen hostiles, wasn't exactly like dress parade. Buchanan wasn't with his men. Instead, he spent his time unsuccessfully trying to induce the tribes to return to their reservations.

On April 26th Buchanan sent Lieutenant Ord and 112 men to destroy an Indian village eleven miles north of Gold Beach and to force the Indians there to go to the reservation. The Lieutenant did a good job, accomplished both objectives after a fight and the loss of one man.

Then Lieutenant Ord with 60 men went to Crescent City, in Northwestern California, to escort a large pack-train of army stores to the mouth of the Rogue River. On April 29th, as he came to the Chetco River, he was attacked, his losses being one killed and three wounded while the hostiles lost six killed and were driven off. The volunteers, be it remembered, were still hard at work in the field and now, knowing that the regulars were also campaigning, sought to drive the Indians in the direction of the Federal troops for final disposition.

Captains Harris, Creighton, and Bledsoe of the volunteers were particularly active in this regard. George H. Abbott and his company surprised a band of Coquilles on the river of that name, killing twelve. On two occasions that band had promised to go back to their reservation and twice had broken their word. They had probably meant it when they had made their promises but Chief John and the half-breed Enos knew how to change their minds.

In the first part of May, Buchanan moved his regulars to a point near the mouth of the Illinois River. As related, some Indian bands had surrendered, some had given themselves up voluntarily, and some, mostly women and children, had been captured. Buchanan used a number of these Indians as messengers to the various groups of hostiles urging the latter to meet with him and Superintendent Palmer for a peace council. Finally, on May 21st, Chief John and his son, Chief George, Chief Limpy, and others came in for a conference. It had been stipulated to the chiefs as a condition of their attendance that they would not be restrained at the council. Chief John finally made a speech refusing to accept reservation life, saying that he would fight instead. He left the council unmolested as promised. The other chiefs, however, consented to lay down their arms on May 26th and be escorted to reservations. Captain Smith and his dragoons were at the appointed meeting place on the 26th but the Indians did not come in. That evening Smith received word from two Indian women that Chief John would attack the next day. Smith immediately began moving his camp to higher ground and sent a courier to Buchanan requesting reinforcements. The dragoons had no rest that night because of moving the camp and preparing for battle. The site chosen was an elevation between two creeks. The south side was steep, the north side even more perpendicular; the west side was less difficult than the south, while the east slope was gentle.

At daybreak the Indians appeared in force to the north and about 40 warriors started up the east slope to the camp. Smith halted them while they were some distance away when they told him that they had come to lay down their arms and wanted to talk with him. But Smith knew too much about Indians and remembered what had happened to Ben Wright and Captain Poland on the Coquille. The howitzer was in position and aimed in the right direction. Seeing that Smith was preparing to fight, and foiled in their design, the warriors withdrew. About midafternoon the Indians attacked from two directions simultaneously, approaching by the east and west slopes. The howitzer stopped them on the east and rifle fire halted them on the west. The hostiles made several attempts and then tried scaling the precipitous north and south approaches. But a number were shot and rolled to the bottom of the slopes. After a day of continuous fighting the engagement ended with nightfall. The troops spent the night in digging rifle pits and erecting breastworks, that being the second night without sleep, and with little food and almost no water.

Next morning, the 29th of April, the Indians renewed the battle. The dragoons were now in bad condition. They were worn out from fighting and laboring at their fortifications as well as suffering from lack of sleep and water. At the council on the 26th Captain Smith had told the Indians that any of them who strayed from their reservations while armed would be hanged. So the Indians now taunted Smith, recalling his threat and saying that they would hang him and all his troopers. They even dangled a rope inviting Captain Smith to hang himself and save them the trouble. They chided the troops about being thirsty. They called the soldiers vile names and occasionally some warrior would work his way under the parapet, reach over with a hooked pole and drag out a soldier's blanket. By late afternoon one-third of Smith's 80 dragoons were killed or wounded and still no news from Buchanan. That night the Indians held council and decided to finish off the troopers the next morning. To the soldiers it seemed that April 29, 1856, would be their last day on earth. Early that morning all the Indians let out a blood-curdling yell and charged up the east and west slopes. To the consternation of the hostiles the troopers met the offensive with cheers and a counter-charge, for the dragoons had seen what the Indians had not seen. Recall, please, that General Wool while at Vancouver, had ordered Captain Augur of the 4th Infantry to reinforce Major Reynolds. On his way to fulfill that assignment, Captain Augur with 75 fresh soldiers came upon the scene of Captain Smith's desperate battle in the nick of time. Captain Augur swung his troops into action, attacking the Indians from the rear. The tables were turned. In fifteen minutes the Indians fled to the hills carrying their dead and wounded with them. Five of Augur's men were killed. Next day their dead bodies, horribly mutilated, were found hanging to trees. Another find was a supply of native-made ropes with which Chief John had expected to hang the dragoons.

Volunteer units still active in the mountains and unaware of Smith's battle came upon a camp of Chief John's tribe on the 29th and routed the Indians who fled down river, only to run into Buchanan's troops, to whom they ultimately surrendered. Those volunteers who constituted Captain Wallen's company continued scouting and picking up many stragglers from Chief John's people. Captain Daniel Keith's company joined Wallen and still other units augmented the volunteer force from time to time. When the volunteers reached Smith's fortification they found Superintendent Joel Palmer there.

He had expected to take part in the surrender of the Indians to the United States regulars. He sent messengers to round up the fugitives and to tell them to come in but most of those who responded were those whom the volunteers delivered. Chief John, instead of coming in to surrender, sent a challenge to the volunteers nearest his location, inviting them to do battle. The volunteers accepted because those who had reached Smith's fort returned to reinforce their comrades. The Indians were under cover in the forest but came out, advancing in two lines. After the first volley from the Indians' first line, the troops opened up with such accurate fire that the line broke and fled. The second line then moved forward and withstood the soldiers' fire somewhat better than had the first line, but they, too, gave way and retreated. Chief John tried without success to rally his warriors. Among his dead was a popular young chief. The warriors wept over their plight and finally Chief John sent word by a squaw that he was ready to give up, provided that his people could retain their arms. That proposal was rejected. He then sent his son to ask that one-half of their arms might be kept. That request was likewise refused. Chief John then reduced his plea to one-third of the arms. He was then notified to stack all arms in a place available to the troops or to come back fighting. As night approached many of John's warriors laid down their weapons. So many kept straggling in to surrender that they were finally told to stay away from the soldiers' lines until daybreak. As the new day dawned, Chief John came in, the last of his band. Twice he raised his rifle as if to fire and twice decided not to pull the trigger, and with reluctance joined the rest of the prisoners.

All the troops, regular and volunteer, in the vicinity, drew together, prepared their wounded for transport, assembled their prisoners, and under command of Captain Smith set out for the coast. The prisoners although disarmed were twice as numerous as the troops, which fact was a cause for concern on the trip. Arrived at the mouth of the Rogue the officers learned that renegades from several coast tribes had banded together and were attacking the miners at Gold Beach. So that band had to be subdued, which job was accomplished by killing 40 and forcing the rest to surrender.

The regulars decided to move to Ft. Orford and enroute gathered in the Indians from the Pistol and Chetco rivers, completing that task by their arrival at Ft. Orford on July 2, 1856. On the 9th of July 700 Indians, which number did not include Chief John's tribe, were taken by sea, in charge of Captain Smith, to Portland, from where they were transferred to the north end of the reservation in Polk County, Oregon. Four hundred more, including Chief John's tribe and the Pistol and Chetco river bands, were taken overland to the south end of the same reservation. This transfer was not without incidents. Numbers of Indians escaped,which meant that eventually they had to be rounded up again.

Life on the reservations was not a happy one. The Indians all complained of being homesick for their old haunts, which was natural. They said game was scarce, which by comparison with southwestern Oregon, was true. Then, the government did not make good its promises of machinery and other benefactions provided in several treaties. Fraud was discovered in the quality of the food furnished for the subsistence of the reservation tribes.

The last of the so-called Rogue River Wars was ended but its repercussions continued for some time. Chief John would not desist from inflaming the Indians, which finally was ended by sending the Chief and his son to imprisonment on Alcatraz Island in SanFrancisco Bay. They were taken there by sea and enroute tried to escape. Detected in the attempt, a fight ensued aboard their ship, *S. S. Columbia,* in which several participants were wounded, among them the Chief's son, hurt so badly that a leg had to be amputated. After several years at Alcatraz a pardon was granted and the bitter old Chief rejoined his wife and daughters.

Military establishments were provided to guard, control, and protect the Indian reservations. Stragglers were systematically rounded up. The regular troops destroyed every Indian camp and village which they found. A blockhouse was erected on the Siletz reservation; Ft. Sheridan was built on the Grand Ronde reservation; Ft. Umpqua was established at the mouth of the Umpqua River, and Ft. Hoskins was built in Benton County. In the process of rounding up the stragglers several skirmishes and engagements occurred but these all ended disastrously for the Indians. Their day had passed in the southwestern part of the territory and white government was in control.

Finally, in July, 1858, it was announced that the subjugation of the tribes had been completed and peace again returned to Southern Oregon.

THE YAKIMA WAR

PART OF THE GENERAL UNREST

In earlier pages we have told about the call for aid from Vancouver Barracks to Ft. Lane when the latter was over-occupied with the Rogue River wars. We also wrote that Superintendent Joel Palmer was in the northern part of the territory with the Indians there; and of the decision to build Ft. Steilacoom in the Puget Sound country. We shall now, in more detail, relate the chain of events which preceded the Yakima War.

Washington Territory had been separated from Oregon Territory by Congressional action on March 2, 1853, but Major Isaac I. Stevens of the United States Army, Washington's first Territorial Governor, did not arrive to take over his office until September 29, 1853. At that time the population of his territory was less than 4000 white people. The new Governor had arrived overland, as he also had the assignment of surveying the right-of-way for a railroad.

Meanwhile, Superintendent Palmer had intended moving the Willamette Valley Indians to some reservation east of the Cascades. Not only were the Willamette tribes opposed to the idea but the Indians east of the Cascades did not want these Western tribes in their midst because of the diseased condition of the Willamettes. So Palmer had placed the latter on the Grand Ronde reservation in Polk County, Oregon Territory, over the objections of the settlers in that district. No treaties had ever been made with the tribes of Washington or Eastern Oregon with two exceptions, namely, those agreements made by Dr. Elijah White under the Provisional Government and such measures as had been engineered by the Military at the time of the Cayuse War.

As Governor Stevens crossed the Pacific Northwest country he conferred with various tribes concerning their attitude toward selling their lands. He reported their willingness to sell and their apparent friendly feeling toward the Government. As a result of his report Governor Stevens and Superintendent Palmer were appointed Commissioners to make treaties with the tribes north of the Columbia River and funds had been appropriated to carry on that work. But a year and a half passed between the time of Governor Stevens' conferences with the northern tribes and the spring of 1855 when the Commissioners were ready to treat, and many disturbing events had occurred in the interval. The Northern Indians had heard of Palmer's plan to send the Willamette tribes east of the Cascades. They knew about the wars in Southwestern Oregon. They were aware of the increase in the white population. They saw Federal troops and new forts. It was not a good time to talk treaties.

Governor Stevens sent James Doty to notify the tribes of a series of councils to be held in May, 1855, the first of which was to be attended by the Yakimas, Cayuses, Walla Wallas, and Nez Perces. Kamiakin, chief of the Yakimas, selected as the council ground a place in the Walla Walla Valley not far from Waiilatpu. Governor Stevens and Superintendent Palmer were escorted there by Lt. Archibald Gracie and 47 dragoons. The presents for the chiefs were stored at Ft. Walla Walla. Comfortable arrangements were made at the council grounds and on May 24th the first of the Indians arrived. They were the Nez Perces under Chiefs Lawyer and Lookingglass. They camped near the Commissioners whom they entertained with tribal dances. On the 26th the Cayuses and Walla Wallas came and they, too, danced for the Commissioners. May 28th came and with it the Yakimas. All told there were about 5000 people present counting commissioners, dragoons, chiefs, warriors, squaws, and children. It took until the 30th to get down to the business of the council.

The speeches dragged on for days. There was almost unanimous sentiment against sale of their lands by the chiefs. Kamiakin, head chief of the Yakimas, and Chief Owhi, his half-brother, opposed the plan as did Old Joseph and Lookingglass of the Nez Perces. The Cayuses were against the sale and even Peu-peu-mox-mox, traditional friend of the whites, refused to be a party to the Commissioners' offer. Lawyer, head chief of the Nez Perces, was alone in his willingness to sell.

Lawyer told Stevens that a plot was afoot to massacre Stevens and his escort and that the attempt only awaited concurrence by more of the tribes. He also said that the contemplated massacre was to be the signal for the capture of the military post at The Dalles and a war of extinction of the whites.

Lawyer offered to move his family and pitch his lodge in the midst of Stevens' camp, which was done. Stevens later credited Lawyer with having prevented the attack. Also, in later years, the tribes accused of this plot asserted that there was no basis for Lawyer's accusation, saying that it had been a political move on

Lawyer's part to share more favorably from the treaty negotiations.

Perhaps the main stumbling block was a provision that after the sale, all tribes represented were to share a common reservation. Finally the Commissioners conceded that point and offered separate tribal reservations and with that concession all chiefs except Kamiakin signed the treaty on June 11, 1855.

The Nez Perce tribe received $200,000 payable in installments over a term of years, and a large reservation tract. The Walla Wallas and the Cayuses combined and accepted their reservation in the Umatilla Valley and $150,000; the Yakimas took as their reservation the best land south of the Yakima River and $200,000. They were all assured of schools, mills, and equipment, and the attitude of the chiefs after the signing was one of friendliness and cordiality. The presents were distributed and W. H. Tappan was appointed Agent to the Nez Perces, R. R. Thompson to the Cayuses and Walla Wallas, and A. J. Bolon to the Yakimas.

On June 16th Governor Stevens departed to treat with the Colvilles, Coeur d'Alenes, Spokanes, and other Northeastern Washington tribes. Palmer went to The Dalles where he purchased land and concluded treaties with the tribes located between the Powder River and the Cascades. As a result of Palmer's treaties the Oregon tribes involved acquired the Warm Springs Reservation between the Deschutes River and the Cascades.

It should be remembered that after the Walla Walla treaty in June, that Governor Stevens went to treat with the more northern tribes of Washington Territory. It must also be recalled that at the time the Territory embraced portions of Idaho and Western Montana. While Stevens was thus occupied far from the seat of government, C. H. Mason was acting Governor.

During the late summer and early fall of 1855 several citizens of the Puget Sound country were murdered by Yakimas while traveling to or from the mines in the Colville district. Occasional travelers from elsewhere were murdered while passing through the land of the Yakimas. News of these outrages reached A. J. Bolon, sub-agent for the Yakimas, while on his way to meet Governor Stevens in the Spokane Indian country. Bolon turned back from his proposed meeting with the Governor, having decided to go to Father Brouillet's mission, near which Chief Kamiakin lived, and ask the Chief first-hand about the murders. Bolon decided to travel alone to show the Yakimas that their sub-agent believed in them. Hence, we do not know exactly what happened except from subsequent stories of less hostile Indians.

From such sources it would appear that Kamiakin was insulting and belligerent. That attitude roused Bolon who told the Chief that the latter could depend upon the United States Government to punish the murderers.

Chief Owhi, half-brother of Kamiakin, had a son, Qual-chin, who was suggested as an escort for Bolon through the Yakima country. Bolon, however, chose to ride alone to show his confidence in the Indians under his supervision. Bolon had told Nathan Olney, sub-agent at The Dalles, that he would return there after concluding his session with Kamiakin. When Bolen did not return, Olney sent a friendly Deschutes chief to learn what had happened.

Kamiakin confided to the Deschutes chief that he intended to war on the whites and that he was prepared to fight for five years unless he killed off all the white people sooner. Kamiakin also said that he would invite all the Indian tribes to join him and that those who were foolish enough to refuse would either be exterminated or enslaved. Father Brouillet also advised Olney that the Yakimas around his mission had talked of nothing but war since the treaty of the preceding June. Olney and others secured all the information they could and it seemed to clearly indicate that the Yakimas had somehow been able to acquire large quantities of ammunition in spite of prohibitory legislation. It also appeared that Kamiakin had already succeeded in rallying several important tribes, including the Walla Wallas, who had previously been friendly.

To revert to Qual-chin, it was well-known that he had voiced the threat to kill any whites passing through his tribal domain and that he had been rebuked for that decision by Eneas, one of the Yakima chiefs. Not to be diverted, Qual-chin rounded up five warrior relatives and the six started riding toward the Kittitas Valley. They crossed a trail showing tracks of shod horses, which fact identified the trail as that of white men. The Indians followed and murdered the six white men constituting the party.

These murders, coupled with the offer to assign his son, Qual-chin, as Agent Bolon's guide, have probably been the bases for the accusation that Qual-chin murdered Bolon. As a matter of truth Qual-chin had not seen Bolon on the occasion of Owhi's offer and knew nothing about the meeting between Bolon and the other Indians a few days later.

Bolon had left The Dalles on September 20, 1855. On Toppenish Creek, at a point a few miles from Fort Simcoe, he visited the lodge of Chief Show-a-way (also called Chief Ice), a younger brother of Kamiakin. Show-a-way urgently advised Bolon to return to The Dalles without delay, warning that Bolon would be killed if he persisted in going ahead. This chief and Bolon were good friends, each admiring the other's basic good traits. So Bolon accepted the advice and started the backtrail to The Dalles. His trail was crossed by a party of Indians headed for the fisheries above The Dalles, where they planned to trade for dried salmon. This party was led by Me-cheil, a son of Show-a-way. Me-cheil and two others, Wap-pi-wa-pi-clah and Stok-an-chan. These three caught up with Bolon and rode along with him with every appearance of friendship. Me-chiel decided that Bolon knew too much about Qual-chin's murders and that Bolon should be killed. The other two agreed to help do the job. Camp was made and a good fire was burning. Bolon was standing by the fire warming himself when Wap-pi-wap-pi-clah, a powerful man, pinned Bolon's arms and Stok-an-chan calmly pushed Bolon's head back and cut his throat.

The Indians then threw the body into the fire, killed Bolon's horse, and rolled it with its saddle and other gear into the fire.

Tales of men being murdered while going back and forth to the Colville mines continued to receive confirmation. In the absence of Governor Stevens, Acting Governor Mason decided that something had to be done and in September, 1855, he called upon Forts Vancouver and Steilacoom to furnish troops to protect travel to and from the mines. Major G. J. Rains was in charge at Vancouver and honored Mason's request by ordering Brevet-Major Granville O. Haller from The Dalles with a hundred men and a howitzer, and Lieutenant W. A. Slaughter with fifty men from Steilacoom, the two forces to unite. Their purpose was not that of fighting but to learn the reasons for Kamiakin's hostility, and, by a show of strength, to discourage attacks on Colville travelers. Major Haller did not expect to find the Yakimas prepared for war.

At the same time Acting Governor Mason and Governor Curry, of Oregon, and their principal civilian assistants were concerned about Major Haller's expedition because they could foresee a long war if the Major should fail.

Haller left The Dalles on October 2 and had proceeded about sixty miles by the 6th. On that day, and just as his command was emerging from a ravine on the Pisco River, he found himself facing 1500 Indians, who immediately attacked. The fighting was furious and ceased only at nightfall, by which time the troops had succeeded in reaching a hill. There was no water and little food, a situation which seemed to be repeated frequently in Indian wars. The Indians surrounded the hill and at daybreak resumed the attack which continued all day. That night a messenger was sent to The Dalles for help and to acquaint Major Rains with the sad plight of Major Haller's command. On the 8th, which was the third day of the battle, suffering from thirst was intense. Most of the horses were turned loose, only enough being kept to carry the wounded and the ammunition. The howitzer was buried, the baggage and surplus supplies were burned, and the troop prepared to set out on a retreat in the direction of The Dalles. The contingent was divided into two parties, the advance section which included the wounded being in command of Major Haller, and the rear guard, under Captain Russell. Haller's section set out undetected by the Indians but they lost the trail and lighted signal fires to let the rear guard know their location. The fires were, of course, notice to the Indians, and, unhappily, were unseen by Captain Russell's command.

The Indians pursued Haller and his men, who kept up a running fight until within 25 miles of The Dalles where they were met by Lieutenant Day of the 3rd Artillery with 45 men. The forces joined and erected a block-house on the Klickitat River. Lieutenant Slaughter and his 50 men, traveling from Ft. Steilacoom, had crossed the Cascades at Natches Pass. Upon reaching the east side of the range he found large numbers of Indians prepared for war and heard of Major Haller's defeat. So Slaughter retreated, recrossing the range to the west side. Major Haller lost five men killed and 17 wounded, besides a large quantity of supplies. The Indian losses were estimated at 40 killed.

Major Haller considered that 1000 soldiers would be needed to subdue the Indians. From the regulars at The Dalles 19 officers and 315 men, both infantry and artillery, with three howitzers were sent into the field. From Ft. Steilacoom all except a small guard were dispatched under Captain Maloney. Nineteen Dragoons under Lieutenant Phil Sheridan were sent from Vancouver. But the aggregate of all these regulars was not enough for the campaign. Major Rains called upon Acting Governor Mason for two companies of volunteers and upon Governor Curry for four companies. Adequate supplies of arms were obtained at Vancouver Barracks to equip two of the Oregon companies. The rest of the Oregon Volunteers outfitted themselves. Acting Governor Mason petitioned the captains of two government ships then in Puget Sound for assistance. The ships' commanders responded.

Chief Kamiakin of the Yakimas

". . . all chiefs except Kamiakin signed the treaty on June 11, 1855." (page 111)

Chief Peu-peu-mox-mox of the Walla Wallas

"The Walla Wallas, influenced by their Head Chief Peu-peu-mox-mox, had decided to join the Yakimas." (page 117)

The Cascades of the Columbia

"His [Kamiakin's] instructions were to wait until both steamboats were tied up at the Cascades, then attack, burn the boats . . . kill all the whites from the Upper to the Lower Cascades, and then await further orders." (page 138)

Middle Blockhouse at the Cascades

"After the Yakima outbreak . . . a blockhouse had been erected between the two settlements and there a company of troops was quartered to protect the portage of army supplies." (page 132)

One of the Washington companies was deployed at various strategic points west of the Cascades as a defense measure in case of Indian attacks and the other made preparations to go to the relief of Governor Stevens, who was still somewhere in Northern Idaho or Western Montana, unwilling to risk his way through the hostile country.

On October 11, 1855, Governor Curry issued a proclamation calling for the enrollment of eight companies of mounted volunteers. While this was twice the number requested by Major Rains, Governor Curry had required that the Oregon volunteers were to be an independent command, but would work with the regular troops. Just why that restriction was inserted by Governor Curry may be a matter for debate, but it must be borne in mind that the attitude of General Wool toward volunteers was still fresh in the memories of all territorial residents and it was a mark of a changing attitude for a regular army officer to ask for volunteer help.

Governor Curry appointed recruiting officers and enlistments were so numerous that eventually ten companies were enrolled.

Major Rains left for the seat of war on October 30th. With him were all the available regulars and two companies of volunteers who had been enlisted in the Federal service. On November 4th he was joined by four companies of Oregon Volunteers under the command of Colonel J. W. Nesmith. The official name of Nesmith's force was the First Regiment of Oregon Mounted Volunteers. November 7th found them in the Yakima country and on the 8th they engaged in the first skirmishes. The Indians were not favored with overwhelming numbers as was the case in their fight with Major Haller's previous command. Now the number of soldiers equalled that of the hostiles. They went up the Yakima River with the troops in pursuit and took up a position on the heights overlooking a point where the river flowed through rather precipitous walls. A portion of the regulars under Major Haller and Captain Augur charged the position and the Indians fled. Next day contact was again made, followed by an unsuccessful effort by part of the Oregon Volunteers under Major Ambrose N. Armstrong to surround the Indians. The attempt might have succeeded but for the fact that the wrong point was selected for the assault and the Indians escaped.

A few miles farther up the Yakima Valley was a Catholic Mission, called Ahtanahm Mission, and to that place the troops moved. The mission had been vacated, but there Major Rains received a letter from Chief Kamiakin, written by the missionary Father Pandozy. In the letter Kamiakin offered friendship but on terms dictated by himself. On November 13th Major Rains addressed his reply, which was a masterly example of directness as well as of understanding of Indian character. In it he laid down the dictum that he was in the field to exterminate the Yakimas because of the wanton murders and the repudiation of the treaty made with Governor Stevens and Superintendent Palmer. Rains signed the letter with two titles, first as "Major, United States Army" and then as "Brigadier-General Washington Territory." Major Rains had accepted the latter commission from Acting Governor Mason because the Oregon Volunteers had a Brigadier-General of their own, John K. Lamerick, and while Major Rains was acknowledged by all to be the logical commander in the field, embarrassment because of rank was obviated by the Washington commission. Later Major Rains was criticized by General Wool in characteristic fashion for having accepted Mason's commission, General Wool considering it beneath the dignity of a regular army officer to accept a commission from a Territorial official.

The first snows of the winter had fallen to a considerable depth at the higher elevations. The Indians had scattered and Rains decided to return his regular troops to The Dalles, which he did. From there the Major went to Vancouver Barracks to report to General Wool, arriving on November 24th. Colonel Nesmith marched his Oregon Volunteers to Walla Walla.

In the meantime other events of importance had been transpiring.

AFFAIRS OTHER THAN MAJOR RAINS' EXPEDITION

KAMIAKIN was a man of mixed talents and many outstanding characteristics and easily the outstanding Indian personality in the entire Columbia Basin. He was tall, muscular, and very dark, with a bearing that was regal. He had condemned the Cayuses for the Whitman massacre but was true to his race and wanted only the peaceful possession of the country for his people. On the other hand, foreseeing the inroads of the white people and the ultimate consequences, he decided that the only way through which the Indians could continue to hold their lands was by the extermination of the whites. To that end, then, he traveled far and wide, urging all the tribes to join in his effort. He was tireless. His oratory was typical of all great chiefs. When a tribe refused to join with him it was not because he lacked their esteem.

Nathan Olney, as previously stated, was the Indian Agent at The Dalles when the foregoing events occurred. As soon as he learned of Major Haller's defeat he went to Walla Walla to dissuade the Cayuses, Deschutes and Walla Wallas from joining the Yakimas in the war. From his observations he concluded that Peu-peu-mox-mox, the Walla Walla chief, planned to join Kamiakin. He reported that belief to his superior, R. R. Thompson, who concurred. Olney decided to remove the white settlers from the Yakima Valley and notified them that he believed that a general Indian uprising was imminent and told them to be in readiness to leave that country as soon as a military escort which he had requested arrived from The Dalles. He warned the settlers not to attempt a combined exodus without military escort as such a move would, in his opinion, cause an immediate Indian attack. Olney also conferred with the Hudson's Bay Company officials at their Walla Walla post and those men were also convinced of the emergency. At the time there was a large quantity of ammunition at Fort Walla Walla, together with a considerable inventory of Hudson's Bay Company stores and a quantity of supplies which Governor Stevens had left there, not wishing to encumber himself when he set out to treat with the Blackfeet, far to the northeast. The surplus ammunition was dumped into the river, and the other stores were placed in charge of Pierre, one of the Walla Walla chiefs who was friendly.

But Chief Pierre could not stand alone. The Walla Wallas, influenced by their Head Chief Peu-peu-mox-mox, had decided to join the Yakimas. The Nez Perces refused to join and said that they would harbor no hostiles. One of the settlers who had been warned by Olney was Narcisse Raymond. He sent a dispatch addressed to the commander of the escort, presumed to be enroute to Fort Walla Walla. Raymond must have been greatly concerned, for while he told of the daily threats by Peu-peu-mox-mox to kill the settlers, he also advised the military commander that it would be unwise to come with only 150 men, which was his information about the size of the relief force. He told of the pillage of the fort and that the Yakimas 1000 strong were guarding the approach to Ft. Walla Walla. However, no escort from The Dalles was on its way. When Raymond's message was sent there was only a small garrison at The Dalles, the main force being in the field under Major Rains. But while the regulars were unable to send an escort we shall see later that the Oregon Volunteers were on the march.

The critical situation of the Yakima Valley settlers as well as a desire to assist Governor Stevens to return from the country of the Blackfeet, where he was cut off from returning by the Yakima War, was sufficient reason for Governor Curry to have called for enlistments.

General Wool arrived at Vancouver Barracks on November 17, 1855. He proceeded at once to criticize Major Rains saying that Rains had enough troops to defeat all the Indians in the Pacific Northwest and accused the Major of having been afflicted with the hysteria pervading the territory. The General said that there was no occasion for Governor Curry to have called for enrolling a regiment of volunteers to defend the inhabitants of Oregon. Yet, General Wool in a subsequent report on the Yakima War, said that he had ordered all available troops into the campaign and that he had called upon the War Department to furnish an additional regiment. Thus we are aware of a typical General Wool paradox. By his report there was no need for Governor Curry to recruit a regiment, part of which was in the field in ten days, but the General, himself, called for at least an additional regiment of regulars, which could hardly have been furnished in less than a year.

We have seen that four companies of Oregon Volunteers under Colonel Nesmith had arrived in time to accompany Major Rains on his expedition. Other companies followed soon. Major Mark A. Chinn arrived at The Dalles with three companies and started for Walla Walla on November 12th. On the 17th he was met by Raymond's messenger. Acting upon the advice that 150 men were insufficient, Major Chinn proceeded only as far as the Umatilla River where he camped and erected a fortification and decided to stay there until reinforcements came up. He named his fortification Ft. Henrietta in honor of Major Haller's wife. On November 27th Captain Connoyer arrived with his company. Two days later Lieutenant-Colonel James K. Kelly came with two more companies commanded by Captains A. V. Wilson and Charles Bennett. The force now numbered 350 men and late in the day on December 2nd, under the command of Lieutenant-Colonel Kelly, set out for Ft. Walla Walla.

It was Kelly's hope that he would reach the fort before sunrise, but a heavy rain set in, continuing through the night, and the troops delayed in arriving until mid-forenoon. They found the fort pillaged, defaced, and the Indians gone.

Kelly set out on the morning of December 4th with most of his troops unencumbered by baggage, proceeding up the Touchet River hoping to locate the Indians. Major Chinn, with the remainder of the soldiers guarding the baggage train, started for the mouth of the Touchet where he was to camp and await orders. Upon reaching a point about 15 miles upstream, Kelly's command saw a party of five or six Indians approaching. Upon meeting it was discovered that the group was led by Peu-peu-mox-mox. An interview was held, the Indian chief opening the discussion by asking why armed men had come into his country. Lieutenant-Colonel Kelly replied that he had come to chastise the chief and his followers for their crimes against the white people. To that statement Peu-peu-mox-mox answered that he did not want to fight and that he had done no wrong, whereupon Kelly recounted a long list of crimes in answer to which the chief said that he could not restrain his young warriors. Kelly then told the chief that the latter had been seen to distribute some of the stolen goods and that he had laid out a pile of blankets as an inducement to the Cayuses to join the war, and, further, that Howlish Wampool, a Cayuse chief, had so testified. Peu-peu-mox-mox then said that he would require his people to restore whatever goods could be recovered and make restitution for the remainder. Kelly replied that the offer was not sufficient; that the Walla Wallas would have to give up their arms and ammunition, furnish beef cattle for the troops, and supply remounts so that the volunteers could pursue the other hostiles.

The chief agreed to all of Kelly's terms, saying that he would surrender the arms and ammunition the next day. But Kelly could recognize Indian deceit and concluded that the chief only wanted time enough to move his tribe and that the chief, himself, had no intention of returning the next day. So Kelly stated that he had come for the sole purpose of waging war and that for the chief to return to his village would precipitate an immediate attack there because he had no confidence in the promises made. Then Kelly said that if the chief was really dealing honestly that he should have no objection to remaining with the troops, and carry out his obligations through messengers to his people. Kelly next instructed his interpreters to make it clear to the chief that he was at liberty to leave under the flag of truce which he carried but that if he did the troops would attack the village at once. As an alternative, Peu-peu-mox-mox was told that if he and six of his escort would remain with the soldiers and carry out the promises that the people would be spared. The chief, thus outsmarted, consented to remain. He made a high-sounding speech stressing the point that his principal concern was the keeping of his promises; that he was interested in the safety of his people; that next forenoon he would lead the troops to his village and conclude the terms imposed by Kelly; and, moreover, that none of his followers would go away during the night. Nevertheless a guard was placed over him and his six fellow hostages. The chief then suggested that the troops move towards the Indian village to secure the beef cattle as the soldiers were hungry. The command set out, the main part of the chief's escort marching along with the troops. The village was in a canyon of the Touchet River and after marching about half a mile and it being late afternoon, Kelly decided that it would be unwise to enter the canyon where they might readily be ambushed. His suspicion had been heightened by Peu-peu-mox-mox's concern over the hunger of the soldiers. So Kelly marched his command back two miles to open ground and camped for the night.

That evening the chief asked leave to send one of his fellow hostages to the village for the purpose of acquainting the tribe with the terms agreed upon. Kelly agreed but thought that the messenger would not return, in which belief he was quite correct.

On the morning of December 6 the troops marched into the village. It was deserted. The only Indians to be seen were those along the ridge of the hills from where they appeared to be fully armed and interested in the movement of the troops. Kelly tried to get the Indians to come in and comply with the terms of the agreement, sending out a flag of truce for that purpose, but the Indians showed no interest. Deciding that further effort in that direction was useless, Kelly moved his command to the mouth of the river where Major Chinn was camped with the supply train. Of course the hostages were taken along. That night one of the Indians made an unsuccessful attempt to escape so Kelly had all of them tied up until morning. When they were unbound Kelly told the chief that the latter was acting in bad faith and that if he, or any of the other hostages, tried to escape that sure death by shooting would be the answer.

Kelly decided to march to Waiilatpu and establish headquarters there. To that end preparations were proceeding on the morning of December 7th. It was noticed that mounted Indians, all armed, were appearing along the hills about a half mile distant from the camp, but even then no attack was anticipated. As the advance guard moved out the Indians opened fire on a detail driving up some beef cattle and the fire was immediately returned. Soon the shooting became general and as the troops got under way a running battle ensued, continuing for ten miles, or within two miles of Waiilatpu, at which point was located the farm of a French-Canadian settler named LaRoche.

At this point it would be well to describe the respective situations of the combatants. As the ten-mile battle had proceeded with its noise of firing and characteristic war-whoops, hundreds of Indians in the vicinity were attracted to the scene. Not all of them, perhaps not more than half, actually engaged in the battle. The rest were interested onlookers, but by the time the troops had reached the LaRoche farm it is certain that the number of Indians actually engaged in the fight outnumbered the troops three to one. The volunteers were between a range of hills on their left and the Walla Walla River on their right. To check the advance of the troops the Indians deployed across the level land from the hills to the river. Part of their line was protected by a thin growth of trees. As a part of the panorama the Indians set up poles on each prominent hill. From the poles dangled the scalps of white people and around each pole danced a howling mob of hostiles. It was clear that the warriors had worked themselves into a high degree of excitement and that they believed that the victory would be theirs.

The troops advanced and were met by a withering fire which caused them to fall back. Several of the volunteers were wounded, two mortally. Lieutenant J. M. Burrows, with a detachment, was ordered to flank the Indians. Advancing, the Lieutenant was almost instantly killed and several of his men wounded. Company A, under Captain A. V. Wilson, came up at a gallop in response to a call for reinforcements. They dismounted and made a bayonet charge through the underbrush driving the Indians before them. Quickly Company F, Captain Charles Bennett, joined Company A and together these troops chased the hostiles about a mile up river. At that point there was an abandoned house surrounded by a tight fence. The Indians turned it into an improvised fortification. The troops attempted to take the place. CaptainBennett and one of Wilson's men were killed. The troops took cover as best they could. A howitzer was brought up and exploded at the first shot, wounding Captain Wilson but chasing the Indians from their shelter. The soldiers took possession, recovering the bodies of the dead and removing the wounded. A field hospital was established in LaRoche's house, a mile away.

While the fighting raged the hostiles became greatly excited. Peu-peu-mox-mox yelled cheering words to his warriors. The few men comprising the prisoners' guard, through one of their number, reported to Lieutenant-Colonel Kelly that they feared the hostages would try to escape. Kelly instructed the guard to bind the prisoners and if they offered resistance or tried to escape to kill them. The hostages did resist. One of them stabbed a sergeant-major in the arm. Peu-peu-mox-mox tried to seize a gun from another of the guards but the guard, clubbing his gun, knocked the chief to the ground and killed him. Five of the remaining prisoners tried to escape and were shot.

Meanwhile the battle continued and only ceased at night-fall. The troops were tired and hungry. Their losses had been considerable, including two officers killed and one wounded. They tried to cook supper but the camp fires only made targets for the Indians and had to be extinguished. All night long the troops were on the alert. Here and there a few exhausted men snatched a few minutes of sleep. At daybreak breakfast was prepared but in the midst of the meal the Indians attacked. They had evidently persuaded many of the previous day's onlookers to join in the active fighting. It had been established that 1000 warriors had been engaged in the battle of the previous day and now there were many more. The hostiles regained all the points they had lost the day before. They fought furiously, convinced of victory.

Kelly called a hasty council of some of his officers. As a result Companies A and H, commanded by Lieutenants Charles B. Pillows and A. B. Hannah, respectively, were ordered to dislodge the Indians from the timber and to hold the positions if humanly possible. Companies F, B, I, and K, commanded by Lieutenants A. M. Fellows, Lieutenant Jeffreys, Lieutenant Charles B. Hand, and Captain N. A. Connoyer, were ordered to take the hills from the hostiles and to generally harass the enemy. The battle continued all day without a major decision. The Indians were driven from the woods and brush and at nightfall withdrew. The troops were tired and while they had made some gains they had not administered a defeat. That night Kelly sent a messenger to Fort Henrietta requiring Companies D and E to reinforce him at once.

Next morning, which was December 9th, the battle was resumed. But the troops were worn out and did not take the offensive all day, preferring to absorb the Indian attacks, which was done with heavy losses to the hostiles.

When the morning of the 10th came the Indians were in better position and had erected a breastwork and their reserves were in strategic positions. They had dug rifle-pits and in all respects seemed to be prepared for a fresh fight.

Lieutenant James McAuliff, with Company B, was ordered to to take the breastworks. Companies A and H were ordered to clear the woods and overrun the rifle-pits. From the rest of the troops those with the freshest horses were sent to the hills from where they were to charge the Indians on the plain below. All objectives were accomplished. The Indians fought bravely but the tide of battle flowed in favor of the troops; the hostiles fled and the four days of battle were over.

The volunteers lost eight officers and men killed or dead of wounds and eighteen others wounded. The Indians' losses were estimated at 100 killed and wounded. The troops built a new fort two miles above Waiilatpu, naming it Fort Bennett in memory of Captain Charles Bennett, killed in the battle. Colonel J. W. Nesmith resigned his command of the regiment and Thomas R. Cornelius, who had commanded Company D, was elected Colonel. Lieutenant-Colonel Kelly was a member of the legislature and returned to participate in its deliberations. He was welcomed signally by the people of the Willamette Valley as a fitting conclusion to the second phase of the Yakima War.

THE WINTER OF 1855-1856

It will be recalled that Governor Stevens of Washington Territory had been marooned to the northeast by the war. Fort Bennett received him late in the day on December 20, 1855. He had exhibited a rare insight into Indian character in his masterly conduct of treaty negotiations.

Governor Stevens had left Walla Walla in June, 1855, with an escort of Nez Perces and had spent some time in establishing a spirit of cooperation with the Kootenai, Pend Oreilles, and

Flathead tribes before visiting the Blackfeet. In October, having concluded a treaty with the latter tribe, he prepared to return home. His messenger, W. H. Pearson, had carried the news of the treaty to Olympia and then immediately retraced his steps to report to the Governor that the Yakima War was in full swing and that it would be impossible for him to traverse the hostile country. In fact, Pearson brought a recommendation from regular army officers that Stevens return to Olympia via New York!

The Governor, meanwhile, had actually started for the Columbia River and was two days on his way when met by Pearson. Stevens delayed long enough to send back to Fort Bennett for additional arms, ammunition, and horses, and then, with one white man and an Indian interpreter, rode post-haste to the Bitterroot Valley to confer with R. H. Landsdale, agent in charge of the Flatheads there. He then proceeded to Fort Owen, on the Bitterroot River where he overtook the Nez Perce escort which, in the meantime, had learned of the Yakima War and that the Cayuses and a disaffected faction of their own tribe were likely to join with the warring tribes. In the delegation were three of their war chiefs, Lookingglass, Three Feathers, and Spotted Eagle. It is a compliment to Stevens' ability that he not only persuaded them to stay out of the war but that he received from them an offer of an escort of young Nez Perce warriors to see him safely through to The Dalles should he elect to take the route through the Nez Perce country.

At Hell Gate Pass he was met by Special Agent James Doty with the horses and munitions from Fort Bennett, on November 11th. On the 20th he crossed the Bitter Root Mountains through three feet of snow. His plan called for a bold entry into the country of the Coeur d'Alenes, not knowing how that tribe might be disposed toward the hostiles allied in the Yakima War. When about two hours' ride from the Coeur d'Alene Mission he left his escort and rode ahead with Pearson, Special Agent William Craig and four Nez Perces. Without slackening their pace they rode into the midst of the Coeur d'Alenes, but were prepared for any emergency which might ensue. Stevens had told the four Nez Perces to immediately regale the Coeur d'Alenes with an account of his treaty with the Blackfeet stressing the importance of that treaty to the Coeur d'Alenes in having halted the raids which the Blackfeet had periodically made. Stevens' psychology was good. The Coeur d'Alenes were pleased with the prospect. Before there was any time for the tribe to reconsider, Stevens' escort and supply train arrived and the entourage set out at once for the country of the Spokanes. The event had transpired so quickly that the Coeur d'Alenes had no time to compare what Stevens had to offer through the Blackfeet treaty and that which Kamiakin's ambassadors had told them a week earlier.

The Governor next stopped at the home of Antoine Plante, a French-Canadian settler who lived midway between the country of the Coeur d'Alenes and that of the Northern Spokanes. He sent messengers to the Colvilles, the Pend Oreilles, and the Spokanes to meet him at Plante's place. Also invited were Angus McDonald of Fort Colville, Father Ravelli of the Colville Mission, and Father Joset of the Coeur d'Alene Mission.

In a few days all had assembled and a council was held. At the end of several days it looked as if the whole matter would end without affirmative result because the Indians held out for a guarantee that United States troops would not cross to the north side of the Snake River. Of course Stevens had no authority to make that promise and did not. Eventually he won the Indians over to his opinions, after which the Spokanes warned him that the Nez Perce chief, Lookingglass, was up to some treachery, which fact Stevens confirmed by his Indian interpreter, who was a Delaware, and who had heard Lookingglass attempting to persuade the Spokanes to join in his treachery, which probably meant the liquidation of Stevens and his associates. The Spokanes refused to join in the Lookingglass plot and Stevens prepared to move towards Lapwai.

He sent William Craig and some of the Nez Perces ahead to arrange for a council and to make arrangements for an escort to The Dalles. The Governor, himself, enlarged his party by adding a group of miners and others who were waiting for a chance to get through the hostile country. His personal escort then numbered fifty men. Not knowing what dangers he might encounter, he procured fresh horses from the Spokanes, reduced the packs to a minimum, and set out. It rained and snowed, but Stevens pressed on and in four days reached Lapwai. Craig had assembled the Nez Perces tribe for the council. While it was in progress a messenger arrived with the news of the battle between the Oregon volunteers and the Yakimas and also about the death of Peu-peu-mox-mox. Two points were thus made clear. Stevens now understood that it had been possible for him to come through hostile country only because the warriors were away at the scene of the fighting and he also knew that a large escort to The Dalles would not be needed. So the next day he set out with

69 Nez Perces and the others of his party and reached Fort Bennett on December 20th.

He stayed in the Walla Walla Valley for ten days during which he paid tribute to the Oregon volunteers, as their presence in the region was undoubtedly responsible for his escape. He also met Indian Agent B. F. Shaw, who was also a Colonel in the militia of Washington Territory. He ordered Shaw to form a company of home guards and to prepare fortifications adjacent to the winter quarters of the French-Canadian settlers and friendly Indians in the Walla Walla Valley. His instructions to Shaw also included similar protection for the settlers in the Colville and Spokane districts and the admonition to assist Colonel Thomas R. Cornelius, the new commander of Oregon volunteers, in any way the latter might direct. The Governor also conferred with the Oregon officers and agreed that it would be well for them to hold the Walla Walla Valley until the regular troops arrived and in the meantime that there should be no relaxing of the war effort. He sent Craig to Lapwai with the 69 Nez Perces to muster them out of service and to see that the muster rolls were prepared in such a manner that there would be no doubt about payment to the Nez Perces for their services. Craig's duties also entailed taking measures for the protection of the Nez Perce tribe against raids by hostiles. These measures included the use of young Nez Perce braves as patrols and guards for which service they would be paid. The tribe was pleased at the interest shown in their welfare and as a token of appreciation offered to outfit the Oregon volunteers with fresh horses.

Governor Stevens then returned to Olympia where he received a rousing welcome, not only for his achievements and safe return, but because Indian troubles had broken out in the Puget Sound district nearby and his presence at home was important.

INDIAN TROUBLES OF PUGET SOUND

Governor Stevens soon learned that, as an adjunct to the Yakima War, there had been serious outbreaks in the Puget Sound country and that there was every prospect of more to follow soon.

Often designated as "The Battles of Puget Sound" they were really a part of the Yakima War and are detailed here not alone for their intrinsic historical interest but also to show the widespread disaffection of the Western Washington tribes. Kamiakin, principal chief of theYakimas, was adept in his use of emissaries to incite and to threaten reprisals on any tribe which did not cooperate with him.

The Indians who lived on several of the Puget Sound rivers, namely, the Snoqualmie, Nisqually, Puyallup, Cowlitz, Cedar, Green, and White rivers, were all related to the Yakimas and the Klickitats. Chief Leschi of the Nisqually tribe was half Yakima and a willing lieutenant of Kamiakin. In the summer of 1855 much information reached the authorities in Washington Territory to the effect that an Indian war was imminent. The news was conveyed by friendly chiefs and by the Indian wives of white men. Some treaties had been made by Governor Stevens, others were contemplated or in process, but seldom was any tribe unanimously for peace. Usually a part of each tribe favored war. The situation in the Puget Sound Basin was no different in that respect than the rest of the Territory.

On September 27, 1855, the home of A. L. Porter on the White River was attacked. Porter had anticipated such an event and had hidden in the underbrush, escaping capture. Next morning he spread the alarm and the settlers from that district all hastened into Seattle. In the absence of Governor Stevens, Acting Governor Charles H. Mason requested soldiers from Fort Steilacoom.

A detachment under Lieutenant Nugent was sent and the soldiers marched through the district where they were met with nothing but assurances of friendliness on the part of the Indians. Returning to Seattle, Nugent, with Mason's assistance, advised the settlers that there was no cause for alarm and that they should return to their homes, which advice most of them followed. On October 28th those who had returned were massacred. Three children were saved by a friendly Indian known as Old Tom, who placed the children under a bearskin in his canoe and paddled down to Seattle. Chief Kitsap, the elder, for whom Kitsap County, Washington, is named, warned the whites living in the Puyallup Valley, and they escaped at night while the Indians were waiting for daylight to kill them.

Acting Governor Mason asked the Hudson's Bay Company for arms and ammunition. Immediately fifty guns and a large supply of ammunition were sent. This act puzzled the Indians who thought that the British would help in the extermination of the Americans.

Captain C. C. Hewitt, with his company of volunteers, went to the White River Valley to bury the dead and to rescue any who might have escaped by hiding. None was found to rescue. In November this company was again ordered into the White River Valley to cooperate with troops being sent from Fort Steilacoom under Lieutenant W. A. Slaughter. On November 25 Slaughter's force was attacked during a dense fog by Klickitats, Nisquallies, and Green River Indians. One soldier was killed and forty horses belonging to the troopers were stolen. On December 4th Lieutenant Slaughter and Captain Hewitt were conferring at a cabin near the junction of the White and Green rivers, when Lieutenant Slaughter was shot and instantly killed by a lurking Indian. Later a town was to be located at that site and named "Slaughter." The name Slaughter was satisfactory for a settlement, but when the town started to boom, with the coming of the Northern Pacific Railway, the citizens of Slaughter became name-conscious. It was embarrassing to have the hotel runner board the train and cry, "This way to the Slaughter House!" By special act of the legislature in 1893, the name was changed to Auburn, from Oliver Goldsmith's opening line in "The Deserted Village": "Sweet Auburn, loveliest village of the plain."

The sloop-of-war *Decatur* was in Seattle harbor when Governor Isaac I. Stevens returned to Olympia on January 19, 1856. Friendly Indians gave warning of the approach of hostiles by way of Lake Washington on January 25th. The men from the *Decatur* remained ashore on guard that night and returned to the sloop next morning for a breakfast they were destined not to eat. An alarm sounded and the men went ashore, taking a howitzer with them. They sent a shot where the Indians were supposed to be hiding and immediately received a volley of rifle fire. That circumstance initiated the Battle of Seattle which raged until ten o'clock that night. Two white men were killed and, as usual, the Indians concealed their losses. The hostiles were defeated but sent word that they would return with a force sufficient to take Seattle even with the support of a battleship. A strong stockade was built and Governor Stevens kept the volunteers constantly scouring the country. Captain Maloney was in the White River Valley with 125 men and in February Lieutenant-Colonel Casey came up from Fort Steilacoom with two companies and joined with Maloney's force. Two companies of volunteers also headed in the same direction, established depots at two points and built a blockhouse and constructed a ferry at the Puyallup River crossing. Meanwhile depredations broke out anew south of Fort Steilacoom. On March 4 Lieutenant Kautz, with a detachment of regulars, was busy opening a road from the Puyallup River to Muckleshute Prairie when they were attacked by a large force of Indians. One soldier was killed and nine, including Lieutenant Kautz, were wounded.

The Battle of Connell's Prairie occurred on March 8th. Two small companies of volunteers had been sent to the White River crossing to establish a ferry and build a blockhouse. They were vigorously attacked by 150 Indians. The volunteers charged, putting the Indians to flight. The total casualties for the volunteers were four wounded while the Indians lost thirty killed and many wounded. That result encouraged the white men and discouraged the hostiles. It was the last battle west of the Cascades in which the Indians appeared in force in the Puget Sound area. Subsequent attacks were confined to surprise raids by small bands.

The U. S. S. *Massachusetts* arrived in Seattle harbor on February 24, 1856. A month later the U. S. S. *John Hancock* put in its appearance, which arrivals did much to convince the Indians thereabout that they were on the losing side. However, hostiles came down from the north and upon refusing to return whence they came, were attacked by men from the ships. Twenty-seven Indians were killed and twenty-one wounded out of a total of 117 warriors. Their canoes and supplies were destroyed and the survivors surrendered. They were transported to Victoria Island aboard the *Massachusetts* and the episode took all idea of fight out of the Northern Indians.

As an additional safeguard two new forts were built, Fort Townsend across the strait from Victoria, and Fort Bellingham, on the mainland east of the San Juan Islands. The ringleaders among the hostile chiefs were hunted down and executed. The volunteers of Washington Territory had proved their mettle. They had built 35 stockades, blockhouses and forts; other citizens had built 23 more; and the regular troops, seven. Roads and trails had been finished and the entire cost was defrayed by the auction of animals captured from the Indians.

Through the fine efforts of Governor Stevens, attention of the nation was focused on the Territory and it was on its way to eventually take its place in the roster of states.

COLONEL WRIGHT ARRIVES WITH HIS REGULARS

On December 21, 1855, the volunteers in the Walla Walla Valley were faced with a new snow-fall followed by a temperature of 20 degrees below zero. Their equipment and clothing did not conform to the needs of the weather. Shoes were worn out and many of the men improvised moccasins from rawhide. Blankets and jackets had worn thin. Camp was moved from Fort Bennett to a location several miles north of present-day Walla Walla. There was plenty of beef and ample supplies of potatoes in the new camp and these provisions were supplemented by recovered caches of Indian food with sometimes a ration of something less common. Meanwhile, two companies under Major Ambrose N. Armstrong were busy recovering property stolen from immigrants. But the volunteers were anxious to return home. They had been in service for several months and the comfort of a home fireside was certainly preferable to a thin tent in sub-zero weather. So Governor Curry, on January 16, 1856, issued a proclamation calling for the recruiting of five companies to relieve the veterans. Recruiting moved quickly and the new troops arrived at Walla Walla on March 1st.

When the Walla Wallas had vacated their village on the night of December 5-6, they had gone to the country north of the Snake River. The volunteers could not pursue them because there were no boats, so several weeks were spent in constructing six craft to be used in crossing the river. On March 9, 1856, the reorganized regiment crossed the river about 30 miles southwest of the junction of the Palouse. A few Indians congregated to oppose the crossing but they were repulsed with some casualties and the loss of their horses. The horses were slaughtered for food and the command proceeded northeast to the falls of the Palouse where it was decided to camp and await the arrival of supplies from The Dalles. The commissary train reached them on March 23rd when the troops again set out. The weather had turned unusually hot. Their course was due west for 60 miles to what is now the site of the town of White Bluffs on the Columbia River. The country traversed on this march was poor land having little water or grass. Many of the horses died. Several days were spent in rounding up enough Indian horses to remount the troops. On March 30th the soldiers again started out, swinging around and returning to the valley of the Walla Walla. There was a recurrent shortage of food and part of the force was detached to go into the Umatilla country and forage for food. It was a poor existence and the troops were often hungry. Also their period of enlistment was about to expire.

Colonel Cornelius — concerned about the inadequate commissary service and the further fact that he had received no news about potential relief by regular soldiers — decided that he should confer with Governor Curry. Accordingly, on April 6 he set out for The Dalles with a part of his command. His route was along the north bank of the Columbia and on the 4th day he was attacked by Kamiakin, Chief of the Yakimas, with about 300 warriors. The Indians were repulsed, only one soldier being wounded. The troops could not follow up their victory because of short supplies and continued their march. On April 28th they were camped five miles from The Dalles. There the Indians stampeded the horses leaving the command one of foot soldiers instead of mounted infantrymen. In the meantime Lieutenant-Colonel Kelly, with the remainder of the regiment at Fort Henrietta, had suffered a similar raid, on April 21, a large band of Indians having surprised the guard and driven off 45 head of horses.

Colonel Cornelius conferred with Governor Curry, as a result of which the regiment was mustered out of service. For those who wished to continue their enlistment, two companies were organized. One was assigned to protect the Walla Walla Valley and the other the Tygh Valley. In May an additional company was sent to the latter section, the provisional battalion being commanded by Major Davis Layton.

Meanwhile, the regular army was finally taking affirmative measures to move into the war.

It will be recalled that General Wool had been at Vancouver during the winter. With the mail steamer from San Francisco on January 11, 1856, came word of the Indian troubles in Southern Oregon and Northern California, necessitating the General's return to San Francisco. Starting his trip down the Columbia his vessel met a transport headed for Vancouver. Aboard was Colonel George Wright and eight companies of the 9th United States Infantry. General Wool assigned Colonel Wright to the command of the Columbia River district. The General's ship proceeded to sea and later met another vessel northbound, aboard which was Lieutenant-Colonel Silas Casey with two companies of the 9th United States Infantry. The General ordered Casey to the command of the Puget Sound district.

Among Colonel Wright's orders were these: he was to establish his headquarters at The Dalles and to assemble there all the troops which he might find it necessary to use in the Yakima War; to set up a military post at Walla Walla; another on the Yakima River; another midway between The Dalles and the Yakima River post. The strategy called for preventing the Indians from fishing, thus threatening their food supply and advancing the probability of capitulation.

Arriving at Vancouver Colonel Wright took his time, remaining there several weeks after the first five companies of the First Regiment of Oregon Mounted Volunteers had reached the upper hostile country. By early March, Colonel Wright began moving his troops to The Dalles, in the course of which movement a large quantity of army supplies were piled up at the Cascades of the Columbia River about 40 miles west of The Dalles. The Cascades were caused by a large number of rocks and rocky islands, with swiftly rushing water in their many channels, making it necessary to portage freight along the shore for a distance of several miles. Small steamers carried the army's supplies from Vancouver to a point just below the Cascades where unloading occurred. The goods were then transported around the dangerous rocks and re-loaded on other small steamers above the rapids, then completing the transport to The Dalles. There was a small settlement on the north bank of the river at both the lower and upper ends of the cascades. After the Yakima outbreak of the preceding October, a blockhouse had been erected between the two settlements and there a company of troops was quartered to protect the portage of army supplies. By mid-March all the troops left at Vancouver were ordered to Fort Steilacoom and the company at the Cascades was ordered into the field except eight men under Sergeant Matthew Kelly who were left to garrison the blockhouse. The settlement at the upper end of the Cascades included the store of Bradford & Company. On March 26th, two days after the main body of the garrison had left, the little village was awake bright and early for there was work to be done. A wooden railroad track was being built to replace the mule-power portage; a bridge was being built from Bradford's store to one of the rocky islands. The steamer *Mary* was tied up nearby waiting for cargo, and the steamer *Wasco* was moored on the south side of the river. Suddenly the residents were startled by the Indian war-whoop. The settlers were taken by surprise. Indians were everywhere. The miller, his wife and brother-in-law were killed, scalped and their bodies thrown into the river. Some of the crew of the *Mary* were ashore and their return to their ship was cut off by the Indians. The hostiles attacked the boat but in spite of wounds and a reduced crew the *Mary* was swung into the stream. The *Wasco,* sensing the trouble, started moving across the river. The two boats picked up several men who had fled from the Indians. Others were not so fortunate, but all who survived made their way to Bradford's store, which was a strong log building of two stories. About 40 people reached that haven, 19 of them men. One of the 19 was shot as he opened the door to see if he could observe any signs of three men marooned on the island. Some government rifles and ammunition had been left at Bradford's for forwarding to Vancouver. The guns were too few to arm the remaining 18 men but all of them could not give their attention to shooting because the Indians began throwing combustibles onto the roof. While some of the defenders shot at any Indian coming within range, others put out the fires by shoving the burning embers off with sticks forced through the roof or by tossing cups of brine from a barrel of pickled pork, or by chopping out a burning section.

However, the gunfire from the store inflicted casualties among the hostiles and they became more cautious though there was still no respite for the besieged. There was no water in the store and none dared venture to the river without the risk of almost certain death as a reward for the attempt. Night came and the Indians set fire to several buildings, thus lighting the area so that escape was impossible. Some of the occupants had been wounded. The few bottles of ale and spirits in stock were soon used. All agreed that if the store should burn that they would run to a flatboat tied up nearby and go over the falls, preferring that kind of death to torture by the Indians. A young Spokane Indian, brought up by whites in the neighborhood, did succeed in getting one bucket of water but the risk was too great and he did not try again. The night dragged itself into another day. Neither steamboat was in sight. There was not only no water but little food. The second night came and the Indians burned more buildings. Towards morning the young Spokane again volunteered to get water and at the same time the body of the man who had been shot the day before was slid into the river.

Meanwhile word had reached the settlement at the lower end of the falls. Among others living there was George Griswold who learned from the Cascade Indians that the Yakimas were attacking. The neighborhood was quickly alerted and men, women, and children jumped into boats and headed for Vancouver. A few men stayed by to unmoor a schooner and some smaller boats and succeeded in getting them into the stream only after one man was wounded.

Some of the Yakimas with a few Klickitat allies moved down from Bradford's to the small fort or blockhouse midway to the lower Cascades. The soldiers at the blockhouse ran out a small cannon, thus succeeding in keeping most of the Indians at a distance. All up and down the north shore of the Cascades things were in confusion. No one knew what was happening except in his immediate neighborhood. All were sure that someone must have reached Vancouver with an appeal for help. Their hopes were gratified on the morning of March 28 when the steamers *Mary* and *Wasco* nosed into the landing at the Upper Cascades, having come down from The Dalles. Soldiers poured off the boats and at once began searching for Indians who had taken to the woods.

These soldiers were of Colonel Wright's command, which was on its way from The Dalles to Walla Walla to establish a military post. When the steamer *Mary* had arrived at The Dalles a messenger was sent to the Colonel who was encamped at Five-Mile Creek. As soon as Wright heard the news he marched his command, comprising 250 officers and men, back to The Dalles and boarded the two steamers on the night of the 27th, but difficulties with the boiler of the *Mary* delayed sailing until the following morning. Immediately upon landing Colonel Wright organized a relief force which he placed under the command of Lieutenant-Colonel Edward J. Steptoe, whose subordinates were Captains Winder and Archer, with two companies of the 9th Infantry, a detachment of dragoons from the 3rd Artillery under Lieutenant Tear, and a small group under Lieutenant Piper to handle a howitzer. They were to advance on the blockhouse at once and from there move down to the lower landing.

In the meantime events were transpiring at Vancouver. It will be recalled that one company of regulars had been left there when the main force had started for The Dalles and that the remaining company was under orders to go to Fort Steilacoom. As soon as news of hostilities at the Cascades was received, the post commander, Colonel Morris, took several measures. First, believing that Vancouver might be attacked, he moved all women and children to the Hudson's Bay Company's old fort. Then, obeying his orders from General Wool, he refused arms and ammunition to the volunteer home guard. At the same time he detailed 40 regulars, commanded by Lieutenant Phil Sheridan, to proceed by the steamer *Belle* to the Cascades. This detachment sailed on the morning of the 27th. The *Belle* met the schooner and smaller boats, which had succeeded in getting away the previous day, and accepted the offer of their crews to join his expedition.

The steamer reached the lower Cascades, found the settlement there destroyed, and proceeded to land on the south shore. Sheridan reconnoitered the upper settlement from the south shore and learned from the Cascade Indians what had been happening. He then crossed to the north shore and while disembarking was attacked by the Indians, two soldiers being killed. Sheridan then withdrew out of range but could not advance because of the intense pressure from the Indians.

While these events were occurring, other affirmative action was being taken. A volunteer company had been hastily recruited in Portland, the commander being L. G. Powell. He had about 60 men, equally divided between those from Portland and those from Vancouver. They sailed on the steamer *Fashion* and arrived at the lower Cascades shortly after the *Belle,* but like Sheridan's force, were unable to advance up river because of the intensity of the Indian attack. However, they did land and took up a defensive position. The *Fashion* went back to Portland and returned next day with 40 more volunteers under Captain Stephen Coffin, together with a detail of regular replacements and a supply of ammunition.

Lieutenant Sheridan placed his howitzer on a barge and occupied the attention of the Indians on the river bank as Lieutenant-Colonel Steptoe's force approached from the north. Then one of those things happened which upsets opportunity. With the Yakimas between the troops of Steptoe and Sheridan, surprise and defeat for the Indians seemed certain, when a bugle call sounded from Steptoe's command and the Indians vanished into the forest. Instead of heavy casualties for the hostiles, there was one dead Indian and one dead soldier.

Two companies of Oregon Volunteers returned home on the 29th and Colonel Wright arranged for the erection of two blockhouses, one on the cliff north of Bradford's store and the other at the lower Cascades. There were 15 white people killed or died of wounds in the attack on the Cascades and the wounded who recovered numbered twelve.

Colonel Wright ordered the arrest of a number of the Indians but since the Yakimas had fled and with them certain of the Klickitats and a few of the Cascade Indians who had chosen to join the hostiles, those arrested consisted only of Chief Chenoweth of the Cascade tribe and eight of his warriors. They were tried fairly and the verdict resulted in the execution of all nine. Others of the tribe were also arrested and sent as prisoners to Vancouver. An island was set aside for the Cascades and the Colonel issued orders to shoot any Cascade Indian found off the island.

Again the controversy between the volunteers and the regulars was revived. The ubiquitous General Wool quickly reported on the errors of the volunteers and the expense incident to placing Oregon and Washington volunteer units in the field, and even went so far as to fabricate property losses caused by the volunteers, which had never occurred. Actually, Major Haller, Major Rains, and Colonel Wright, the latter under the direct orders of General Wool, all of them regulars, suffered appreciable losses of government property, and in the case of Colonel Wright, who was responsible for leaving the Cascades settlement virtually unguarded, there was ample blame for the massacre and destruction there.

Colonel Wright collected his forces and returned to The Dalles late in April, from where he again set out. Snow was two feet deep in the mountains but by April 30 the command was camped on the north shore of the river 25 miles east of The Dalles. Lieutenant Davidson, with a detachment, was sent ahead to look for Indians but none were seen. The troops moved on and May 6th found them in camp seven miles north of Ahtanahm Mission on the creek of the same name. Here a few Indians were seen but none were killed or captured. On the night of the 6th the camp was attacked and the prairie set afire. The Indians were vigorously repulsed, but next morning great numbers of the hostiles were seen on the hills near camp. On the 7th the troops overtook a party of Yakimas under Chief Skloom. This chief would make no promises of peace or consider any terms without first consulting Kamiakin and others of the leading chiefs. A messenger was sent to invite them to parley.

Colonel Wright waited all day on the 8th without results and on the morning of May 9th set out to the north with his command. Indian messengers followed him but he moved on to the Naches River, from where he sent word that he would receive the chiefs in his new location. The Colonel's courier found Chiefs Skloom, Showaway, Owhi, Teies, and Kamiakin holding council and being addressed by young Peu-peu-mox-mox, Chief of the Walla Wallas, who urged that the tribesmen continue the war until autumn. The council decided against visiting Wright that day although several messengers were sent to the Colonel. Finally Wright notified Kamiakin that unless the Indians wanted to treat for peace that there was no point in interchanging messages and, further, that unless peace purposes were indicated that he would begin firing on any Indians who approached within range. Thereupon Kamiakin sent word that all the chiefs wanted peace and that they would call upon the Colonel the following day, first sending their warriors away. The morning of May 10th came and a large movement of Indians was observed traveling northward but no chiefs appeared at Wright's camp.The Colonel sent a detachment of dragoons to locate a place where the Naches River could be forded but the stream was high and the search was unsuccessful. That night a friendly Klickitat told Wright that only two chiefs, namely Skloom and Showaway, wanted peace, that the majority favored war, and that the camp would be attacked either that night or early on the 11th. At this information Wright sent a courier to Lieutenant-Colonel Steptoe asking for a joining of the two forces on the Columbia River.

Affairs remained in status quo until the 15th when a number of Indians came to the opposite bank of the Naches River with the information that most of the chiefs were assembled and wished to talk. Several days passed during which a number of chiefs came into camp to talk with Wright but Kamiakin was not one of them.

It began to seem clear that the Indians were stalling for time, their purpose being to lay in a supply of salmon for the coming winter. The salmon run up the tributaries of the Columbia had not started and Wright wanted to conclude a peace treaty when the Indians were without assurance of food for a long campaign.

On May 27th Steptoe's troops came up, the combined regular force thus numbering 500 plus those necessary for the ammunition and supply trains. Earth fortifications were erected on the Naches River to protect the reserve supplies and to shield the 60 or more men to be left as a guard. A temporary bridge was thrown across the river so that the troops could reach the Indians' favorite fishing places on the nearby streams. Joel Palmer was still Superintendent of Indian Affairs. Wright sent the friendly Klickitats to reservation and advised Palmer to similarly dispose of the Cascade Indians, Wright's plan being to clear the region of all but hostiles and then crush them in a single battle.

The chiefs continued to spar for time. Many messengers expressing a desire for peace filtered into Wright's camp and finally about mid-June Wright sent word that if the chiefs really wanted peace they would have to come in and talk it over. Chiefs Owhi and Teies complied and said that the cause of the war was the treaty of Walla Walla which had been more or less forced on them by Governor Stevens, Superintendent Palmer, and the military officers who had accompanied them. Wright replied that the Indians had nothing to gain by war; that if they continued fighting all the braves would be killed and their women and children would starve. The Colonel said that he was their friend and informed the two chiefs that it was his order that all the chiefs come into his camp within five days during which the property plundered from immigrants should be turned over to the troops and a peace talk held. But the order was not obeyed. All the chiefs did not come in. The Oregon Volunteers were still in the Palouse country and Skloom and Showaway had gone there, leaving their women and children with Chief Owhi.

So, the five days having passed, Wright took the field. He moved to the Yakima River leaving Steptoe at the Naches fortification with three companies and a howitzer. Wright marched about 200 miles and collected a number of Indian women, children, and old men and sent them to the reservation in Oregon. Aside from that task he accomplished little except perhaps for the fact that he met with an old chief named Nikatani who told him of the role played by Kamiakin and others in the attack on the Cascades. From that information it appeared that Kamiakin had sent about 30 of his young warriors to the Klickitat tribe, ordering them to influence the Cascade Indians to join in the attack. His instructions were to await until both steamboats were tied up at the Cascades, then attack, burn the boats, thus cutting off escape and aid, kill all the whites from the Upper to the Lower Cascades, and then await further orders. It developed that about 20 young Klickitats joined the Yakimas and all proceeded on the mission to influence the Cascade Indians. Most of the Cascade chiefs refused to cooperate but many of their young warriors joined in the attack with the results already detailed. Nikatani said that two Cascade chiefs, Chenoweth and Banahi, had set fire to their own houses to make it appear that they had been attacked and then took part in the massacre.

In the meantime, as indicated elsewhere, Governor Stevens had been busy west of the Cascade Mountains. In mid-April, 1856, there had been the general uprising in the Puget Sound country, inspired by Kamiakin's agents. The settlers in the valleys all fled to the more populous centers. Seattle was besieged and was saved only by the providential appearance of United States gunboats. The Indians murdered anyone caught out alone. Conditions were serious. Fortunately, Stevens knew what to do and lost no time about it. Having cleared up the Seattle situation with the aid of the navy, he sent a battalion of Washington Volunteers under Colonel B. F. Shaw to reinforce the Oregon Volunteers east of the mountains. Again General Wool had instructed his officers to oppose the volunteer plan but Stevens understood the current needs as well as he understood the character of General Wool.

Colonel Shaw crossed the Cascade Mountains at the Naches Pass and joined Colonel Wright's force on the Naches River, but Wright declined Shaw's services so the latter marched to the valley of the Walla Walla with his command except for 75 men who joined the Oregon Rangers under Major Davis Layton. The latter force marched through the John Day country capturing Indians and sending them to the reservation, keeping the Indians' horses. These expeditions under Wright, Shaw, and Layton gradually deprived the Indians of their means of livelihood, the taking of the horses, particularly, minimizing the opportunities for depredations or aid to the active hostiles. More than 900 of the Wasco, Tygh, DesChutes, and John Day tribes surrendered and all of them were placed on the Warm Springs Reservation in Oregon. However, the Cayuse, Walla Wallas, and a few sympathetic Nez Perces were still fighting.

Governor Stevens, as will be remembered, was also Superintendent of Indian Affairs for Washington Territory and prepared for the annual distribution of goods to the tribes who had remained friendly. He sent word to William Craig, Indian Agent, to invite the Coeur d'Alenes and the Spokanes to join the main body of Nez Perces in the latter's country for a council. Craig was also still a Lieutenant-Colonel of Washington Volunteers and currently in command of a picked force of Nez Perce chiefs and principal men numbering about 60. On May 27, 1856, he sent a letter to Stevens giving a personal appraisal of the situation in his district. In effect the report recited that most of the tribes had joined in the war, their goal being to exterminate the whites and any Indians who remained friendly to the settlers. Craig pointed out that promised supplies had not reached him and that ammunition was in short supply. He said that he would be compelled to flee with his Indian allies if help did not arrive soon and begged for at least two companies of volunteers.

This appeal resulted in immediate action. Captain Goff's command escorted a supply train from The Dalles to Walla Walla. On July 8th there were 290 men under Shaw and 60 Nez Perces under Craig and Chief Spotted Eagle in the Walla Walla Valley. A pack train of 100 animals was sent to the Nez Perce country under the charge of Special Indian Agent Robie.

Shaw's instructions from Stevens were to overlook no opportunity to subdue the hostiles. So Shaw, learning that a large force of hostiles had congregated in the Grand Ronde country, decided to attack them. This he did on July 17th, defeating the Indians decisively and inflicting heavy casualties. He captured many horses and some ammunition, and destroyed the Indians' food supplies. Meanwhile Major Layton was on the Snake River fighting small bands of hostiles wherever found. All of this campaigning had the effect of nullifying the influence of the Spokanes over the Nez Perce tribe, but it was a fact that the Spokanes had been successful in considerable measure with the Nez Perces in the absence of the 60 chiefs and other principal men under Craig. So great, indeed, was that influence that when Special Agent Robie arrived with his pack train he was ordered out of the Nez Perce country and marched back the 100 miles without a halt.

After Shaw's victory at the Grand Ronde he sent an emissary to the Nez Perces saying that he was their friend but that if they wanted war he would see that they got it. As a result the Nez Perces sent messengers insisting that their friendship for the whites was firm.

The Oregon Volunteer units finished their service in August and the Washington Volunteers in early September, which marked the end of the active participation of volunteers in the Yakima War. Colonel Wright notified Governor Stevens that four companies of regulars under Lieutenant-Colonel Steptoe would be sent to occupy the Walla Walla country.

When Governor Stevens learned that the Nez Perces had refused the supplies sent to them and that only Chief Lawyer of the leaders remaining at home would acknowledge treaty obligations, he instructed Shaw to send messengers to all tribes, friendly or hostile, to meet the Governor on September 25th, but with the condition that the hostiles would surrender unconditionally. Stevens asked Wright to be present with three companies of regulars but Wright refused.

So Stevens set out on August 19th from The Dalles. He had 30 wagons, 80 oxen, and 200 other animals, and no escort except the supply train employees. About 48 hours behind him came the baggage and supply train of the regulars under Steptoe. Stevens arrived in the Walla Walla Valley on the 23rd and immediately sent messengers to all the tribes telling them of his plan to meet with them for final settlement of their difficulties. Several days passed before the first Indians appeared. They comprised a group of Nez Perces accompanied by Agent Craig. A week later others of the Nez Perces came in. Following them was Father Ravelli, whose station was at the Coeur d'Alene Mission and who said that Kamiakin, Owhi, and Qualchin, all Yakima chiefs, refused to come to the council. Kamiakin's home bordered the land of the Spokanes, who were much influenced by him and who also refused to attend. The rest of the northern tribes followed the pattern set by the Spokanes. On September 10th the Cayuses arrived with some of their allies and camped near the Nez Perces but did not extend the courtesy of the usual ceremonial visit to Governor Stevens. The Cayuses had recently captured a pack train on its way to Colonel Shaw's troops and had burned the grass off the country through which they had traveled so that any mounted troops would find no subsistence for their horses.

Stevens moved his camp six miles to be near to Steptoe's command as the Governor feared an attack. The council, vastly smaller than had been hoped, opened on September 11th and lasted until the 18th. Nothing was accomplished, partly because the regular army officers, under General Wool's direction, refused to back up Governor Stevens, so the latter decided to return to The Dalles. He was escorted by some of Colonel Shaw's troops under Captain Goff. On the 19th and on the 20th the Indians attacked them several times and the result would have been disastrous except that Lieutenant-Colonel Steptoe brought up his troops and turned the tide, losing two of his soldiers in the battle. Subsequently General Wool reprimanded Steptoe for acting as an escort to volunteers.

Governor Stevens went back to the Puget Sound country. General Wool wrote his superiors of the Governor's return saying that he hoped the Governor would remain at home but that he anticipated that Stevens would attempt to renew the war. The General wrote a long report, often departing from the facts, and placing all the blame he could on Governor Stevens for the unsettled conditions of the territory.

Colonel Wright went to Walla Walla and called a council. Only five chiefs obeyed the summons, three of them being Cayuses and two Nez Perces. All the Yakima, Spokane, Walla Walla, and DesChutes chiefs ignored the summons entirely. Wright held his abbreviated council and reported that he was well satisfied with the statements of the chiefs present that they wanted only peace and quiet and that the treaty which Stevens had made in December, 1855, had caused all the hostilities.

Governor Stevens also made a report to the Secretary of War in which he criticized Colonel Wright for usurping the duties of the Superintendent of Indian Affairs and accused Wright of weakening the influence of the Bureau of Indian Affairs.

By November 20th Colonel Wright had established Fort Walla Walla. He placed Lieutenant-Colonel Steptoe in charge, Wright himself returning to The Dalles. There Wright arranged for water transport of supplies on the Upper Columbia, the forerunner of commercial navigation enterprises there. He strengthened military defenses of The Dalles and redistributed his forces, all of whom spent the winter of 1856-57 without further Indian trouble.

THE COEUR D'ALENE WAR

THE FINAL PHASE OF THE YAKIMA WAR

A MATTER to be remarked is the variation in designations of the names of Indian wars of the Pacific Northwest. In some cases there is complete acceptance of a single designation. In those instances the fighting was entirely between the whites and a single tribe, or tribes which were blood relatives. Under other conditions the transition from one to another was not clearly defined, the blending of one series of hostilities often being overlaid by periods of inactivity or witnessing the passing of the warfare from the initiating tribe to some other tribe or combination of tribes.

Hence it has been rather common practice to call the final phase of the Yakima War, the Coeur d'Alene War. Actually it might just as readily have been known as the Palouse War or the Spokane War because the first major engagement was precipitated by Indian allies in which the Palouse predominated numerically and the more important battles were fought in the country of the Spokanes. It is true that the Coeur d'Alenes were always among the warring Indian allies and were probably the most reluctant to treat for peace and that much of the diplomatic strategy hinged upon bringing the Coeur d'Alenes under treaty. So it is this author's opinion that the so-called Coeur d'Alene War was, in fact, the final phase of the Yakima War, as shown in the chapter heading. All of which has no effect historically, except that the count of Pacific Northwest Indian Wars would become seven instead of eight.

In the spring of 1857 an economy wave struck the Bureau of Indian Affairs. The job of Isaac I. Stevens as Superintendent of Indian Affairs for Washington Territory and the similar position of Joel Palmer for Oregon, were combined under J. W. Nesmith of Oregon, who had back of him a fine record as Colonel of Volunteers. A change, welcomed generally, also occurred in the high command of the regular army, through the replacement of General Wool by General Newman S. Clarke, who arrived in the Columbia River in June, 1857.

General Clarke was, of course, familiar with the reports which General Wool had forwarded to the War Department from time to time, and accepted them as factual. Clarke increased the number of regular troops and re-assigned them. Three companies of the 9th Infantry under Major R. S. Garnett were stationed at Fort Simcoe among the Yakimas. Three more companies of the 9th were sent to The Dalles where Colonel Wright was in charge. Four companies were assigned to Lieutenant-Colonel Steptoe at Walla Walla. These four companies were a company each from the 4th and 9th regiments, a company of the 1st Dragoons, and a company of the 3rd Field Artillery. To Steptoe's force another company was added in the fall, that of Captain A. J. Smith, which had been stationed in Southern Oregon.

General Clarke gradually became aware of the facts surrounding conditions, concluding at last that there was a side to the story which differed from that of General Wool and that instead of the peaceful attitude of the Indians as stressed by his predecessor, that it would be necessary to take aggressive action against the erstwhile hostiles.

Thus things drifted along during the winter of 1857-58. In April of the latter year Steptoe reported that an expedition into the Colville country was indicated. Two white men had been murdered by Palouse Indians while traveling to the Colville mining district. The Palouse had raided the Walla Walla Valley and had driven off government cattle, and a petition signed by 40 settlers in the Colville district had urged that troops be sent there.

On May 6, 1858 Steptoe set out with 130 dragoons intending to make a leisurely trip here and there to impress the tribes with the fact that United States regulars were stationed in their country. Anticipating no trouble and not setting out as a punitive expedition, his troopers were armed only with light weapons. He first went to the Nez Perce country. There the Nez Perce chief, Timothy, agreed to act as guide and, with his tribesmen, assisted in ferrying Steptoe's command across the Snake River. They soon came across a party of Palouse who reportedly were the murderers of the two white men on the Colville road, but those Indians fled. Proceeding northward Steptoe received word on the 16th that the Spokanes were gathering to intercept him. He gave little credence to the report and kept going until he discovered that he had been surrounded by 600 Indians stationed close to a ravine through which his line of march would take him. These Indians were Palouse, Spokanes, Coeur d'Alenes, and a few dissident Nez Perces. Steptoe halted and held a parley with the Spokanes, who told him that they understood that he had come to make war and that they would not permit him to cross the Spokane River. Steptoe believed that the Indians meant what they said and concluded that no matter what he did he was in for trouble. He avoided the ravine and camped on the shore of a small lake. The Indians traveled at his flank and tried by abusive language and signs to provoke a fight. No shots were fired, each side waiting for the other to commit the first overt act. Steptoe was unwilling to start anything because of the light armament of his troopers.

About four o'clock in the afternoon several chiefs rode up to the soldiers' camp and asked Steptoe what his business was in their country. He told them that he was on his way to Colville to look into recent depredations there. The Chiefs departed leaving the impression that they believed the explanation but actually pointing out to each other and to Father Joset, their priest, that Steptoe was off the regular route to Colville. While that was a fact, Steptoe was unaware of it, having trusted his guide to lead the way.

Steptoe considered his situation. He was sure that should he attempt to cross the Spokane River that the Indians would fight. He knew that he was not equipped for a battle so he decided to retreat. On the morning of May 17th, he started for Walla Walla. But the Indians had ideas of their own. Before starting Father Joset had talked with Steptoe, offering to explain the hostile attitude of the Indians, but Steptoe wanted to get started and invited the priest and the principal chiefs of the Spokanes and the Couer d'Alenes to ride along and talk as they rode. None of the Spokane chiefs accepted the invitation but the head chief of the Coeur d'Alenes, Vincent, joined Steptoe and Father Joset. Then some Palouses began firing at the dragoons and Chief Vincent was called to his people. Immediately firing became general.

The battle followed an old pattern. Troops guarding the supply train as they rode; Indians dashing up or riding by and firing; troops returning the fire. The soldiers reached a creek and prepared to ford. The Indians closed in on the head of the column. Steptoe ordered Lieutenant Gregg with one company to occupy a hill. This was done but the Indians took a position on a higher hill. Gregg divided his company, one platoon driving the Indians from their hill. The fighting became general and more intense. Company A tried to reinforce Gregg's position. The Indians decided to prevent that effort. Lieutenant William

Gaston saw this maneuver and though 1000 yards away dashed to intercept the Indians. He was joined by Gregg's platoon from the hill and the Indians lost nine killed, one of whom was Chief Vincent's brother-in-law. Chief Victor of the Coeur d'Alenes was mortally wounded and many others less severely. Instead of stopping the Coeur d'Alenes or slowing them up, fighting was harder. Captain Oliver Taylor and Lieutenant William Gaston were killed. With the loss of these officers the troopers became confused but succeeded in carrying off the bodies of their dead.

By this time it was noon. The nearest water was the Palouse River, many hours away. Steptoe occupied a broad hill, since known as Steptoe Butte. The dragoons picketed their horses and then, from prone position, defended their hill. Toward evening the ammunition began to run out. The men were tired and very thirsty. Six would never fight again; eleven others were wounded. Darkness came. The dead were buried. The best horses were selected and stealthily Steptoe and his dragoons slipped away. On the morning of May 19th they crossed the Snake River, thence to Walla Walla. The regular army had lost face.

When Steptoe's retreat started, Father Joset told him that for three years the Coeur d'Alenes had sworn that no white settlers could stay in their country and that no road could be built through it. They had heard of the road to be built by Lieutenant John Mullan, the report of which project enraged them and they then determined that they would oppose any troops sent to Colville. General Clarke, through Father Joset, offered to treat with the chiefs. The Coeur d'Alenes were elated over the defeat of Steptoe and refused to listen to overtures of peace. The other tribes followed the lead of the Coeur d'Alenes.

In June, 1858, General Clarke held a conference with his officers, Wright and Steptoe being present. The General decided that he would settle the issue at once and for all time. He brought three companies of artillery from San Francisco, a company of infantry from Fort Jones in California, and another infantry company from Fort Umpqua in Oregon as additions to his existing force. Two expeditions were prepared. The main force, under Colonel Wright, trained at Walla Walla. Most of the artillery was instructed in infantry tactics, the rest as mounted artillery. The second expedition was commanded by Major R. S. Garnett. That force numbered 300 men and was to move on August 15th through the Yakima country to Colville and drive the hostiles it

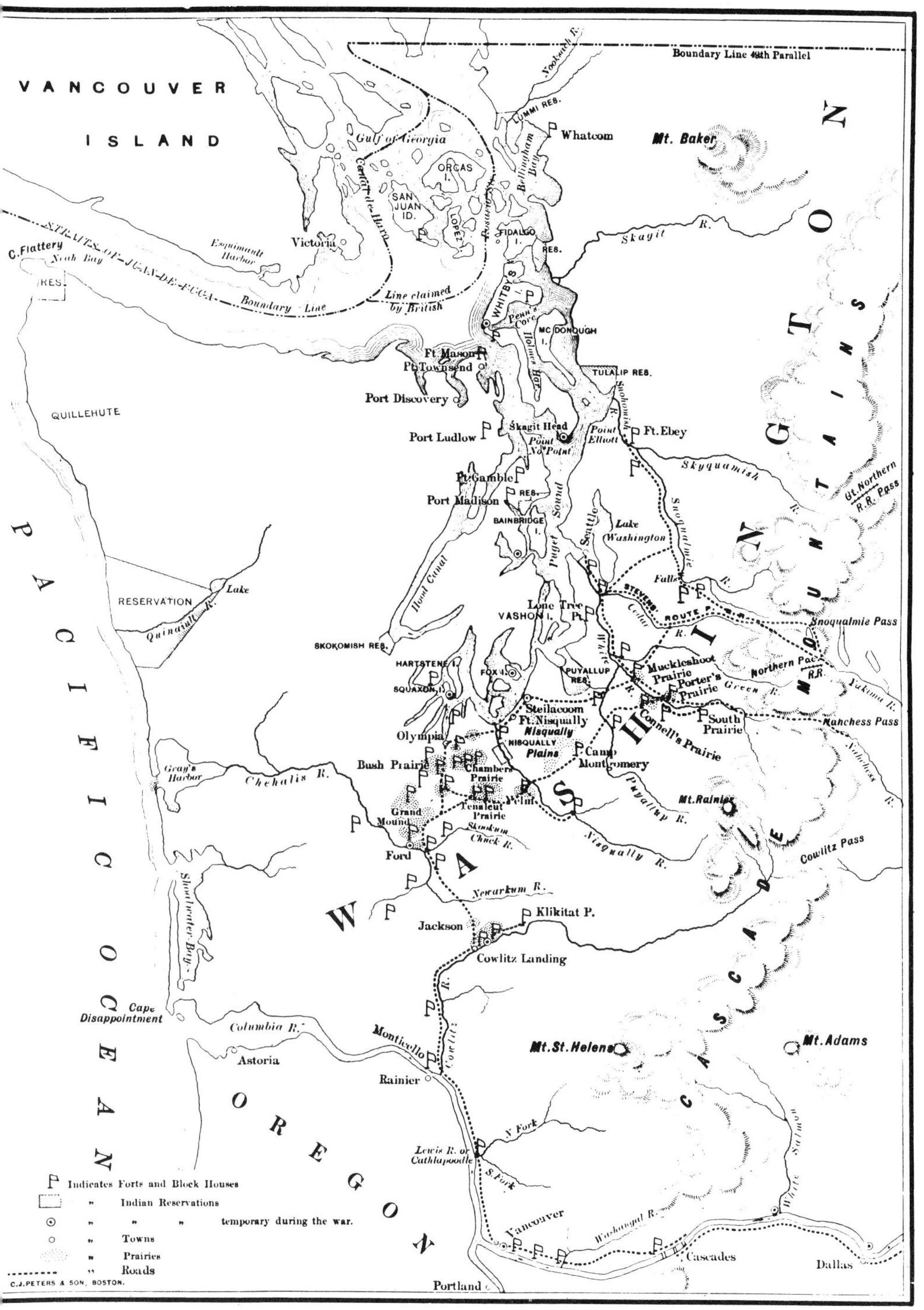

Theater of Indian Wars of 1855-56 on Puget Sound and West of the Cascades

"Often designated as 'The Battles of Puget Sound' they were really a part of the Yakima War. . . . The Indians who lived on several of the Puget Sound rivers, namely, the Snoqualmie, Nisqually, Puyallup, Cowlitz, Cedar, Green, and White rivers, were all related to the Yakimas." (page 127)

General George Wright

"As Wright's men approached, the Indians set fire to the grass, the wind carrying the flames and smoke towards the troops." (page 148)

Lt.-Col. Edward J. Steptoe

"When Steptoe's retreat started, Father Joset told him that for three years the Coeur d'Alenes had sworn that no white settlers could stay in their country and that no road could be built through it." (page 146)

encountered southward toward Wright's force, which strategy would catch the Indians in a pincers movement.

On August 7th Captain E. D. Keys was sent ahead with a force of dragoons to erect a fortification where the Tucannon River empties into the Snake. The place was named Fort Taylor in memory of Captain Oliver H. Taylor killed during Steptoe's retreat. On the 18th Wright arrived at Fort Taylor with his command. He had 400 artillerymen trained as infantry, a rifle brigade of 90 infantrymen, and 200 dragoons. Moreover, the riflemen were armed with the new Sharp's rifles, which the Indians knew nothing about and which were to cost them dearly because of the increased range of this new weapon.

Before starting his march, Colonel Wright had concluded a treaty with the Nez Perces, signed by himself for the United States, and by Chiefs Timothy, Richard, Three Feathers, and Speaking Eagle for the tribesmen. Thirty Nez Perce warriors volunteered for service as scouts and were outfitted in army uniforms and placed under the command of Lieutenant John Mullan, whose road-building had been interrupted by the war.

Wright moved northward. On August 31st he was within 20 miles of the Spokane River. Bands of hostiles appeared along the hillsides and exchanged shots with the Nez Perce scouts. The hostiles tried to set fire to the grass but without much success.

Concluding that the main force of the enemy was not far distant,Wright decided to rest his men and camped at Four Lakes. Again the Indians had ideas of their own. On the morning of September 1st they assembled on a hill about two miles from the camp of the troops. Wright wasted no time. He left one company of artillerymen and 54 infantrymen with a howitzer in camp under the command of Captain J. A. Hardie. The rest of his force advanced. It consisted of two squadrons of dragoons under Major W. N. Grier; four companies of artillerymen armed as infantry under Brevet-Major E. D. Keyes; two companies of riflemen under Captain F.T. Dent; and the Nez Perce scouts commanded by Lieutenant John Mullan. Major Grier took his dragoons around to the northeast of the hill. The foot soldiers advanced by the easier slopes to drive the Indians toward the cavalry. No one knows how many Indians had assembled but they were everywhere—in the ravines, in the woods, on the hills, on the plain. One officer later reported that "they seemed to cover the country for two miles." They were gaudily painted, their horses were decorated with strings of beads and eagle feathers. Most of them carried muskets, but some of them were armed only with bows and arrows or spears. They rode about, brandishing their weapons and yelling defiance.

The troops advanced. When within 600 yards they opened fire. The Indians would ride forward, fire, and ride away. But they had not reckoned with the Sharp's rifles and minie balls. Their warriors began to fall, only to be picked up and carried away as was the Indian custom. The soldiers kept advancing and firing with telling effect. The Indians broke toward the plain. The dragoons charged and in the best tradition of trained cavalrymen, cut the hostiles down with their sabers. The Indians fled for the wooded hills, this time leaving their dead. In the woods they were in less danger from the cavalry and besides the dragoons' horses were worn out, not only from the furious charge but also because of almost a solid month on the march. The foot soldiers came up, passed through the ranks of the cavalrymen and drove the Indians for two miles, until the soldiers, too, were exhausted.

The troops lost neither man nor horse. They stayed in camp for three days and on September 5th again resumed their march toward the north. After moving five miles they came upon the hostiles who had taken a position at the edge of the timber and evidently were prepared to attack. As Wright's men approached the Indians set fire to the grass, the wind carrying the flames and smoke towards the troops. In great numbers the Indians came out upon the plain, forming a huge semi-circle. Wright assigned a strong guard to the supply train; the foot soldiers deployed to the flanks, dashed through the burning grass and drove the Indians back to the woods. Then the howitzers cut loose, driving the hostiles deeper among the trees. The soldiers followed. These tactics were repeated several times until the Indians had been driven four miles. The forest ended there and the braves were chased out into the plain again. It was once more the cavalry's turn. The dragoons charged. Their sabers ran red with the blood of Indians. The hostiles were driven back but they courageously fought at every backward step. Again they reached trees. From this advantageous cover they harassed the troops from many points of concealment but the soldiers were not to be denied. Again the howitzers went into action. Again the chase was resumed. This running battle continued for 14 miles until the Spokane River was reached. The river was welcome. The troops had been without water since morning. The only soldier casualty was one man slightly wounded. The Indians suffered heavily but, as was always their custom whenever possible, they carried away their dead to prevent their enemy from taking scalps. However it was known that two Coeur d'Alene chiefs were killed as were two chiefs of the Spokanes; and the ring-leader, Kamiakin, Chief of the Yakimas, was injured when a tree-top, dislodged by a howitzer shell, fell on his head. The Indians also burned one of their villages rather than permit it to suffer that fate at the hands of the soldiers.

Wright rested his troops for a day. They were not attacked but many Indians appeared on the far side of the river. About to resume his march on September 7th, the Indians let it be known that they wished to hold a parley, to which Wright consented. The Indian delegation was headed by Chief Garry of the Spokanes, Garry always having been known as a peace man but who had been overruled by the majority of his people in their decision to wage war. Again let it be emphasized that Indian chiefs were not absolute monarchs, at least in the Pacific Northwest country. Their tribesmen could overrule their decisions by popular vote. While Wright knew Garry's reputation for peace he nevertheless was stern and unrelenting. He told Garry that the soldiers were there to fight, not to talk; that as often as the hostiles chose to fight, just that often would he defeat them; that whenever they tired of fighting the surrender would be on Wright's unconditional terms, namely, the surrender of all arms and property, and all the women and children. Otherwise, said Wright, he would continue to engage the hostiles until they were exterminated.

Garry took the ultimatum back to the tribes but he did not return with an answer. Instead, another chief of the Spokanes, Polatkin, appeared with nine warriors to argue for terms. Wright told him the same conditions as had been outlined to Chief Garry. Knowing that Chief Polatkin had helped to defeat Steptoe, Wright kept Polatkin in custody and sent some of his braves back to tell the hostiles to come in to surrender. This brought no affirmative result so Wright took up his march on the 8th. After nine miles the Indians were to be seen driving all their live stock toward the mountains. Wright engaged them and captured 800 horses which were taken into camp 16 miles above Spokane Falls. There one of Polatkin's braves was tried for certain murders, convicted and hanged. Most of the captured horses had never been saddled, so Wright determined to kill all the animals not immediately useful, and this was done on September 9th and 10th. Thus the Spokane Nation was largely dismounted and the Spokane chief, Big Star, surrendered with his people on

Wright's announced terms. The Coeur d'Alenes decided to do likewise and they were instructed to assemble for their surrender at the Catholic Mission on Lake Coeur d'Alene, where a council was held on September 17th. Father Joset was present and Chief Vincent was the official spokesman for his tribe. Wright demanded the surrender of the warriors who started the attack on Steptoe, they to be sent to General Clarke; one Chief and four warriors, with their families, to be sent to Walla Walla; the return of all property taken from Steptoe's command; agreement that white people could pass safely through the country; that they forever refrain from hostilities against the whites; and that they remain at peace with the Nez Perces. These terms being accepted, the treaty was reduced to writing and signed. The peace pipe was smoked and Wright next called another council, this time for the Spokanes for September 23rd, to which he also invited Kamiakin. But that wily Chief of the Yakimas failed to appear. Next day the Yakima chief, Owhi, came into camp. Wright had him arrested for breaking his agreement made two years earlier and ordered him to send for his son Qualchin, warning that if Qualchin did not appear that Owhi, himself, would be hanged. Before Owhi could send for his son, Qualchin rode into camp and was promptly seized and hanged.

Wright started his return march taking Owhi with him. Near the Snake River Owhi tried to escape and was shot by Lieutenant Morgan, the chief dying in a few hours. The only high chiefs of the Yakimas who were now left were Kamiakin and Skloom. Kamiakin abandoned his people and fled to British Columbia. Skloom, having lost his prestige, was gradually forgotten.

Colonel Wright refused to make a treaty with the Palouses. He considered them to be incapable of living up to the terms of a treaty. Instead he hanged several of them. Wright ordered Fort Taylor abandoned on October 1st, and its garrison, together with the rest of Wright's command, all returned to Walla Walla on October 5th.

On October 9, 1858, Wright ordered the Walla Wallas assembled. They came in and the Colonel ordered all who had participated in the recent fighting to stand. Only 35 arose, but from that number Wright selected four, who were delivered to the guard, and peremptorily hanged.

This Walla Walla episode closed the war. By military order the Yakima country was closed to settlement until the following year, 1859, when General Harney succeeded General Clarke and reopened the Columbia country to settlers.

THE MODOC WAR

THE GATHERING STORM

THE Modoc Indians called themselves MAKLAKS, meaning "the people," and Captain Jack, their principal leader in the war of 1873, was KIENTEPOOS in their own language. His name has several variations, among which are Kientepoos, Kintupash, and Kintpuash. The Modocs comprised a branch of the once powerful Pacific Coast tribe known as LALACAS and belonged to the LUTUAMIAN linguistic stock, the same as the Klamaths. The Lalacas inhabited the country around the Klamath lakes and in the Lost River basin as well as a large area drained by the Klamath River. Their country extended inland from the Pacific Coast about 300 miles and included what are now parts of Curry, Josephine, Jackson, and Klamath counties in Oregon, and Del Norte and Siskiyou counties in California.

The Lalacas were warlike, and at about the time of the American Revolution underwent a rebellion which resulted in division of the nation into two tribes, the Klamaths and the Modocs. In their native condition Indian nations were divided into tribes, the tribes into bands, and the bands into families. At the time of the rebellion the Modocs were living in a rather restricted area in the Lost River Basin in extreme Northern California near Tule Lake and just southeast of Klamath Lake in Oregon. Their country abounded in fish and game, edible plants and roots. For Indians their lot was an easy one. The head chief of the Lalacas made a demand upon Mo-a-doc-us, the chief of the Lost River tribe, not only for fighting men to go on the warpath —but also for supplies of Lost River fish being furnished. The first part of the demand was a normal one but that for the fish was not and Moadocus issued a declaration of independence and renounced all allegiance to the head chief of the Lalacas. A great internecine war ensued in which Moadocus and his tribesmen ultimately triumphed.

At the time of the earliest white immigrations into Oregon and California, the Modocs numbered about 600 souls with Schonchin as head chief. There seems to have been some dispute among the various bands regarding his chieftainship on the ground that he was not a legitimate descendant of Moadocus and hence not of royal blood. But Schonchin, known as "Old" Schonchin, to distinguish him from his brother John, had won his place by great personal bravery in battle. He had also fought the whites in early battles but by the time of the Modoc War he was tired of fighting and had settled down at Yainax Reservation with a part of the tribe and kept strictly neutral while his brother John and Captain Jack were fighting the Federal troops. On the other hand, Captain Jack was of royal blood. His father had been chief of the Lost River Indians and had lost his life in a battle with the Warm Springs and Tenino Indians near the headwaters of the Deschutes River in Oregon when Jack was a small boy. Captain Jack received that name in 1864 from Elisha Steele, Acting Superintendent of Indian Affairs for Northern California, because of Jack's resemblance to a miner known as "Captain Jack." Kientepoos (Captain Jack) was born on Lost River and said that he would never speak any language but Modoc and apparently kept his word, though it is believed that he later came to understand a considerable number of English words and phrases.

The Modocs had a history of major troubles with immigrants and settlers for 20 years prior to their final war. There remain the usual differences of opinion between those who represent the Modocs as wanton killers and the apologists who insist that there was plenty of provocation by the whites. Old Chief Schonchin said that the trouble arose because the whites did not distinguish between the Modocs, the Snakes, and the Pit River Indians. It seems that in passing through the Snake River country the Snakes stole or captured horses and mules from the immigrants and either sold the animals or lost them in gambling to the Pit River Indians. In turn the latter, through the same processes, transferred the horses and mules to the Modocs. Later, some of the animals in possession of the Modocs were identified and retaken, thus giving cause for bloodshed and war.

At any rate, in September, 1852, a wagon train with 65 men, women, and children was approaching the point on Tule Lake where the emigrant road had to touch the shore by reason of the contour of the land. The Modocs were hidden in the rocks overlooking the trail. With typical suddenness the Indians attacked. Sixty-two whites were massacred with all the savagery known to the hostiles. In fact they outdid themselves in fiendishness and tortures of unprintable character. Two young girls, aged 12 and 14, were held as captives by the Indians, and one man somehow escaped. The location of the massacre has ever since been known as "Bloody Point." The two girls survived for several years, became reconciled to their fate and adopted the manners and customs of their captors. However, eventually the Modoc women became jealous and threw the two white girls to their deaths from a cliff.

Ben Wright, an esteemed citizen and natural leader of Yreka, California, was chosen to command a company of volunteers to punish the Indians. While the Bloody Point massacre was reason enough to launch a punitive expedition, it was merely the culmination of a series of lesser attacks, murders and robberies

Again we are faced with two versions of an episode in history, this time over what was thereafter to be known as the "Ben Wright Affair." Wright's friends always contended that he committed no act of treachery, but the preponderance of evidence would seem to be on the other side. There were persons who stated positively that Wright purchased strychnine with the avowed intention of poisoning the Indians. Be that as it may, he set out with his company of volunteers and after reaching the Modoc country invited the Indians to come in to a parley under a flag of truce. A feast was prepared but the Indians declined to eat until the volunteers first partook of the food. Wright thereupon ordered his men to fire and about 40 Modocs were killed, the rest escaping. Had Wright exterminated the Modocs in battle, or had he ambushed them and killed all, no one would ever have censured him, but to violate a flag of truce under the pretence of a peace parley was something roundly condemned by the fair-minded public generally and his act was to bear bitter fruit in the Modoc War to follow 20 years later.

Hostilities continued for several years. In 1855 the pioneers with the Shastas as allies fought a battle with the Modocs. In that fray Joaquin Miller, later to be known as the Poet of the Sierras, was wounded in the head by an arrow and through the body by a bullet. He was nursed back to health by Sutatot, a Shasta maiden, who had lost two brothers in the battle.

In 1864 a lull occurred in the sporadic warfare, when Elisha Steele, of Yreka, who, at the time, was Acting Superintendent of Indian Affairs for Northern California, made an informal treaty with the Modocs. By its terms reference was made to the localities wherein certain tribes, including Modocs and Klamaths, might reside. The several tribes mentioned also agreed to keep peace with each other as well as with the whites. It was at that treaty council that Kientepoos was first recognized as a chief and it was then that Steele gave him the name "Captain Jack."

For some reason the Steele treaty was never recognized by the Federal Government. It has been suggested that the reason lay in the fact that the Oregon-California line bisected the Modoc country. Captain Jack and Old Schonchin lived on the Oregon side and each state had a Superintendent of Indian Affairs. At any rate, the Oregon Superintendent received orders to negotiate a treaty with the Indians in the Klamath country, including the Modocs. The council met in 1864, the Modocs being represented by Old Chief Schonchin and his brother John, afterwards known as Schonchin John. Captain Jack was given recognition as a sub-chief and thereafter he and Schonchin John were to be closely associated, although usually holding opposite points of view. Captain Jack signed the treaty by his Indian name Kientepoos. By the treaty terms the Klamaths and the Modocs were to be joint-occupants of the territory hence known as the Klamath Reservation. All other territory previously occupied by the two tribes was ceded to the United States in return for certain benefits which were to follow.

Captain Jack almost immediately regretted having signed the treaty and persuaded a part of the Modoc tribe to leave the reservation and return to the old home on Lost River. He at once began a series of efforts to convince various citizens, among them Acting Superintendent Steele, that the terms of the treaty had been misrepresented to him. Jack had confidence in Steele but subsequently took advantage of that confidence by saying that Steele had said that Jack was justified in leaving the reservation. As a matter of fact, Steele probably limited his statement to a promise to see what could be done. He did write several letters to the Department at Washington on the subject and even gave letters to Jack and other Modocs, but these letters merely recited Jack's own contentions and commended him to the friendly consideration of white people. There was nothing in any of this correspondence to indicate that Steele ever said anything which could have been construed to mean that Jack should have repudiated the treaty, or even that it could be repudiated.

So Jack and his followers stayed on Lost River, and Old Schonchin with the rest of the tribe remained on the reservation about six miles from Fort Klamath at the north end of Klamath Lake. In 1865 the white settlers of the Lost River Basin requested Captain MacGregor, the commandant at Fort Klamath, to return Jack and his tribesmen to the reservation. An effort to that end was made but it was unsuccessful, although no hostilities ensued. In 1866 Lindsay Applegate, sub-agent, tried to persuade the tribe to again move to the Klamath Reservation but his efforts also failed. In the following year, 1867, Superintendent Huntington went to confer with Jack for the same purpose. Upon Huntington's approach Captain Jack and his warriors took up a position on the far side of Lost River and yelled that if Huntington attempted to cross that they would fire on him. The Superintendent was not accompanied by troops and made no attempt to cross the river. He reported the incident, as had those engineering the previous attempts, but the Department failed to order any action. Captain Jack and his tribesmen stayed on Lost River.

In 1869 Alfred B. Meacham was Superintendent of Indian Affairs for Oregon. Late in that year he made an official visit to the Klamath Agency and after a talk with O. C. Knapp, the Indian Agent there, it was agreed that another attempt to relocate Captain Jack and his tribe should be made. Accordingly a courier was sent to Captain Jack notifying him that Meacham and Knapp would meet him at Link River. Jack told the courier that if they wanted to see him they would have to come to his country and that, furthermore, he had no wish to see the government's representatives.

Nevertheless, Meacham and Knapp decided to visit the Modoc country and, recognizing the possibility of attack, requested a guard of soldiers from Fort Klamath. The new commander, Captain Goodale, demurred, saying that he had no men to spare for that purpose but finally assigned a small squad under the command of a non-commissioned officer. Also in the party were I. D. Applegate and W. C. McKay, as well as teamsters, guides, interpreters, and two prominent Klamaths and two Klamath women. The party set out, the soldiers following. Instructions to the latter required that they stop at Link River, there to await further orders. On the morning of December 22, 1869, the principal members of the group quickened their pace, leaving the supply wagons to follow as rapidly as they could. From Link River they cut across country to the west bank of Lost River, which they were to follow to the Modoc village.

It, perhaps, would be well to explain that Lost River acquired its name from the fact that for a part of its length it disappeared underground, emerging again after several miles. This is not an uncommon trait of streams in lava country. Porous rock, subterranean caverns and tunnels are common and contribute to this quirk of nature. Lakes revert to marshes or go dry. There are many dry lakes today in the Pacific Northwest, which were sizeable bodies of water in pioneer times. A few have been drained by irrigation projects but most of them have disappeared naturally. Lost River connected Clear Lake with Tule Lake in Northern California, it being the outlet of the former and the inlet of the latter. It was narrow and deep with few places shallow enough for fording. One crossing was known as Natural Bridge, but was really a ledge about 20 feet wide, situated a mile downstream from Captain Jack's village. Depending upon the water stage of the stream it was alternately slightly above or below the surface of the river. As the party came within a few miles of the Indian village they saw four Indians approaching on ponies. Each was armed with a rifle and a pistol and the white men were ordered to halt. These Modocs demanded to know the purpose of the visit. Meacham told them that their mission was to see Captain Jack on important business. The Indians told him that the Modocs did not want to see anybody and warned the white men to turn back. Meacham and each of his men were armed with a Henry rifle and a navy six-shooter. Knowing that a bold front was often the best defense they swung around the Indians and, at a brisk pace, approached the Modoc town, consisting of 13 houses, each about 30 feet long and 12 feet wide.

The village seemed to be deserted, but one of the intercepting Indians, all four of whom had followed the white party to the town, ran up the crude steps outside the largest lodge and went inside. That was the home of the chief. Meacham's party dismounted and prepared to follow when an Indian look-out yelled, "One man come; no more." Meacham was ahead and knew that he could not turn back without indicating fear, although thoughts of Indian treachery occupied his mind. He entered, not knowing what to expect. Captain Jack stared at him, refusing to shake hands, speak, or smoke. A number of Indians were present. Meacham calmly lit his pipe and prepared to face a bad situation as best he could. Finally, Scarface Charley spoke, asking what Meacham wanted and telling him that Captain Jack would come to Meacham's home if he ever wanted to see him; that Jack did not want to talk; and that the white men should go away.

Meacham took the opportunity to tell the Modocs that he was the newly appointed Superintendent, sent by the President to talk about new subjects; that whether or not they were his friends, he was their friend; that he was neither afraid to talk nor to listen and emphasized the statement that he was indeed a big white chief. Then Captain Jack spoke saying that all whites were liars and swindlers; that he would not believe half that he heard, but that he would listen. Meacham then asked that other members of his party be admitted, which request was granted. Jack ordered a camp prepared for the white men but said that he had no provisions to share. The Indians selected a site, constructed a shelter, and brought in a plentiful supply of sage-brush for fuel. They caught fish in the river, roasted the fish for their visitors and left the white men for the night. One of Meacham's party was posted as guard and the others pretended to sleep but felt that they dare not.

Next morning the supply wagons came up and a feast was prepared to which the Indians were invited, but no Modoc would touch the food until the white men had eaten. The Indians explained that procedure in their remembrance of the Ben Wright affair. But filled with beef, bacon, hard bread, and coffee with sugar, the Modocs prepared to parley. Captain Jack had considered that as a probable outcome because he had sent for Frank Riddle, a white man who had married a Modoc girl, Winemah, known as Tobey, and Jack would not open the council until Riddle and Tobey had arrived. Meacham made the first speech, telling of the purposes of his visit, and produced the treaty of 1864 which Captain Jack promptly declared he had never signed. However, that statement was immediately disproved by the testimony of Old Schonchin and sub-chief Blo of the Klamaths, who were in Meacham's party.

The talk continued, Meacham pressing the point that Captain Jack should observe the treaty which he had signed and agree to go back to the reservation. Jack began to waver, asking what part of the reservation he was to occupy. The white men began to breathe easier, sensing agreement, when the Modoc medicine man arose and said in Modoc that "we will not go there." Immediately the whole aspect of things changed. The Indians announced that they were finished with talking. The whites expected attack. But Tobey arose and urged acceptance of Meacham's point of view. Captain Jack started to leave. Meacham intercepted him saying, "Don't leave me now; I am your friend but I am not afraid of you. Be careful what you do. We mean peace, but we are ready for war. We will not begin, but if you do, it shall be the end of your people. We came for you and we are not going back without you. You must go." Jack then asked what would happen if he refused. Meacham pointed to his own group and told Jack that if the latter refused that "we will whip you until you are willing." Jack replied that he would be ashamed to fight so few white men with all his warriors.

The argument waxed and waned until it was finally agreed that

Captain Jack should have until the following morning to give his answer. Jack withdrew for a pow-wow with his tribesmen and the white men were left to consider their plight. All knew that it was fraught with great danger. Under the pretense of looking for the horses a courier got away for the camp of the soldiers on Link River 25 miles away, with orders for them to move up to a point within hearing of gunfire should it occur at the Modoc village, but that unless they heard the noise of combat they were not to come in to Meacham's camp until the next morning.

The white men inspected their firearms and prepared to undergo another sleepless night. Captain Jack began his pow-wow and the medicine man "made medicine." The night wore on. Suddenly the soldiers burst into camp. Fortified with whiskey acquired at Link River they did not stop at the appointed place but rode headlong into camp. At once all was confusion. The council broke up. There Schonchin John had urged treachery and Captain Jack spoke against assassination, in fact he was speaking at the time the soldiers rode in. The Modocs took to the sagebrush with their rifles. The white men encircled the whole camp. Sunrise disclosed about 200 souls within the guard lines but some of the Modocs were not there, among them Captain Jack and Schonchin John. They had gone to the lava beds.

Meacham ordered the Indians to form a line, assuring them that no harm was contemplated, but the Modocs did not obey. Then a detail of soldiers was ordered to seize the Modocs' firearms. It was a tense moment but the arms were secured. Provisions were issued to the Indians and instructions given to bring in their ponies and prepare to move to the reservation.

Then Meacham met Captain Jack's sister. The white people had named her "Mary, Queen of the Modocs." She was very intelligent, probably leading the tribe in that respect, but had lived with five or six white men—with each only long enough to get hold of all the money and valuables she could. Mary appeared before Meacham to plead for her brother and said that if permitted she would go to the lava beds and persuade Jack to return. It was agreed that she should go, but accompanied by Meacham's guide, Gus Horn, to assure Captain Jack that no one had been harmed at his village and no harm would come to him.

A whole day was devoted to rounding up the Indian ponies, removing the food supplies from the caches, and the interchange of messages with the runaways who did not return. The following morning the village was abandoned and the cavalcade started for the reservation. By late evening they were at Link River. Ample provisions were provided for the hungry travelers and by nine o'clock the camp was snug and quiet. Messengers had been going back and forth all day between the reservation party and the lava beds. The camp did not move for three days, during which negotiations with Captain Jack continued; then on the third day he and his fellows came in after being assured that the Klamaths would not be permitted to make sport of him and call him a coward for running from such a small white force.

Upon Captain Jack's arrival it was decided to move on towards the Klamath reservation and on the morning of December 27th the start was made. At Jack's request the soldiers had been sent ahead. It was a face-saving gesture for Jack even though he had given as his reason for the request that the women and children were afraid of the soldiers.

The next day saw the group at Modoc Point on the reservation where they were met by a large delegation of agency Indians. The meeting was punctuated by an order from Meacham prohibiting gambling. The agency Indians resented the order but Meacham knew the mania for gambling which was characteristic of Indians and did not choose to see the consolidation nullified by the chance transfer of property which often included wives and daughters.

The second day following was set apart for a meeting of reconciliation between the Klamaths and the Modocs. Boundaries were established between the camps of the two tribes and a site designated for the meeting, which was well planned. Meacham knew the values of ceremony among Indians as well as the importance of spotlighting the principal personalities.

The proceedings were dignified and colorful. The Klamaths congregated beneath a huge pine tree and awaited the Modocs, who approached slowly. Arriving, Captain Jack took his stand a few feet from Chief Allen David. Meacham said, "You meet in peace today, to bury all the bad past, to make friends. You are of the same blood, of the same heart. You are to live as neighbors. This country belongs to you, all alike. Your interests are one. You can shake hands and be friends." A hatchet was then laid in the space separating the two chiefs, each of whom was given a pine branch. They advanced, each covering the hatchet with his pine bough, then placing his feet upon the boughs. They gazed at each other, shook hands, and stepped back. The sub-chiefs and other principal men of both tribes then advanced, two at a time, exchanging the pledge of friendship as had the head chiefs. Then Chief Allen David made a brilliant speech urging eternal friendship, to which Captain Jack replied with equal fervor and honesty.

Following that ceremony preparations were made to distribute goods to the Modocs as specified in the treaty of 1864, the agency Indians having previously received theirs. The distribution was made and the Modocs moved away to their camp to stow their new possessions and to prepare a feast from their new supplies of flour and beef.

The Klamaths visited the camp of their new neighbors, Meacham's teamsters built a big bonfire and the reunion of the two tribes of the once proud Lalacas was marked by an auspicious beginning.

An old man known as "Link River Joe" approached the bonfire where Meacham and an interpreter, Old Chief Schonchin, Captain Jack, Allen David, and others were smoking and chatting. Link River Joe had heard a sermon by the Methodist missionary Reverend A. F. Waller 20 years before and asked to have the white man's religion explained to him. Meacham undertook the explanation, which was followed by another question inquiring how the white men could predict an eclipse. Meacham made a good effort to explain that phenomenon when he remembered that it was New Year's Eve. Exhibiting his watch he told the Indians that when both "little sticks, the hands, were together at the top that the old year would die in the west and the new year would be born in the east. All the Indians present were interested and the news spread. Chief Allen David requested that since all could not be looking at the watch when the time arrived that Meacham fire a pistol at the great moment. At the pistol shot the crowd slowly dispersed and thus the year 1870 was ushered in at Klamath Reservation.

The following eleven weeks were trying ones for the Modocs. In spite of the good intentions of Chief Allen David and his peace-promoting speech, he did not have control over his tribesmen, particularly the younger men. Having selected a site for a permanent settlement at Modoc Point the Modocs began hewing logs and splitting rails. It had been thoroughly agreed between Agent Knapp, the Klamaths, and the Modocs that the latter were to share equally with the Klamaths in the use of timber, and the location of the village had been mutually agreed upon. But the Klamaths took some of the logs and rails saying, "the timber is ours. You may use some of it but it is ours and we want part of it." The quarrel continued until Captain Jack appealed to Knapp who told Jack that the matter would be made all right. But the quarrel was renewed, the Klamaths becoming more overbearing by reason of the fact that they were not reprimanded.

Captain Knapp was an excellent military man but with no liking for the duties of an Indian Agent, and, perhaps, an incomplete undertanding of the Indian character. Again Captain Jack appealed to Knapp who advised a change in site for the village, this time a few miles away on the Williamson River. The Modocs obeyed and were soon starting building operations all over again. There the Klamaths repeated their taunts and their appropriation of logs and rails. For the third time Jack appealed to Knapp, who proposed still another move to a location to be selected by Captain Jack. Jack started his search, but either because he could find none suitable or whether the Modocs were overwhelmed by their treatment by the Klamaths and the unsatisfactory administration by the Indian Agent, Jack decided to call a council of his people. The tribe voted by a large majority to leave the reservation. Some of Jack's Modocs elected to remain but most of them returned with Captain Jack to their old home on Lost River early in March, 1870. Jack renewed acquaintance with the less desirable element in the Yreka district and immediately received and accepted their sympathy, strengthening and confirming himself in justification for having left the reservation.

During the spring of 1871 the Indian Department and Old Chief Schonchin tried to induce Jack to return. In fact, a new location at Yai-nax, near the southern edge of the reservation, was offered. Old Chief Schonchin with his tribesmen and a few of Captain Jack's people did move to Yai-nax and remained there. Jack, himself, visited the place and seriously considered moving there. But while Jack was turning the subject over in his mind another incident occurred to upset a good idea.

Among primitive Indians the medicine man occupied a most important place. To him was attributed great power. He was credited with ability to render his callers invulnerable to bullets or arrows; to foretell events; to cause a personal enemy to sicken and die, as well as to cure those who were ill. In this latter field of endeavor, however, he often ran the risk of losing his own life. Such a situation developed while Captain Jack was considering moving to Yai-nax. Jack had employed an Indian doctor to treat a sick child and paid the doctor in advance. The child died and the life of the doctor was in the hands of the friends of the dead child. Captain Jack either killed the doctor or ordered him to be killed and, under Indian tribal law, that should have ended the matter, but friends of the dead doctor decided to invoke the white man's law. An unsuccessful attempt was made to arrest Captain Jack and the whole matter came to the attention of Superintendent Meacham. The country was in a state of alarm and Meacham knew that war might result. Captain Knapp had just been relieved as Indian Agent at Fort Klamath and Meacham, as Superintendent of Indian Affairs, had been instructed by the department to place someone in charge. Meacham decided to make an effort to prevent bloodshed and made some quick moves. His brother, John Meacham, was the commissary at Klamath Agency and the Superintendent appointed him in Knapp's place as Agent.

About that time Superintendent A. B. Meacham received a letter from Jesse Applegate in regard to the Modoc problem. Jesse Applegate was a prominent citizen of many capabilities, among which was that of a surveyor, and he was well versed in the Indian character. Applegate suggested that the only way to permanent peace with the Modocs was to give them a small reservation on Lost River, and furnished Superintendent Meacham with a small map of the proposed site. Meacham forwarded the letter and map to General Canby together with a recommendation that military action to arrest Captain Jack be delayed. General E. R. S. Canby was then commander of the Department of the Columbia and issued the necessary order revoking the one calling for Captain Jack's arrest.

Superintendent Meacham wrote a long letter of instructions to his brother John and arranged for Ivan D. Applegate, then agent in charge of Yai-nax Station, Klamath Reservation, to accompany John as the second commissioner. A. B. Meacham had also requested Jesse Applegate to be a member of the commission but the latter was occupied with other duties and could not participate.

The two commissioners arranged through messengers to meet Captain Jack and five or six of his men. The commissioners were accompanied by only two other men, all four being well armed. They moved into the Modoc country where they met Captain Jack with almost all of his men and all armed, instead of the five or six agreed upon. Again it had been urged that the commissioners' party be assassinated. Schonchin John, Hooker Jim, and Curly-haired Doctor urged the murders and were prevented by the insistance of Captain Jack and Scarface Charley.

It is to be noted that this was the second time that Captain

Jack had halted the murders of official white commissioners. The fortunate outcome resulting from Jack's attitude on each of these two occasions is to be remarked since it subsequently became known that the Modocs, generally, were always suspicious that Captain Jack would not carry out the wishes of the majority of his people. At this point it is also well to understand that all the Modocs were accustomed to contacts with white men and were somewhat acquainted with the white man's idea of representative government. In the light of events which follow this was troublesome knowledge, for Jack was thereby a representative chief, empowered only to exercise the will of the majority of his tribe. Had the Modocs been unaware of the white man's system, Jack might have been endowed with absolute power as was sometimes the case among primitive aborigines.

Under the foregoing restrictions of authority Jack attended the council. He recited the grievances of his people—their mistreatment by the Klamaths while on the reservation; the failure of government to protect them according to A. B. Meacham's promise of December, 1869; the argument that since the government had failed to keep its promises that Jack could not be held to answer to the white man's law for the killing of the Indian doctor who had failed to cure the sick child. He further said that his people had made two honest attempts to live peaceably with the Klamaths without reciprocity and that the Modocs had made up their minds not to try again. He agreed, however, that white people might settle in his country and that he would keep his people away from the white settlements and would prevent his men from causing trouble with the whites.

The Commissioners again offered the Modocs a home on any unoccupied portion of the Klamath Reservation, which offer Jack declined. He was assured of protection and again pointed to previous broken promises. He was then told that the Commissioners would be willing to recommend a small reservation near the mouth of Lost River if he would not molest the white settlements while the Indian Department was reaching a decision on the recommendation. The whole matter was carefully explained even to a possible long delay before a decision would be handed down and the further possibility of a refusal by the department to approve the location on Lost River. Jack agreed to the whole proposal and in addition said that if the proposed home on Lost River were disapproved that his tribe would move to Yai-nax.

On the above theme the council closed. The Commissioners returned home and made their recommendations as promised.

That they had avoided assassination was due entirely to Captain Jack's refusal to condone the event.

Superintendent A. B. Meacham made a full report to the Indian Department at the national capital, pressing the desirability of the small reservation on Lost River and urging fair treatment for the Modocs. He also reported in detail to General Canby. As far as the department at Washington, D. C. was concerned it again temporized and that characteristic delay can, with reason, be held accountable for the ultimate conflict.

The spring of 1872 came. The Modocs were growing impatient because of no department decision. They began to annoy the white settlers in many ways, thus breaking their agreement with Commissioners John Meacham and Ivan D. Applegate, and thereby forfeiting their right to gentle treatment. The settlers complained to both the Indian and Military Deparments and asked for relief.

There was a new Chief of the Department of Indian Affairs in Washington, D. C. and A. B. Meacham was displaced as Superintendent of Indian Affairs for Oregon by T. B. Odeneal. Neither of the new officials was well acquainted either with Indian character or with the Modoc question. On April 11, 1872, Superintendent Odeneal was instructed by his superior to place the Modocs on the Klamath Reservation, or locate them on a new home site. Odeneal reported to the department that since the Klamath Reservation had been designated, that it was the proper place for the Modocs. On September 6, 1872, he received orders to remove the Modocs to the Klamath Reservation, "peaceably, if you can; forcibly if you must." Of course Captain Jack learned of the order. There was no secret about it and some of Jack's white sympathizers kept him posted.

Captain Jack conferred with Judges Steele and Roseborough of Yreka, who advised him not to resist the authority of the government but promised, as Jack's attorneys, to assist in getting lands for the Modocs, provided the latter would dissolve tribal relations. This offer of assistance as attorneys may have emboldened the Modocs to treat government officers with less respect but we have the word of A. B. Meacham that Steele and Roseborough never held out any promise beyond that of assisting as best they could in the capacity of attorneys. Meacham makes that statement in his lengthy published volume covering the Modoc history and war and if any man would have had excuse to attach ulterior motives to the promises of the two judges it would have been A. B. Meacham, as subsequent events were to prove.

On November 26, 1872, Superintendent Odeneal sent messengers to the Modoc camp on Lost River ordering Captain Jack and his people to go to the Klamath Reservation. The messengers were instructed, in the event of Captain Jack's refusal, that they arrange with Jack to meet Odeneal at Linkville, 25 miles from the Modoc camp. Captain Jack refused either to move to the reservation or to go to Linkville, telling the messengers that he did not want to talk with Odeneal; that he did not want any white man to tell him what he had to do; and that his white friends advised him to remain where he was.

When Superintendent Odeneal received Jack's reply he immediately applied to the military commander at Fort Klamath for a force to compel the Modocs to go upon the Klamath Reservation. Major John Green of the First Cavalry was then in command at Fort Klamath and on November 28th officially notified Odeneal that Captain Jackson with about thirty men would leave the post about noon on the same day, camp on Link River that night, and be at Jack's village on the morning of November 29th. As a matter of fact they did not arrive at Jack's camp until daybreak on the 30th.

The troop movement was intended to be made without the knowledge of the Modocs but Superintendent Odeneal sent messengers to warn the settlers of the possibility of trouble and the nature of the expedition. Somehow several settlers were not warned, among them one named Miller, who had been helpful to the Modocs and who knew almost every man in Captain Jack's band personally. Failure to notify Miller, and others, was a fatal error as will be seen presently.

While Captain Jackson and his men were enroute to the Modoc camp, a group of about 25 citizens of Linkville prepared to accompany the military expedition. They proceeded toward Captain Jack's village, taking the east bank of Lost River while Jackson with his troops approached on the west bank. The river divided the Modoc camp. Captain Jack and 14 of his men with their families occupied the west bank. Among those were Schonchin John, Scarface Charley, Black Jim, One-eyed Mose, Watchman, Humpty Joe, Big Ike, Old Tails, Old Tails' Boy, and Old Longface.

On the east bank were Curly-haired Doctor, Boston Charley, Hooker Jim, Sholax, and ten others with their families.

As Jackson and his troopers arrived at the camp early in the morning of November 30th, the citizens group reached a point near Curly-haired Doctor's camp on the east side. The Modocs were taken by surprise. Their friend Miller had told them that no soldiers were coming. They had gone to his homestead the day before to ask that specific question. Miller had not been notified by Odeneal's messengers.

While Jackson was deploying his men, an Indian who was out hunting discovered the presence of the soldiers and discharged his gun. The camp was curious about the gunshot and upon looking about, the soldiers were seen to have the camp under their control. The Indians grasped their guns but Jackson calmly told the Modocs to lay down their arms. Captain Jack complied and ordered his men to do likewise.

A parley was held. Jackson explained the order under which he was there. Captain Jack begged Jackson to withdraw his troops saying that Superintendent Odeneal's messengers had said that they would come again and try to bring the Superintendent along. It is too bad that Odeneal did not accompany the messengers originally or after they had reported back to him at Linkville. Captain Jack said afterwards that he would not have resisted had Odeneal, himself, come to him and made everything clear. Who knows but that for his mistake in a long list of errors, the Modoc war might not have occurred. The parley seemed to be accomplishing the desired results and Ivan D. Applegate, who had accompanied the troops, walked down to the river bank and called across to the regular Indian Department messenger, known as One-armed Brown-who was on the east shore with the citizens' party-that everything had been settled. Brown immediately prepared to carry the news to Linkville where Superintendent Odeneal was waiting.

During the discussions all the Indians had laid down their arms except Scarface Charley, who was apparently dissatisfied with the trend of events. He was swearing and uttering threats and waving his gun. Jackson ordered Charley to put down his gun and when Charley refused, Jackson told Lieutenant Boutelle to disarm him. The Lieutenant advanced to fulfill the order, at the same time calling Charley a number of vile names. The Indian became enraged at the verbal abuse and drawing his pistol shot at the officer. The Lieutenant's pistol cracked at the same split-second and immediately the soldiers began firing into the Indian camp, the Indians returning the fire. The west bank battle lasted for three hours. The Modoc, Watchman, was killed, and the Indians took cover in the sage-brush taking Watchman's body with them. Ten of the soldiers were killed and five wounded. The Modocs reorganized and upon their return to renew the fray some hours later, Jackson withdrew his troops from the immediate vicinity.

Meanwhile things were happening on the east bank. Messenger Brown had started for Linkville, but hearing the firing returned to see what was happening. The Indians on the east side had grabbed their guns and headed for the river to reinforce Captain Jack. The citizens' group scrambled down the bank to keep the east-bank Modocs from getting into their canoes. A spirited fight at once ensued, the citizens retreating, leaving three or four of their number dead, while the Indian casualties were one dead squaw with a dead infant in her arms.

Up to that moment Captain Jack had not fired a shot although he did direct the battle, but when Jackson dispatched a messenger, Captain Jack ran after him and fired an ineffectual shot or two.

Instead of following up his advantage, Captain Jack assembled his people and led them to the lava beds. That is, all but Scarface Charley, who now gave an example of the unpredictability of the Indian character. Charley remained behind to warn any friendly white people traveling that way and did, in at least two instances, tell white men of the neighborhood's dangers, actually taking the riders' horses by the bits, turning them around, and pointing in the direction of approach, told the riders to ride for their lives. These men heeded the warning and notified the settlers of the hostilities. Among those notified was John A. Fairchild, a stock rancher, who for ten years had grazed his horses and cattle in the Modoc country. Near Fairchild's ranch house 14 Modoc families were living. The ranch was located on Hot Creek, near its source, on the high land dividing the Modoc and Shasta Indian countries. Adjoining the Fairchild place was another ranch belonging to Press Dorris. These two ranchers called the Indian men together and told them of the battle on Lost River and persuaded them to permit Fairchild and Dorris to conduct them to the Klamath Reservation. Among these Modocs were Bogus Charley, Shacknasty Jim, Steamboat Frank, and Ellen's Man George, all of whom were then anxious to avoid trouble but who later were to be prominently identified with tragic events. The two ranchers sent word to the new Indian Agent Dyer at Fort Klamath, telling him of their plan and requesting that the Agent meet the group and take charge of the Indians.

Dyer set out at once and passed through Linkville on his way to meet Fairchild and Dorris with the Hot Creek families. News of the battle had reached Linkville and the bodies of the dead troopers were brought there. Demand for vengeance was rife and a party of citizens had set out before Dyer's arrival. This group of citizens intercepted Fairchild and Dorris with their charges at Robert Whittle's homestead, but found the two ranchers prepared and determined to protect their Modocs. When Dyer reached Whittle's place he stated to Fairchild that he feared an effort would be made to annihilate the Indians in Fairchild's care. Some of the Indians overheard the conversation and all becoming frightened, hurriedly set out, riding straight to the Lava Beds, thus adding 14 warriors to Captain Jack's force.

While the foregoing events were taking place something more sinister was happening elsewhere. After the Lost River battle the survivors of the Linkville citizens' party went to the ranch home of Dennis Crawley. As stated, Jackson had gone to Linkville, taking his dead and wounded there. The Modocs held a pow-wow and some of them, urged by Hooker Jim, Curley-haired Doctor, Steamboat Frank, and others decided upon a raid of vengeance. They went through the district killing the white ranchers and taunting the white women, saying that "Modocs do not kill women and children, but your husband's body will be found in the woods," and other statements of like import. Thus died 13 white men—Brotherton, Schieire, Boddy, Miller, and others. Miller, who for ten years had voluntarily paid rent to the Modocs for grazing his live-stock; who had furnished the Modocs with provisions and ammunition; who had been particularly generous to Hooker Jim. Hooker Jim killed him. Jim later declared that he did not recognize Miller when he shot him, but A. B. Meacham declared that he thought the murder was deliberate because Hooker Jim felt that Miller had purposely withheld information from the Modocs about the coming of the soldiers.

The raiders loaded their ponies with plunder and joined Captain Jack in the Lava Beds. Captain Jack denounced the murderers, particularly for the killing of Miller and said that the raiders should be surrendered to the government authorities for trial. But Captain Jack's will did not prevail. Curly-haired Doctor promised to "make medicine" to protect them, and the warriors, by a large majority, voted that the murderers would not be surrendered. The total number of fighting men in the group was then 53, including Captain Jack himself. November

30, 1872, had been a sad culmination to the mishandling of Indian relations. But the die had now been cast. There could be no turning back from war to a finish.

THE WAR IN THE LAVA BEDS

The portion of the Lava Beds important to the Modoc War is a relatively small fraction between Tule Lake and Clear Lake in extreme Northern California and in sight of the Oregon-California boundary. The entire Cascade Range is volcanic. The section which today comprises Lava Beds National Monument is particularly rugged and probably represents the most recent lava flows in the entire Cascadian plateau. Here is the roughest kind of lava, known as "aa." It is scoriaceous lava which flowed from great fissures in the earth's crust like thick, frothy molasses. It billowed and traveled slowly, some sections cooling more rapidly than others, forming caves and tunnels. Many of these remain today. Others have caved in and are seen as deep trenches 20 to 100 feet deep and 50 to 250 feet wide. There are old fumaroles or vents from which steam and gases once escaped. There are cinder cones and craters. It is a rough country.

The particular section chosen by Captain Jack as his place of refuge, and known ever since as Captain Jack's Stronghold, was at the extreme northern edge of the present-day monument. The place was a maze of winding paths, of changing levels, and caves—an ideal place of concealment, most difficult to attack, but easy to defend.

From the half dozen nearest small military posts regular soldiers were dispatched to concentrate on the Modocs. Oregon recruited two or three companies of volunteers and California sent one. Some of the troops camped at Fairchild's ranch from where they observed a few Modoc women and children camped on a nearby creek and proposed capturing them. John Fairchild stopped that move at its inception. All units were busy with preparations for an early attack. There was a lot of bantering and joking about how easy the job was to be. To get it over quickly and get home was the slogan. The plan of attack called for half of the troops to approach from the north, the other half from the south, converging and encircling the stronghold.

On January 16, 1873, the two assault detachments were only a few miles apart, ready to march at daylight the next morning in accordance with orders already issued.

General Frank Wheaton was there in over-all command, and Colonel Bernard and Major Jackson. All were old Indian fighters. John Fairchild and Press Dorris, the cattle ranchers, were present. They knew the beleagured Modocs personally and they also knew the lava beds, for they had looked for stray cattle there many times. None of these men discounted the difficulties of dislodging the Indians. The veterans among the enlisted men in the regular army also knew what they were up against. Only the recruits and the inexperienced young-bloods among the volunteers considered the coming fray a mere exhilarating pastime. As a matter of fact, the troops were not to be encumbered by blankets and knapsacks, expecting to be back in camp by nightfall.

At four o'clock on the morning of January 17th the bugle sounded, arousing the troops. The weather was cold and foggy—so foggy that no visible signal could be given to Colonel Barnard, in command of the contingent on the southern wing. But his orders had been coordinated with those of the northern wing and the two columns began their converging approach to the Modocs' rocky fortress.

The cavalrymen were dismounted, their horses left at camp. The volunteers moved forward rapidly until cautioned by their officers. The regulars were steadier for Major Jackson's command had been in the fight on Lost River and had respect for the Indians as fighters. Advancing some distance over the rough terrain without raising a Modoc gave cause to some of the men to remark that the Modocs had fled. Presently firing was heard which the northern contingent identified as coming from Colonel Bernard's troops.

Suddenly streaks of flame spurted through the fog from directly in front. A soldier fell, blood pulsating from his neck. Then another dropped. Colonel Green ordered his troops to fire and that order was repeated up and down the line. The troops began firing heavily but without a target. Not a Modoc had thus far been seen. Colonel Green ordered a charge. The men advanced for several hundred yards, climbing rocks, jumping crevasses, but still no Modoc had been sighted nor had there been a cry of agony from the Modoc side. Soldiers were being hit frequently. Green tried to close up his lines and mounted a cliff, calling on his men to follow. Bullets whizzed all around Green, who, miraculously, was not hit. But others were. The Modocs let loose their blood-curdling war-whoop. The fog began to lift. The soldiers continued to move forward, their casualties mounting. However, they gradually tightened the circle around the stronghold. Then the Modoc fire broke the army line again. The wounded cried for rescue.

General Wheaton called a council of his principal officers as the fighting continued. That part of the line nearest the lake also gave way. Almost everywhere the soldiers faltered. Retreat was sounded and as the notes of the bugle reached the ears of the wounded they again cried out for rescue. The retreating soldiers turned to save their wounded comrades. The Indians intensified their fire. At one point a wounded man was reached by two comrades. When they lifted the casualty one of the rescuers fell. Fairchild's men now tried to save both wounded men. They failed.

The soldiers fell back—all the soldiers—400 of them. The voices of the wounded pleading that they be not left to the savagery of the Modoc women were dimmed by distance. The troops which had advanced with confidence only a few hours before did not stop at camp. They kept on retreating. Thirty-five troopers did not answer roll-call. Many more were wounded.

What of the Modocs? They had numbered 53 warriors, one of whom had been wounded in a skirmish on the 15th. There were not more than 53, probably only 52. Not one Modoc had been hurt in the battle. Their women brought in the clothing and personal effects of the fallen soldiers. The braves brought in the scalps. Curley-haired Doctor, the Medicine Man, boasted of his powers of protection. Schonchin John praised the powers of the Medicine Man. And Captain Jack knew that he might be deposed as chief. However, he made a speech saying that the white men were many and that they would come again but that he, their Chief, would not make peace until "the Modoc heart says 'peace'. " He also said that they would not again go on the war-path.

The squaws brought in huge heaps of sage-brush and the tribe prepared for the scalp-dance. The native drum beat started. The dance began, each successful trophy hunter carrying, tied to the ramrod of his gun, such scalps as he had taken. The Chief took no part in the ceremony.

Meanwhile the troops were resting and talking, attempting to explain and excuse their defeat. The only result of all the talk was the ultimate recall of General Wheaton. True, he was in command and the effort had failed. But where was the officer who could have succeeded? With more of the troops untrained in Indian warfare and an impregnable stronghold to storm?

THE NEXT THREE MONTHS

SEVERAL DAYS after the battle Captain Jack sent word to John Fairchild and Press Dorris suggesting a talk and guaranteeing safety should the white men agree to meet him at the foot of the bluff near the Modoc camp. The meeting was held, the substance of Captain Jack's talk being that he did not want to fight any more and asking that the old home on Lost River be restored to the Modocs. Fairchild and Dorris had no authority to promise anything and so informed Jack, promising only that they would do what they could to stop further hostilities. That meeting brought much unwarranted criticism of the two white men from wagging tongues belonging to men who would not have ventured to such a meeting themselves. Fairchild and Dorris were men of integrity and their reputations withstood the slander.

News of the January 17th defeat had, of course, reached the nation's capital. E. L. Applegate, of Oregon, was in Washington, D. C. at the time, as were other Oregonians. Applegate conferred with Attorney-General Williams about the Modoc troubles. The Attorney-General requested Applegate to submit a memorandum covering their conversation, which was done. That resulted in notice to Applegate from the Attorney-General that Secretary of Interior Delano would be glad to discuss the Modoc question with the Oregon delegation, and that meeting was held on January 25th. Secretary Delano requested a written rocommendation for his use at a cabinet meeting and that document was furnished. It contained a recital of the history of the Modoc affairs, the reasons for incompatibility between the Modocs and the Klamaths, a recommendation that several of the related tribes, including the Modocs, be placed on a reservation on the Oregon Coast, and suggested that A. B. Meacham, who was then in the capital, be selected to head a peace commission to treat with the Indians. Meacham was invited to accept the appointment and only did so upon the earnest insistance of the Secretary of the Interior.*

Albert B. Meacham was qualified. He had managed the various Indian tribes successfully while Superintendent of Indian Affairs for Oregon and possessed an unusually complete understanding of the Indian character. Besides he was anxious to see an end to the Indian troubles in the Pacific Northwest. The other men appointed to the Commission were Jesse Applegate, a first citizen of Oregon and well qualified in every way for the task, and Samuel Case, who, at the time, was Acting Indian Agent at Alsea, Oregon. General E. R. S. Canby, U. S. Army, Commander of the Department of the Columbia, was to act as counsellor to the commission.

Commissioner Meacham arrived at Fairchild's ranch on February 19th. General Canby had established his headquarters there and Jesse Applegate and Samuel Case were waiting. The Commission went into session, its first job being that of reestablishing communication with the Modocs. This was motivated by the selection of Robert Whittle, his Klamath Indian wife Matilda, and a Modoc woman living nearby who was known as One-eyed Dixie. They were asked to go to the Modoc stronghold. It was a dangerous mission in view of the popular belief that the Modocs were elated over their recent victory and the failure of the troops to renew hostilities. In fact, the messengers all expressed doubt of survival as they left Fairchild's on the morning of February 21st. The ranch was located about 25 miles from the Lava Beds and late the same day the trio returned safe and sound. They brought the news that the Indians were willing to meet John Fairchild and Robert Whittle the next day at the foot of the bluff beneath their camp. The two men with the two Indian women left the next morning. Fairchild was instructed to tell the Modocs about the Commission, stating its purpose and giving the names of its members, and to arrange, if possible, for a meeting between the Commissioners and the principal men of the Modocs. Fairchild was also told that he should explain the meaning of an armistice, in the event that a meeting was acceptable, and that the meaning of that term was that "no act of war would be committed by us, or permitted by them, while negotiations for peace were going on."

---

* In a reminiscent article of January 30, 1926, Captain Oliver C. Applegate thus designates the official composition of the Modoc Peace Commission: Alfred B. Meacham, formerly Superintendent of Indian Affairs for Ore-

The meeting was held, Fairchild following his instructions explicitly. Captain Jack told his visitors that he was ready to make peace; that he did not desire to fight; that he understood the terms of the proposed armistice; that the white people would be safe to come and go while peace negotiations were in progress; that he was unwilling to leave the Lava Beds to talk peace but that he would be glad to meet the Commissioners at the foot of the bluff; that he did not want soldiers to accompany the commissioners because soldiers frightened his boys. He may have meant that soldiers excited his warriors. Jack ended his talk by saying that his men would remain in the rocks while peace was being discussed and that "we will not fire the first shot." He also said that he would like to talk to his friend Squire Steele.

Two Modocs, Boston Charley and Bogus Charley, accompanied the emissaries back to headquarters at Fairchild's to convey the Commissioners' answer to Captain Jack. The Commissioners decided to go to the foot of the bluff without a military escort but told the two Charleys to tell Jack that the meeting would have to be held on open ground with both delegations either armed or unarmed. General Canby received permission to add Judge A. M. Roseborough to the Commission and on the morning of February 23rd both Steele and Roseborough arrived.

Meanwhile communication continued between the Commissioners and Captain Jack, the messengers being Frank Riddle and his Modoc wife Tobey, whose tribal name was Winema. No plan offered seemed to meet the approval of Captain Jack. A few Modocs drifted into the Commissioners' camp. These Modocs

---

gon, Chairman; General [Edward Richard Sprigg] Canby, Department Commander, U. S. Army; Reverend Ezekiel Thomas, a Methodist minister; LeRoy S. Dyer, U. S. Indian Agent of the Klamath Falls Agency, Oregon; Interpreters: Winema, or Toby Riddle, a Modoc woman and second cousin of Captain Jack; and her husband, Frank Riddle, a Kentuckian. For the Modocs: Captain Jack; Schonchin John, sub-chief, and brothers of Old Schonchin (Sconchin) who was chief of the friendly Modocs, then at their Camp Yainax on the Klamath Reservation; Black Jim, half-brother of Captain Jack; Boston Charley and Hocka (Hooker, Hocker) Jim, headman.

Also (Captain) Oliver C. Applegate, officer in charge of the Modocs, Piutes and Klamaths at Camp Yainax, was detailed by General Canby to assist the Commission and at Canby's request brought loyal Old Schonchin to the Lava Beds to assist in negotiations but particularly to observe the conduct of the hostiles to determine whether they were acting in good faith. However, after several days word was received that Captain Jack had emissaries at Yainax trying to get the Modocs there to join the impending war. Thereupon, Old Schonchin asked General Canby that Applegate escort him back to Yainax to head off disaffection among his people, which request was granted.

learned from squaw men about the general feeling against the Indians; of the grand jury indictments in Jackson County returned against the Lost River murderers; of the adverse attitude of the newspapers; all of which information was carried back to Captain Jack. Bogus Charley and Boston Charley were not above embellishing what they heard with plausible additions.

Judge Steele agreed to visit the Modoc camp. There was no unanimity of opinion regarding Steele's instructions. Commissioners Applegate, Case, and Roseborough agreed that Steele should offer peace terms. Chairman Meacham demurred believing that it was unwise for a third party to intervene in that duty. However, as a result, Steele was authorized to offer amnesty to all Modocs upon their agreement to be moved to some distant reservation to be selected by the Modocs themselves, but that pending such transfer the Indians were to surrender as prisoners of war and be taken to Angel Island in San Francisco Bay where they would be kept at Government expense. With Mr. Steele went John Fairchild and a few newspaper reporters, with Frank and Tobey Riddle as interpreters.

The party was welcomed by Captain Jack, and Judge Steele outlined the peace conditions as instructed. The Modocs appeared to favor the plan and it was agreed that several of the tribesmen would accompany the emissaries back to the headquarters of the commission. Those selected were Queen Mary, who was Captain Jack's sister, Bogus Charley, Boston Charley, Hooker Jim, Shacknasty Jim, Duffy, William, and Curley-haired Jack.

When the party came within hailing distance of the Commissioners' camp, Steele raised his hat in salute and shouted "They accept peace." Immediately the camp was astir with newspaper correspondents hurriedly preparing news articles for their papers; aides writing dispatches to the war and interior departments — an atmosphere of relief pervaded the camp.

As the party dismounted, Fairchild stepped forward and said that he did not concur in Steele's statement. He expressed the opinion that Steele's peace talk had been well received but he was sure that the Modocs did not understand that they were to surrender. The Modocs present were interrogated but declined to comment, saying that they had come to listen and not to talk. Steele was so sure of his statement that he offered to return to the Modoc camp the next day to secure confirmation of his understanding. Both Fairchild and Riddle declined to accompany him but Tobey agreed to go as did the correspondent for the *Sacramento Record,* and, of course, the visiting Modocs. The latter rode ahead and when Steele and his newsman companion arrived it was completely clear to Steele that he had been mistaken. There was every evidence of hostility and the situation was saved only by the fact that Steele remained calm and appeared not to notice the changed attitude. Events moved quickly. Steele extended his hand to Captain Jack who cautiously managed to tell Steele that he was still a friend. Captain Jack then made a speech in which he said that Steele had misunderstood him. Steele replied that he was their friend and that he would not intentionally have misquoted them. Schonchin John accused Steele of betraying the Modocs and clearly indicated that Steele would not live to misrepresent them again. Steele, grasping the situation, said that he would not talk with a man "when his heart is bad" and that they would resume the council the following day.

Captain Jack and Scarface Charley took Steele and the newsman to Jack's quarters for the night, where the two Indians and Queen Mary stood guard over them until morning. The council was then resumed and it was evident that the danger was still very real. Steele proposed that he and his companions return to the headquarters of the Commission and bring back with them all of the commissioners on the following day. The ruse worked only because some of the Indians saw in the proposal a chance to trap the commissioners.

When Steele returned he frankly acknowledged his error and explained the strategy behind his escape. With equal candor he gave as his opinion the statement that if the commissioners visited the Modocs that all of the commissioners would be murdered. Meacham, as chairman, wired Secretary Delano the details of the situation, concluding with the statement that he believed treachery was intended and that the mission could not succeed. General Canby concurred. But on March 5th Secretary Delano replied by telegraph via Yreka, California, that he did not think the Modocs meant treachery; said he thought he understood the unwillingness of the Modocs to place confidence in Meacham; ordered negotiations continued; and ended by saying he would consult the President the following day and ask the War Department to communicate with General Canby.

The camp was dejected. The troops who had fought under Major Jackson at Lost River and those who had been under

General Wheaton in the January defeat in the Lava Beds had no desire for another go at the Modocs.

The situation stagnated until one evening a small group of Modocs came into the camp at Fairchild's. One of them was Queen Mary who brought a proposal from her brother that if General Canby would send wagons half-way that all of the Modocs would meet them and surrender. The Commissioners discussed the proposal, Meacham voting against the offer and the other three voting affirmatively. Thus the Commission relinquished its primary authority to General Canby who accepted the new responsibilty. He concluded a clear understanding with Queen Mary and those with her, all of whom returned to the Lava Beds. The agreement stood that the wagons would be sent without a military escort and that on the following Monday all the Modocs would move out and surrender.

Two or three circumstances, each unimportant when considered separately, are worthy of mention at this point. For some reason never explained, General Canby now refused to use Riddle or Tobey as interpreters although they were still employed by the Commissioners as such. This fact was observed by the visiting Modocs, one of whom, Boston Charley, indicated to Tobey that she would not see him again by saying, "If you ever see me I will pay you for the saddle I borrowed." Tobey, who resented the treatment she and her husband were receiving in not being used as interpreters, kept silent about her understanding of the meaning of Boston Charley's remark. The day preceding that set for the surrender, a messenger arrived from the Modocs saying that they would need two more days because they were burying their dead. General Canby accepted the delay and assured the messenger that the teams would be on hand two days hence, as now requested. In the meantime news that the war had ended began to spread.

The day before the postponed surrender was to have occurred Riddle and Tobey told Meacham that, in their opinion, one of two things would happen—either the Modocs would not put in an appearance or, if they did, it would be only for the purpose of capturing the wagons. Meacham conveyed that information to General Canby who interviewed the Riddles and also consulted General Gillem (often mis-spelled "Gilliam") . Canby reached the conclusion that either Tobey did not have a basis for her suspicions, that she was being fooled by the Modocs, or influenced adversely by those opposed to peace. So the appointed morning arrived and the teams were sent out under the supervision of Mr. Steele.

So sure were Generals Canby and Gillem of the good intentions of the Modocs that they designated the individual tents to be occupied by the Modoc families. Oliver C. Applegate, with equal certainty, left for home reporting enroute that the war was ended and that the Modocs had surrendered. Fairchild thought otherwise as, of course, did the Riddles. Hours passed and just at nightfall the cavalcade returned, Steele riding at the head of the column of empty wagons.

Next day another delegation of Modocs arrived stating that the tribesmen had failed to agree; that they needed more time. The truth, as subsequently proved, was that the subject on which they disagreed was whether or not to capture the wagons. Captain Jack and Scarface Charley opposed the capture.

Washington, D. C. was notified of the failure and orders came back at once for the Commission to continue negotiations. At that time the Commission consisted of A. B. Meacham, former Superinendent of Indian Affairs for Oregon, General Edward Richard Sprigg Canby, commanding the Department of the Columbia of the United States Army, Samuel Case, Acting Indian Agent at Alsea, Oregon, and Judge Roseborough of Yreka, California.

Upon receiving the instruction to continue negotiations Mr. Case resigned from the Commission and Judge Roseborough returned to his regular judicial duties. LeRoy S. Dyer, Indian Agent at Klamath Agency, Oregon, was appointed in place of Case, and Reverend Eleazar* Thomas, a Methodist minister from California, was selected in place of Judge Roseborough.

General Canby notified the Modocs that there would be no more temporizing. Recruits were pouring into camp. One company of newly enlisted men while passing near the Lava Beds captured 30 Modoc ponies. Canby moved his headquarters to Van Bremen's ranch, several miles nearer the Lava Beds. He sent out scouting parties to obtain a better knowledge of the terrain surrounding the Modoc stronghold. On one of these trips Reverend Thomas accompanied the troopers and meeting several Modocs re-opened communications. A delegation of the Indians then visited the new camp but all efforts made through them to arrange a meeting with their leaders were fruitless. General Canby notified Captain Jack of the General's

* In A. B. Meacham's book, *Wigwam* & *Warpath,* he refers to Thomas as Ezekiel.

Captain Jack of the Modocs

"Next day when the verdict was announced it recited that the death penalty had been fixed for Captain Jack . . . and October 3, 1878, was designated as the day of execution." (page 204)

Jack's Family: Lizzie (young wife), Mary (his sister), Old Wife, and Daughter

"Captain Jack's sister . . . was very intelligent, probably leading the tribe in that respect." (page 158)

Scarface Charley, Modoc Warrior

"Scarface Charley . . . now gave an example of the unpredictability of the Indian character. Charley remained behind to warn any friendly white people traveling that way . . . of the neighborhood's dangers." (page 167)

Schonchin John of the Modocs

"Schonchin John had urged treachery and Captain Jack spoke against assassination, in fact he was speaking at the time the soldiers rode in." (page 158)

Lava Beds in Modoc Country

"The particular section chosen by Captain Jack as his place of refuge and known ever since as Captain Jack's Stronghold was . . . a maze of winding paths, of changing levels, and caves—an ideal place of concealment, most difficult to attack, but easy to defend." (page 169)

Fort Klamath

"At the conclusion of the trial A. B. Meacham left Fort Klamath, first visiting the prisoners and shaking hands with them as evidence of his forgiveness. Captain Jack told Meacham that but one side of the story had been told and that he had no one to speak for him." (page 204)

Chief Joseph of the Nez Perces

"... on the fifth day Joseph went to General Miles and gave up his gun, saying, 'From where the sun now stands I will fight no more.'" (page 222)

Lookingglass, War Chief of the Nez Perces

"With Joseph were Chiefs White Bird, Lookingglass, Black Eagle, other lesser chiefs and about 300 warriors, all armed with the most modern breech-loading rifles." (page 215)

intention to change the position of the troops in the interest of better communications, and that the soldiers would not begin hostilities unless the Modocs provoked an attack. Captain Jack sent a reply saying that the Indians would not fire the first shot and asked that the stolen horses be returned. Then a few Modoc women came to ask the return of the ponies. The request was denied; in fact some of the ponies had already been appropriated by young volunteers for their own use when returning home.

On March 31, 1873, the army started to move to the Lava Beds. The movement consumed four days. The new camp was on the lake shore at the foot of the bluff which overlooked the stronghold.

It was quite apparent to Meacham that any attempt to storm the hideout would be costly in soldiers' lives and it was decided to try at once for a council with the Modocs.

Boston Charley came into camp and through him arrangements were made for a meeting, which was held the day after the Commissioners arrived at the new camp of the army. Attending the council were General Canby, General Gillem, Reverend Thomas, Messrs. Meacham and Dyer, with Frank and Tobey Riddle as interpreters. With Captain Jack and his principal men were six or seven Modoc women, the latter tending a bonfire in a low, rocky basin. The place was out of view from the soldiers' camp, which fact, of itself, suggested treachery. However, the pipe of peace was smoked and then each of the white men made a short speech favoring peace, to which Captain Jack and Schonchin John replied in preliminary talks. A heavy rainstorm came up and General Canby suggested that a tent be erected at a half-way point where subsequent meetings could be held, and that idea met with Modoc favor, although a definite time for the next meeting was not fixed.

Next day the council tent was erected at a place not quite a mile from army headquarters and slightly more than a mile from the Modocs' stronghold. Care was taken to select a site as free as possible from the dangers of ambush. The signal corps established a station about half way up the bluff in plain sight of the tent. Colonel Mason's command was beyond Captain Jack's camp on the opposite side from General Canby's headquarters and a telegraph line was installed between the two bodies of troops. The Modocs were invited to visit the General's camp during daylight hours and did so, being encouraged to mix freely with officers and men. This was done for the two-fold purpose of convincing the tribesmen of the friendly intentions of the army as well as to make an impression of might. The Indians were even permitted to examine the mortars and the heavy shells.

One day Bogus Charley and Hooker Jim observed the telegraph line and asked that it be explained. General Gillem told them that it was used to talk to Colonel Mason's camp, also saying that Colonel Mason would move his camp closer to the Modocs in a few days and that Gillem would move his own camp to a flat area very near to Captain Jack, and further that within a few days 100 Warm Springs warriors would arrive. All this news greatly excited the Modocs who sought out John Fairchild to whom they expressed great dissatisfaction because of the telegraph and the coming of the Warm Springs Indians.

On April 4th Captain Jack sent Boston Charley with a request that Meacham and Fairchild meet him at the council tent. The two white men went, taking the Riddles along as interpreters. Soon after reaching the tent Judge Roseborough arrived in camp and learning of the conference also went to the meeting place. Captain Jack was already there, accompanied by seven or eight of his men and some of the Modoc women. The talk lasted seven hours and was, in fact, the only full and free discussion between the Modocs and the Commissioners during the life of the Commission.

The whole history of the Modoc troubles and complaints was reviewed. Captain Jack insisted that he wanted peace. He asked for his old home on Lost River. Meacham told him that since blood had been spilled there that the tribe could never return. Jack expressed his faith in Meacham and Fairchild, saying, "I know your hearts." Jack then asked that he be given the Lava Beds as a home and that no one else would ever want those rocks. Meacham replied that it would be impossible to grant the request unless the Lost River murderers were first surrendered. Captain Jack then developed a description of Indian law compared with the law of the white man and said that he could never surrender his young men to be hung and insisted that the Indians were not the primary aggressors. Meacham told him that there was no alternative for the Modocs but to leave the Lava Beds, go to another part of the country, acknowledge the authority of the government, and then all could live in peace. Jack refused. He made a long speech recounting the Ben Wright affair, to which Meacham replied with a similar story about Bloody Point. Finally the council closed with a friendly invitation by Meacham for Jack to go to Meacham's quarters for dinner and more talk. Jack replied, "I am not afraid to go, but my people are afraid for me." The fact was that his people would not permit him to go because they were not sure that Jack would stick to the Modoc side. Meacham understood that and upon returning to his quarters talked the whole day's events over with General Canby. Both wanted to make an effort to save Captain Jack and those of his people who stood for peace.

Accordingly, with General Canby's authorization, Meacham found a way to get word to Captain Jack that if he and his peace party would agree to come out of the Lava Beds that the army would be placed in position to protect the withdrawal. Tobey Riddle was the messenger explicitly instructed to deliver the offer privately to Captain Jack, if possible. When she arrived, Jack refused to talk alone saying, "I want my people all to hear." So Tobey told her story and a vote was taken, eleven men voting with Jack to accept. But the vote was useless for the majority warned Jack and the eleven voting with him that any attempt to escape would mean death. So Jack said, "I am a Modoc, and I cannot and will not leave my people." Actually he dared not.

On the trail back to camp one of the peace men had secreted himself and said to Tobey as she passed, "Tell old man Meacham and all the men not to come to the council tent again—they get killed."

When Tobey returned, she stayed on her horse, refusing to dismount until her husband arrived. She was upset as she told her story to Frank Riddle. The Commissioners were called together to receive her report. General Canby said that the Modocs might threaten such action but that they would not attempt it. Reverend Thomas considered the news to be propaganda, wholly for effect. But Meacham and Dyer believed the warning.

The next day Bogus Charley, Boston Charley, and Shacknasty Jim came into camp and proposed that the Commissioners go to the council tent for a meeting with Captain Jack who was waiting there with four other Modocs. Boston Charley was the spokesman and Meacham, distrusting Boston Charley but not showing his distrust, said that the Commissioners were not ready to talk that day. As the conversation was progressing General Canby was handed a dispatch from the signal station reading, "Five Indians at the council tent, apparently unarmed, and about 20 others with rifles are in the rocks a few yards behind them." The message was passed around while the parley continued. At that moment all were convinced that treachery was afloat. Then, as the Modocs departed, Reverend Thomas made a grave mistake by saying to Bogus Charley, "What do you want to kill us for? We are your friends." Bogus Charley pressed Thomas for the source of that idea and Thomas finally said, "Tobey told it." Bogus made it a point to question Tobey whereupon Tobey and her husband both became very much alarmed for their personal safety.

The Modoc trio returned to their camp and almost immediately a messenger was sent demanding that Tobey visit the Modocs at once. Tobey and her husband consulted the Commissioners, all of whom except Meacham considered compliance by Tobey to be extremely dangerous. General Canby agreed to move his troops against the Modocs at once if Tobey were harmed, upon which promise she agreed to go. She had a tearful parting with her ten-year-old son and then left under watchful field-glasses, one pair at the eyes of her husband.

Arriving, demand was made for the source of her information. At first she denied the statement, then she said that the spirits had told her, but finally, when the tribesmen began to threaten her, she pointed to the soldiers' camp and acknowledged the statement and said that a Modoc had told her but that she would not reveal his name and dared them to shoot her, saying that if she were harmed the soldiers would swoop down upon them, killing all. Captain Jack and Scarface Charley interceded and provided an escort for her to the soldiers' camp. Upon arrival there she repeated her warning that none should go to the council tent.

THE COMMISSIONERS GO TO THE TENT

After more than three-quarters of a century it is still difficult to rationalize the reasons leading to the decision to treat further with the Modocs as the circumstances stood after Tobey's second warning. The senior military officers did not agree; the Commissioners did not agree. General Gillem thought the Modocs could be exterminated with small losses to the troops; Colonels

Mason and Bernard felt that the casualties would take one-third of the one thousand soldiers; Colonel Green remembered the defeat of January 17th; the junior officers who had not been in the January battle were eager to fight; the enlisted men who had been through the January ordeal wanted no repetition of it; Colonel Wright wanted to wager that two companies, his own and Lieutenant Eagan's, could whip the Modocs in 15 minutes.

Once again a Modoc messenger came into the soldiers' camp. His request was for Frank Riddle to come to the Lava Beds to advise the Indians. Riddle went but learned nothing new, but again warned the Commissioners not to meet with the Modocs unless fully armed. On the morning of April 10th Mr. Meacham went to the south end of the lake to visit Boyle's camp, leaving Reverend Thomas in charge of the Commissioner's affairs. Upon his return that evening, Meacham learned that a distressing decision had been made in his absence. Modoc messengers had come in to talk with Reverend Thomas, assuring him that they had changed their hearts; that they now wanted only to make peace; that they were willing to surrender; that they merely wanted the Commissioners to prove their faith in the Modocs by coming unarmed to the council tent. The reverend gentleman, believing that his prayers for peace were being answered, accepted the statement of the Modocs at face value. He conferred with General Canby and agreed that the Commission would meet the Indians at the council tent. Meacham was astounded. He stated unequivocally, that should the Commissioners go that they would not return alive.

Next day was Good Friday, April 11, 1873. The Commissioners were at breakfast early. Meacham was slow about leaving the table. Modoc messengers arrived urging haste and saying that Captain Jack and four of his men were waiting. General Canby had issued orders that the signal corps keep a close watch through field-glasses and from the break of dawn the Lava Beds had been scanned. There were several informal conferences around the Commissioners' quarters. Frank Riddle again begged Meacham not to go because of the danger of assassination. Meacham asked him to repeat the warning in General Gillem's tent, which Riddle did, urging that if they were determined to go on the expedition that they go well armed. Reverend Thomas insisted that they go unarmed as agreed. Dyer talked with John Fairchild who chatted with Bogus Charley and reported back to Meacham that he was uncertain about what was likely to occur and offered Meacham a six-shooter, which Meacham declined. Meacham seated himself on a blanket-roll and wrote a note to his wife saying plainly that she might be a widow by evening. He gave Fairchild $650.00 in currency to send to Mrs. Meacham. Mr. Dyer also gave Fairchild a package for Mrs. Dyer. Meacham urged Dyer not to go to the tent, with Dyer feeling sure that tragedy would follow. But Dyer said that he would go if the others went. It was Meacham's own philosophy that since he was chairman he either had to go or be disgraced.

Tobey was holding Meacham's horse. She was weeping and said, "Meacham you no go; you no go. You get kill! You get kill!" But General Canby and Reverend Thomas had started. With them was Bogus Charley carrying his rifle. Meacham called to Canby and Thomas saying that it was his cool, deliberate judgment that all of them would be murdered. Canby called back that Meacham was unduly cautious; that there were but five Indians at the tent. Thomas accused Meacham of lack of faith. Meacham urged that John Fairchild be invited to accompany them and that Fairchild and himself be permitted to go armed. A man walked by Meacham and dropped something in Meacham's pocket. It was a small Derringer pistol and Meacham permitted it to remain. Dyer saw the move and went into his own tent and slipped a Derringer into his own pocket. Meacham had to order Tobey to release his horse. The Commissioners were on their way.

Arriving at the council tent it was at once observed that the council fire was back of the tent and out of the view of the signal station on the slope of the bluff. That was a suspicious circumstance. Captain Jack was waiting, ill at ease. With him were Schonchin John, Boston Charley, Shacknasty Jim, Hooker Jim, Ellen's Man, Bogus Charley, and Black Jim. In addition to Commissioners Meacham, Thomas, Dyer, and General Canby, were Frank Riddle and Tobey. Unknown to the white men, two Indian lads were hidden behind some rocks about 40 paces up the Modoc trail and each had several rifles. The talking began. Frank Riddle translated the Modoc speeches into English and his wife translated the Commissioners' speeches into Modoc. The conversation rambled. It was disconnected and seemed to get nowhere. Bogus Charley walked to Meacham's horse and took the overcoat from the saddle, donned the coat and said, "Me old man Meacham now." Meacham understood the import of the remark and, removing his hat, offered it to Hooker Jim who declined it by saying, "I will by-and-by. Don't hurry, old man." There was no longer any doubt in anyone's mind about the fate which confronted them. Finally, Schonchin John took Captain Jack's place as speaker and ended by declaring that "I talk no more."

Captain Jack gave a signal and the Modoc war-whoop brought everyone erect—everyone but Tobey who lay close to the ground. The two Indian boys, Barncho and Slolux, were seen coming with the rifles. Meacham shouted, "Jack, what does this mean?" Jack answered by reaching inside his coat, drawing a six-shooter and shouting in Modoc, "Ot-we-kau-tux," or "All ready." Steadying the revolver on his left hand he pointed it at General Canby's head and pulled the trigger. It missed fire. He spun the cylinder and again pulled the trigger and the bullet crashed through the General's head. He staggered away, pursued by Jack and Ellen's Man. Canby stumbled. Jack held him down by the shoulders while Ellen's Man slashed the General's throat. Barncho handed Ellen's Man a rifle and the latter sent another bullet through Canby's head. They stripped every vestige of clothing from the body while it still twitched in the throes of death. Two men started to run. The one ahead was Commissioner Dyer. He was pursued by Hooker Jim who fired at Dyer several times without scoring a hit. Dyer turned, pointing his pistol at Hooker Jim who dropped to avoid the shot. Dyer renewed his flight, outdistancing Hooker Jim.

Another man in flight was Frank Riddle. Black Jim was in chase and fired rapidly at Riddle but was not trying to hit him for Scarface Charley had warned all the Modocs that he would kill anyone who harmed either Tobey or Frank Riddle and Black Jim knew that Scarface Charley was watching.

At the very instant that Jack fired at General Canby, Boston Charley shot Reverend Thomas above the heart. Bogus Charley joined Boston Charley. They permitted Thomas to rise, laughed at him as Thomas tried to run and they tripped him. They again permitted him to rise and said, "Next time you believe a squaw, won't you?" But if Thomas heard the taunt it was the last functioning of earthly ears for he dropped over dead. Slolux then came up with rifles and Bogus Charley sent a bullet through the dead man's head. Then they stripped him, waving the clothes aloft.

At the first signal Schonchin John drew his revolver and a knife. He was so close to Meacham that he did not want to trust to pistol alone. But Meacham was quicker. He drew his Derringer, and placed it against Schonchin's breast and pulled the trigger, but the pistol did not fire. He tried again. Once more it did not fire. It was cocked only half-way. By the time that Meacham discovered that fact Schonchin John had thrust his own revolver in Meacham's face. Meacham stooped as the bullet struck. Meacham ran backward, the Derringer now fully cocked but Schonchin John kept firing and emptying his revolver, immediately drawing another and resuming firing. Meacham could have fired but he saw Tobey rushing toward Schonchin John and feared hitting her. She grabbed Schonchin's pistol and shouted, "Don't kill him! Don't kill Meacham. He is friend of the Indians." Slolux joined John and struck Tobey on the head with a gun. Shacknasty Jim came up and snatching up the gun sat down and took deliberate aim at Meacham. Meacham pointed to his breast and yelled, "Shoot me there, you cowardly red devil." Tobey struck down the gun. Shacknasty Jim threatened her and again took aim, firing just as Meacham leaped over a low rock pile. Shacknasty Jim shouted, "I hit him, high up."

Meacham then decided to fire his one shot. He pushed the pistol over the rocks and just as his eye came into range he saw Schonchin John seated with his revolver resting on a knee. Schonchin fired, the bullet striking Meacham between the eyes, but by some freak of circumstances the bullet passed under the eye-brow and out over the left eye. Meacham then fired at Schonchin John, who fell wounded. Meacham was hit twice more and collapsed, twitching. Shacknasty Jim was the first to reach Meacham and without delay proceeded to strip the clothing. Slolux came up and placed the muzzle of a gun at Meacham's head but Shacknasty Jim pushed the gun away saying that it was useless to waste the ammunition; that Meacham was dead. Just then they heard Captain Jack calling and as they left the scene they taunted Tobey with statements to the effect that she was no Modoc; that she was a white-hearted squaw, and "there lies another of your brothers. Take care of him."

Captain Jack gathered his murderous gang and ordered them to get back to the stronghold. They started, carrying the bloody clothing of their victims. Boston Charley handed the garments he was carrying to another and announced that he was going back to get Meacham's scalp. Hooker Jim said, "He has no scalp or I would have it myself," alluding to the fact that Meacham was partly bald. Nevertheless, Boston went over to where Meacham lay and found Tobey wiping the blood from the battered face. Pushing Tobey aside he cut into Meacham's scalp with a knife which he had taken from the pocket of a soldier slain in the January battle. Tobey, remembering that Meacham had befriended her and her husband, rushed at Boston, hurling him against the rocks. He came back threatening to kill her if she again interfered, and resumed his gory job. Placing one foot on Meacham's neck he announced that he would take an ear with the scalp and slashed again. Then Tobey, thinking fast, looked in the direction of the army camp, clapped her hands and shouted, "Bostee-na-soldiers. Kot-pumbla!" meaning "the soldiers are coming." Boston did not pause to verify the statement but ran in the direction of the stronghold. Tobey again wiped the blood from Meacham's face, felt for his heart-beat and decided that he was dead. She glanced at the bodies of the three white men and mounting her horse set out for the camp of the soldiers.

Meanwhile other events were occurring. It will be recalled that the Modocs had planned to assassinate Colonel Mason, in command of the troops on the other side of the stronghold. Accordingly Curly-haired Doctor and one or two others set out toward Colonel Mason's camp under a flag of truce for the purpose of inducing the Colonel to meet them among the rocks. But Mason, an experienced Indian fighter, would not respond. However, Major Boyle and Lieutenant Sherwood volunteered and secured Mason's consent to meet the Indians. They passed through the outer picket line and when within hailing distance the Indians asked where Colonel Mason was. As Major Boyle replied that the Colonel would not come he observed that the Indians were armed and fled, yelling to Lieutenant Sherwood to run for his life. The Indians started shooting and dropped Major Boyle with a bullet through a thigh. The guard from camp came rushing out and the Indians fled. While this was happening the signal station telegraphed the main camp that Boyle and Sherwood were being attacked under a flag of truce. Captain Adams, at the signal station on the bluff, transcribed the message and sent it to General Gillem who was not far away. The General called one of his staff to take the news to the Commissioners at the council tent when Major Biddle, also at Gillem's signal station and who had been watching through field glasses, yelled, "Firing on the Commissioners!"

General Gillem seemed dazed at the news but issued the necessary orders and the men fell into formation quickly.

Colonel Miller and his men were ahead and met Dyer who said that all but himself had been killed. Then they intercepted Frank Riddle who said that all others had been slain. Next Tobey approached with the statement that Canby, Thomas, and Meacham were dead. The troops kept moving forward and came upon Meacham struggling to arise. One of the soldiers was about to shoot when Colonel Miller yelled, "Don't shoot; he's a white man."

Surgeon Cabanis kneeled over Meacham and ordered a stretcher, Meacham murmuring in his delirium, "I am dead; I am dead," and calling for water. The surgeon put a canteen of brandy to Meacham's lips and the lips refused the drink. Even in his plight the temperance principles of Meacham rejected the liquor. But Dr. Cabanis forced the wounded man to drink. The stretcher bearers carried Meacham away and others went on to bring the bodies of General Canby and Reverend Thomas.

The hospital tents were placed in readiness to receive the wounded from the imminent battle, which promised numerous casualties if it followed the pattern of the January fight. But the troops did not pursue the Modocs. Instead, having found Meacham and the bodies of Canby and Thomas, they marched back to camp. Colonel Miller was not under orders to attack because General Gillem had decided to withhold such orders until the arrival of the Warm Springs Indians who were on their way to join the troops.

Official messages announcing the tragedy were sent. The newspaper representatives dispatched couriers to Yreka with the first accounts and the surgeon went to work to save Meacham's life. A messenger was sent to Linkville to bring Captain Ferree, Meacham's brother-in-law, who came post-haste.

MODOC BACKGROUND FOR THE MURDERS

It will be remembered that Tobey Riddle had been the messenger sent to Captain Jack and those of his people who wanted peace; that Jack had declined to listen to Tobey except in the presence of the tribe; that a minority had voted with Jack to accept the offer; that they dared not leave under threat of death by the majority.

Subsequent testimony revealed that after Tobey left the meeting the bloodthirsty majority made its weight felt. A tribal council was held on the morning of April 11th. Captain Jack, Scarface Charley, and a few others opposed the contemplated murders. Jack declared emphatically that the deed should not be done. The murderous majority placed a woman's hat on Captain Jack's head, and threw a shawl over his shoulders, roughly shoving him onto a seat on a rock. They accused him of cowardice, calling him "a woman and a white-face squaw." They told him that his heart had changed and that he had gone back on his own words, by which they referred to majority rule, which system he had instituted. They said that the white man had stolen his heart and that he was no longer a Modoc. Jack could not stand the taunts. He jumped to his feet, tossing the hat and shawl aside and shouted, "I am a Modoc. I am chief. It shall be done if it costs every drop of blood in my heart. But hear me all my people—this day's work will cost the life of every Modoc brave; we will not live to see it ended."

Having reached a decision, Jack planned the assassination with cunning and coolness. He asserted his right to kill General Canby and chose Ellen's Man to be his helper. Schonchin John, next in rank to Captain Jack, chose Meacham as his victim and appointed Hooker Jim to assist. Boston Charley and Bogus Charley selected Reverend Thomas, who had given each of those two unworthies a suit of clothes each only the day before. Shacknasty Jim and Barncho were allotted Mr. Dyer. Discussion then turned to who should take care of Frank Riddle, whereupon Scarface Charley gave notice that if Riddle or his wife were harmed that he would surely avenge them.

There had been a great rivalry among the tribesmen concerning who would have the honor of participating in the killings. The selections having been made, the details of the plan were carefully rehearsed, during which the additional plan for luring Colonel Mason to his death was decided. Captain Jack told his sister and Scarface Charley that he was ashamed of what he was about to do and that he had not thought that he would ever agree to such a thing. Bogus Charley was the first to propose the murders and he had been the one particularly favored by both General Canby and General Gillem, in fact both of them recognized him as interpreter instead of Frank or Tobey Riddle.

At any rate the deed had been done. The soldiers had marched back to camp after recovering the bodies and the Modocs were back in the rocky fastnesses of the Lava Beds. There a bitter quarrel ensued. Shacknasty Jim was roundly criticised for not having killed Mr. Dyer. Those assigned to Colonel Mason's murder were berated for Major Boyle's escape. They quarreled over the division of the clothing which had been worn by Canby, Meacham and Thomas. Captain Jack claimed the uniform of General Canby. The two Charleys divided the clothing of Reverend Thomas. Schonchin John, Shacknasty Jim, and Hooker Jim divided Meacham's effects. But while quarreling they knew that they must prepare for the defense which they felt was to be their immediate problem, for none doubted that the attack by the troops would not be long delayed. So they pledged each other to fight till the last of them was dead. Curly-haired Doctor marshalled his helpers and began the Great Medicine Dance. It lasted all night. Morning came and with it no evidence of the expected attack. The Modocs, except Captain Jack and Scarface Charley, were exultant. The majority thought that the Doctor's medicine had worked its magic; that they had frightened the government which would now grant everything the Modocs asked.

Captain Jack and Scarface Charley could see more clearly and warned the others that the army would come and that it meant a fight to the death.

THE WARM SPRINGS INDIAN SCOUTS ARRIVE

Before daylight on April 12th a picket at Colonel Mason's camp challenged a group of horsemen. Their leader approached and identified himself as Donald McKay, who was a step-grandson of Dr. John McLoughlin, the first Chief Factor of the Hudson's Bay Company, at Vancouver, famous scout and veteran of several Indian wars, a man with Cayuse Indian blood from his mother. With him were 72 Warm Springs Indians, friends of A. B. Meacham since 1871, when Meacham was Superintendent of Indian Affairs for Oregon. They were all dressed in the uniforms of the United States Army, having enlisted with the consent of their Agent on their reservation 250 miles to the north. McKay reported to Colonel Mason's headquarters and returned to his men, to be met with many inquiries about Meacham's condition. McKay had the respect of his charges, and his name was enough to cause a recalcitrant red man to be cautious. McKay, in spite of his part-Indian ancestry, had always been on the side of the white man.

On that day and the following, preparations were made for attack. The Modocs were being inspired by their medicine man who promised immunity from soldiers' bullets. Long Jim, a Modoc who had been under guard in the camp of the soldiers, had escaped and reported the current news to Captain Jack—that Meacham was alive; that McKay and his Warm Springs Scouts had arrived; that preparations for attack by 1000 soldiers had been completed.

At four o'clock in the morning of April 14th, the troops and the Warm Springs scouts assembled. Captain Jack, too, had made his preparations. His old people and the children had been hidden in caves; the young women had been detailed to take water and ammunition to the warriors, each of whom was in his appointed position. The Modocs were armed even better than on January 17th for they had acquired the guns and ammunition from the soldiers who had fallen on that day. Suddenly the artillery opened fire on the stronghold. That was the signal for the troops to advance. The army lines moved forward with no Modocs in sight and no evidence of their presence among the rocks. Then, at an unexpected moment, the Modocs opened fire. Soldiers began falling here and there. Officers urged their men forward. The Indians intensified their firing. More soldiers fell and the bugle sounded retreat. Dead and wounded were carried away, some on stretchers to boats on the lake, by which means they were transported to the hospital tents at camp; others by mule-litters, a sort of stretcher with inclined back-rest, strapped to a mule's back. Five soldiers died, many more were wounded.

The battle was not abandoned. Throughout the day and that night the fight continued, the soldiers working in reliefs, thus securing rest and sleep, while at the same time the Modocs had to remain at their posts.

Immediately to the west of Captain Jack's stronghold was a comparatively level space about a quarter-mile wide. It was absolutely without protection from the Modoc rifles but had to be crossed to invest the stronghold. Lieutenant Eagan and his company were given that hazardous assignment. Eagan led his men and was the first to fall wounded. Then his men began to suffer casualties. Eagan ordered his soldiers to fall back, which they did, but to a position from which they could stop any attempt of the Modocs to capture Eagan and their other comrades who had fallen.

Surgeon Cabanis, hearing that Eagan had been wounded, immediately started to the Lieutenant's aid, dodging a hail of Modoc bullets. He reached the fallen officer and dressed his wound but could not move him out of range.

The Modocs ran out of water. They had even used up the ice often present in some of the caves. Water they must have and they decided to get to the lake to replenish their supply. Concealed behind bundles of sagebrush they started crawling toward the lake, knowing that they had to cut through the lines of the soldiers. As they came close to the troops the Indians opened a terrific firing to which the soldiers quickly replied with equal vigor. The shooting was heavy and while the Modocs did not reach the lake, neither did they retreat. Night came on and through its enduring hours the fight continued. In the morning the Indians abandoned their attempt to reach the lake and also arrived at another decision, namely, that when another night arrived that they would evacuate their stronghold.

Not satisfied to pass the daylight hours inactively, the Modocs sneaked out to the flat area which had been the scene of Lieutenant Eagan's fight the day previous, with the intention of killing any of the civilian teamsters who might be passing, or the stretcher bearers who were bringing in the wounded. Hooker Jim was the only Modoc to crown that venture with successs. He shot a young man named Hovey, who was scalped while still alive. Then Hooker Jim and his fellows crushed Hovey's head to a pulp by battering it with stones, stripped his body, took his horses, and went their way. Emboldened, the Modocs circled towards the army camp, knowing that most of the soldiers were at the job of investing the stronghold. Lieutenant Grier had been left in charge of the camp. When he realized that an attack was imminent he telegraphed Colonel Green that the Indians were out of their camp and attacking the army camp. Grier armed his civilian teamsters to augment his camp guard and prepared to meet the attack. However, the Indians satisfied themselves by firing a few shots and withdrew.

There was considerable ineffectual and desultory firing throughout the day. Curiosity on the part of the Modocs did result in casualties for them. One shell which had landed the previous day had failed to explode. Some of the Modocs decided to see what was inside the projectile, resulting in its detonation and the death of two Modocs.

A few old Indian women passed through the army lines to the lake. With them was a younger Modoc dressed in woman's clothing. After satisfying his thirst he started back to the Lava Beds but his manner of walking betrayed his masculinity and he was shot, a dozen bullets finding their mark. The soldiers scalped him, actually contriving five or six scalps which were subdivided so comrades could share in the trophy taking.

Night came on. The artillery kept up a constant bombardment, but Captain Jack had gathered his people and left the stronghold in the early hours of the night, content that the shells fall near his now empty caves. In the morning the investment proceeded. The soldiers, ever on the alert, converged on the caves only to find that their quarry had escaped—all except one old man whom they incorrectly declared to be Schonchin John. A fusillade killed him and again the soldiers divided an Indian scalp into many pieces. They explored the caves and recesses, finding no more—not even any trace of the Indian cremation which had been given as a reason for delay in surrendering several days earlier.

While the fighting just described was in progress it should be mentioned parenthetically that the bodies of General Canby and Reverend Thomas were enroute to their burial places, and Orpha Meacham, wife of A. B. Meacham, was on her way by stage to be at her husband's side.

Captain Jack and his people found a new hiding place where they were resting from three days of fighting, but they were not so far away but that they could faintly hear the shots which had dispatched the supposed Schonchin John. Actually, Captain Jack's new refuge was within sight of the signal station on the bluff. The Modocs had moved a few miles south into another jumble of lava rocks. With native cleverness their concealment was complete, not even a wisp of smoke to be seen. Their women were at outlook stations while the warriors rested.

Then 14 Modocs were seen to be going for water. A company of soldiers was sent to engage the Indians who had reached a point about a half-mile from the army camp. Firing started at once and the Modoc war-whoop could be plainly heard. The skirmish was a brief one for the soldiers turned back to camp carrying three dead. The Modocs kept coming until they were close enough to fire a few shots which landed among the army tents. Artillery was brought to bear on the Indians who took shelter behind rocks at each round of shells, after each of which the Modocs came out of hiding and patted their shot-pouches in derision. General Gillem ordered the shelling to be discontinued and the Indians insolently mocked the artillery fire by bunching their rifles, elevating the barrels, and firing volleys into camp, Scarface Charley acting as their commanding officer. Tiring of their lethal pastime they went back to their camp. The whole episode reflected anything but credit on the soldiers—14 Indians flaunting their unconcern in the presence of several hundred soldiers.

Meanwhile news dispatches were constantly reaching the nation by courier service to Yreka, California. Most of these accounts were complimentary to the army in that they recited that the Modocs were surrounded; that they could not escape; that the Warm Springs Scouts were on outpost. From every section of the country came demands for the extermination of the Modocs. The score to date was almost wholly to the Indians' credit. About 50 soldiers had died. The hospital tents were crowded with wounded. Almost daily the Modocs waylaid some straggling soldier in sight of camp, killed, stripped, and scalped him. Modoc emissaries visited many other Indian tribes for the purpose of recruiting allies for a general Indian uprising. There were sympathetic ears in all the tribes to listen to the glowing accounts of Modoc successes and, while a major war did not ensue, it was probably closer to realization than most people thought.

Mrs. Meacham had been stopped at Linkville where, on April 19th, she received a message from her brother, D. J. Ferree, to hire an escort and be at the mouth of Lost River at noon the next day when she would be met by a party bringing her wounded husband out of the war zone. However, another day went by because it was feared that Meacham could not survive the trip, but on the second morning he was transported by boat across the lake. A storm arose which almost swamped the boat but finally the crossing was completed and Meacham was transferred to an ambulance which took him back to civilization and convalescence, at Linkville. From there he was moved to Captain Ferree's ranch. There Ferree received a message from L. S. Dyer, Agent at Klamath Reservation, and who had been one of the Commissioners. Under date of April 23rd Dyer wrote that the Klamath Indians had held a war council the night before and that all white women and children had been placed in Fort Klamath for safety. The reason for the war council and the inspiration for Dyer's message stemmed from the fact that word had reached the Klamaths from some of Schonchin John's friends that Meacham had killed Schonchin John during the trouble at the council tent and that Meacham was convalescing at Ferree's ranch. Dyer feared that the Klamaths might attack the ranch for the purpose of killing Meacham. As a result of Dyer's warning Meacham was moved back to Linkville. As subsequent events proved, Schonchin John had recovered from the wound caused by the shot from Meacham's Derringer.

The army was inactive for several days. The reasons for not following up the Modocs are not apparent. By April 26th the Warm Springs Scouts had definitely located the Modoc hide-out. A detachment was organized to reconnoiter for the express purpose of determining whether or not field guns could be placed in position to shell the Indian camp. There were 76 men and officers and Donald McKay and 14 of his Warm Springs Scouts in the contingent. In over-all command was Captain E. Thomas of the 4th Artillery. First Lieutenant Thomas Wright of the 12th Infantry was present in command of detachments from his own company and that of the wounded Lieutenant Eagan. Lieutenants Arthur Cranston, Albion Howe, and Harris, all of the 4th Artillery, Assistant Surgeon B. Semig, guide H. C. Tichnor, Chief Packer Louis Webber and two assistant packers were with the group.

It is well to explain that contemporary historians and newspaper correspondents often elevated the titles of army officers. For example, Lieutenant Wright, who was son of General Wright, the famous Indian fighter of earlier wars, was often referred to as "Colonel" Wright in accounts of the Modoc War written at that time. Sometimes that practice was due to the fact that the officer named was in temporary command of a unit larger than that usually accorded his rank, and sometimes it was due to the practice of bestowing brevet commissions. In the latter case an officer, who, for example, held a commission as a captain, might also hold a brevet commission as a Colonel, which entitled him to command a regiment instead of a company, but still at a captain's pay. It was a method of avoiding internal quarrels because of officer seniority. Lieutenant Wright when styled "Colonel" was in the first of the two categories just described.

These troops were all from General Gillem's camp at the foot of the bluff. The Warm Springs Scouts were encamped in the old Modoc stronghold and were under orders to join the rest of the troops either enroute or at destination, which was a butte on the side of the Lava Beds opposite General Gillem's camp. Captain Thomas was under explicit orders to avoid an engagement. The butte was in full view of Gillem's signal station and about three miles distant.

The detachment set out, with skirmishers forward and on the flanks, until it reached the foot of the butte. No Indians having been seen, Captain Thomas ordered a halt for lunch and called in his skirmishers. Lieutenant Wright advised against removing the precaution, observing to Captain Thomas that when Indians were out of sight was the very time to be expecting them. The men began to prepare their meal except Lieutenant Cranston and 12 men who left to explore the terrain, Cranston remarking that he was going to "raise some Indians." Moving out they soon passed from sight of the main body of the detachment. McKay and his scouts had not yet joined the detachment. Suddenly a withering fire from the rocks on both sides of Lieutenant Cranston's detail struck every man. Hearing the firing, those back with Captain Thomas were thrown into confusion. Thomas ordered Lieutenant Harris with his men to take up a position on the side of the butte. Harris reached his position only to find the Modocs above him, firing into his ranks. Some of his men were hit and Harris ordered a retreat, leaving his dead and wounded, In the retreat Harris, himself, was mortally wounded. The Indians followed up their advantage with appalling results. Every commissioned officer in Thomas' command except Assistant Surgeon Semig was killed and he was wounded. Of the 66 enlisted men only 23 returned to headquarters. Donald McKay and his scouts heard the firing and hastened to the scene, arriving in time to prevent the annihilation of the entire detachment. As a further sad commentary McKay and his scouts were held off for a time by firing from the troops who thought they were Modocs.

The engagement and slaughter lasted three hours in plain sight of the signal station. Some of the 23 survivors were back in camp for more than an hour before Colonel Green and his command were ordered to the rescue. There were 24 Modocs in the fight, not one of whom was even wounded. Fifty-three officers and enlisted men were either killed or wounded. In fact the battle was so one-sided that Scarface Charley called out in English, "All you fellows that ain't dead had better go home. We don't want to kill you all in one day." Charley insisted that the Modocs stop their slaughter saying, "My heart is sick seeing so much blood and so many men lying dead."

Why Captain Thomas called in his skirmishers will never be

known. What circumstances caused Donald McKay to be in no hurry to join Thomas' column will always be a matter of conjecture. How Captain Jack's tribesmen could escape casualties and nullify the efforts of a large body of troops is something to cause wonderment. It is enough to say that the troops again delayed attacking. They awaited reinforcements. Meanwhile, Governor Grover of Oregon had called out volunteers to go into the Modoc country to protect the settlers.

A change in command of the war was deemed necessary and Colonel Jeff. C. Davis of the 23rd Infantry was sent to assume command. He was usually referred to in unofficial circles as "General" Davis while prosecuting the Modoc War. On May 8, 1873, Davis wired the War Department that he had sent two squaws into the Lava Beds on May 6th. The squaws returned on the 7th reporting that they had seen no Indians but that they had found the bodies of Lieutenant Cranston and his men. Davis also informed the Department that he had sent the Warm Springs Scouts out on the 7th and had received a report from them that the Modocs had departed in a southeasterly direction. That report was bolstered by the fact that a supply train had been attacked on the east side of Tule Lake on the 7th, the attack having been made by 15 or 20 Modocs who had whipped the supply train escort of equal number, wounding three of the escort without casualties to the Indians. Davis further said that it was his intention to send troops in search of the Modocs, the soldiers to carry five days' rations.

Accordingly Davis sent two companies, those of H. C. Hasbrouck and James Jackson, under Hasbrouck's command, to find the Indians. On the evening of the 9th these troops camped at a lake where signs of Indians were found. Hasbrouck's orders were not limited to finding the Indians but also covered protection for the settlers, it being feared that since the Modocs had tasted so much blood that they might murder the settlers.

On the morning of May 10th the Indians made a surprise attack just at daylight. While the soldiers were surprised they quickly responded and did so well that the Modocs began a retreat toward the Lava Beds. Heavy firing was exchanged for three miles, which brought the Indians back to their old stronghold, the Warm Springs Scouts being on duty in the field. While Davis' official report gives Hasbrouck's command credit for the first of the Modoc reverses, it is silent on the fact that McKay and his Warm Springs Scouts again arrived at the right time to assist troops in turning the tide of battle. They drove the Modocs back to the Lava Beds and they recaptured the horses that had been taken from the supply train on the 7th.

In that fight Captain Jack participated, wearing General Canby's uniform, and Ellen's Man, sometimes called George, was killed. He, it will be recalled, was Captain Jack's helper in the murder of General Canby. Two Warm Springs Scouts lost their lives in the fray.

The death of Ellen's Man stirred up the quarrel between the factions in Captain Jack's tribe. Jack was accused of placing those not of his immediate family in the forefront of battle. That quarrel culminated in a genuine division of the band. Fourteen Modocs, all of whom had always voted for war, finally turned traitors to Jack and ultimately offered themselves as scouts for the army to run Jack to earth, and without promise of amnesty to themselves. Such was the Modoc character.

The leaders of this traitorous group were Bogus Charley, Hooker Jim, Shacknasty Jim, and Steamboat Frank, none of whom was ever indicted and any one of whom was guilty of more crimes and breaches of faith than any other Modoc with the possible exception of Schonchin John.

At any rate, the quarrel among the Modocs caused a division of the band and both factions left the Lava Beds. The next few pages follow closely the text of Davis' official report.

The troops soon learned of the departure of the Modocs and discovered that the Indians were traveling in a westerly direction. Captain Hasbrouck's cavalry command made a hard march of 50 miles and came upon the faction called the Cottonwood band. A sharp, running fight followed and continued for seven or eight miles, at the end of which the Indians scattered. Night was approaching, the troopers' horses were exhausted, a few Modocs had been captured and Hasbrouck withdrew to Fairchild's ranch a few miles away for food, forage, and rest. Their captives said that the Cottonwood band would like to surrender, if given the opportunity. Such an opportunity was provided through friendly Indians, whereupon the Modocs tried to bargain for terms. Davis refused, guaranteeing nothing but safe conduct to his headquarters. On May 22nd the Cottonwood band came in and laid down their arms. Counting men, women, and children they numbered about 75 persons.

Colonel Davis now decided to accept the services of the traitors but made no promise of amnesty. The four Modoc renegades set out and on the third day found Captain Jack's camp on Willow Creek, east of Wright Lake and about 15 miles from the Applegate ranch, to which place Davis and his staff had moved and where he was to await the return of the four Indians and the cavalry.

On May 28th the four Modocs reported to Davis, saying that Captain Jack had denounced them, had called them "squaws," and had said that he intended to attack Applegate's ranch that night. Davis immediately sent an aide, Captain E. V. Sumner, back to the rendezvous at Tule Lake with orders for Hasbrouck's and Jackson's commands to hasten to Applegate's ranch and to bring three days' rations in haversacks and ten days' rations on pack mules. The cavalrymen arrived on the morning of May 29th under command of their regular leader, Major John Green.

Only one hour's rest was granted the men and horses after which they started in pursuit of Captain Jack's band. About one o'clock in the afternoon of the same day the troops surprised the Modocs on Willow Creek. This creek formed the headwaters of Lost River. The Modocs fled in the direction of Langell Valley, a place just across the California-Oregon boundary on the Oregon side. The end of the campaign seemed near and each detachment of troops vied with the others to be the one responsible for Captain Jack's death or capture. Lieutenant-Colonel Frank Wheaton of the 21st Infantry had reported to Colonel Davis on the 22nd at Fairchild's ranch. Davis placed Wheaton in command of the District of the Lakes. Wheaton moved up to Applegate's ranch together with Perry's detachment of cavalry and these troops were ordered to join in the hunt. Meanwhile many of Jack's band had been picked up by the several detachments of troops but Jack himself and several of his most noted warriors were still on the loose. It fell to the lot of Perry's cavalrymen to capture Captain Jack on June 1st. At the moment of capture he had only two or three braves with him and excused his plight by saying that his "legs had given out." These prisoners were brought in to Davis' headquarters and orders were issued that all prisoners would be concentrated at Boyle's Camp on Tule Lake.

By June 5th all of the important Modocs had been assembled at Boyle's Camp. Davis received orders to hold them under guard pending further instructions. Davis recites in his report that until then it was his intention to execute eight or ten of the ringleaders, and that he understood that to have been implied in the orders issued for the guidance of the Commander of the Modoc Expedition immediately after the murders of the Peace Commissioners, as well as by his own judgment as Commander in the field. He then received instructions from the Attorney-General to assemble a military tribunal to try the Modocs, and to that end all prisoners were eventually moved to Fort Klamath.

For the sake of avoiding the accusation of inaccuracy in some of the details, it should be pointed out that General Davis' report differs somewhat in the non-essentials from the news article in the *New York Times* of June 17, 1873. That article was written by Samuel A. Clark of Salem, Oregon, who was the Oregon correspondent for the *Times* and who was on the scene of these activities with every opportunity to learn the facts and circumstances. He says that General Davis had sent Major Trumble with his squadron and some Warm Springs Scouts—and with young Applegate and Jesse Applegate's nephew, Charles Putnam, as guides—to intercept Captain Jack, and that this force and not Perry's cavalry made the capture. Be that as it may, the Chief of the Modocs had been run to earth.

One fact stands out, and it is that four of the Modocs most guilty of all offenses, subsequently charged to Captain Jack and his fellow defendants, were Bogus Charley, Hooker Jim, Shacknasty Jim, and Steamboat Frank. Not only were they traitors to Captain Jack but Hooker Jim was the guide for Hasbrouck's command in the final phases of the round-up, while Steamboat Frank, with the assistance of Shacknasty Jim and Bogus Charley, guided Major Green's detachment. And in spite of their characters it must be recorded that they performed their services as guides in perfect good faith. Again, therefore, we point out that there were many facets to the Modoc personality.

SOME INCIDENTS PRECEDING THE TRIAL

On the evening of his capture, Captain Jack underwent a deep humiliation. General Davis ordered that Jack and Schonchin John be shackled together with leg-irons. As the two were led out under guard to the blacksmith's forge Jack showed considerable apprehension until John Fairchild explained through Scarface Charley, as interpreter, what was about to transpire. The two Modocs protested that the indignity was unnecessary, but when they realized that the order would be carried out they submitted quietly.

As a part of the fulfillment of the order to concentrate all captives at Boyle's Camp on Tule Lake, some of the less important Modocs were to be moved from Fairchild's ranch to Boyle's Camp on June 8th. The party consisted of John Fairchild, his brother James, and 17 Modocs, the latter including Bogus Charley and Shacknasty Jim. Before reaching Lost River the party divided. James Fairchild drove the 4-mule wagon in which were 15 Modoc men, women, and children, and took a longer route in order to utilize a wagon ford on the river. John Fairchild, Bogus Charley, and Shacknasty Jim, on horseback, took a shorter route. The latter three, anticipating no trouble, made no effort to rejoin James Fairchild.

When James reached the river he encountered a group of Oregon Volunteers under the command of Captain Hizer. The volunteers gathered round the wagon and questioned Fairchild who convinced them that his charges were unimportant Modocs, none of whom were guilty of murder, nor had they had a part in the assassination of the Peace Commissioners. Fairchild proceeded on his way and after traveling a few miles saw two horsemen who evidently intended to intercept the wagon. The Indians begged Fairchild to turn back but while he sensed danger he also knew that the horsemen could overtake the heavy wagon should he attempt to turn back. So he drove on to a point where the two men were waiting, Fairchild in vain scanning the countryside for his brother John and the two Indians with him.

The two men ordered Fairchild to halt, one of them pointing a pistol at Fairchild's head and saying that he was going to kill Fairchild as well as the Indians. The second man cut the mules loose from the wagon and Fairchild jumped to the ground still holding the lines. The Indians in the wagon were, of course, unarmed. The women raised their hands imploringly, crying, "Don't kill! Don't kill!" The four Indian men said nothing. They knew words were useless. The first shot killed Little John, his brains scattering over the women and children. Next, Te-he Jack died, floundering among the occupants of the wagon. Then Poney's blood spurted over his wife and children, and Mooch was the fourth to die. Not satisfied, they shot Little John's wife through the shoulder. Blood dripped through the wagon bed. A cloud of dust was seen in the distance and the two bloody brutes of white men decamped in haste. The dust was caused by Sergeant Murphy and ten men of the 4th Artillery who speedily approached the wagon. Fairchild quickly told the story but the murderers were not pursued. No effort was ever made to indict them though many people knew who they were.

Before orders had been received limiting Davis in his punishment of the criminals, construction of a gallows had been started. That greatly excited the Indians once it began to take shape and its purpose became known. Captain Jack and Schonchin John were photographed with the gibbet as a background. It was their first experience with a camera, and when ranged in front of it, had expected to die, for they thought it was some new type of big gun.

General Davis invited the settlers to come into camp to identify the Modocs who had participated in the murders of November 29, 1872, and to indicate their personal belongings recovered from the Indians. Two of the widows from that bloody day, Mrs. Boddy and Mrs. Schiere, attempted to kill Hooker Jim and Steamboat Frank whom they identified as participants in the murders of their husbands. Mrs. Boddy lunged at Hooker Jim with a knife and Mrs. Schiere drew a pistol to shoot Steamboat Frank. General Davis personally disarmed both women, accidentally receiving a slight cut from the knife.

Construction of the gallows was suspended when Davis received his orders to try the prisoners by military court — whereupon he decided to move the proceedings to Fort Klamath, as previously mentioned. Enroute, Curley-haired Jack committed suicide by shooting out his brains. He it was who had murdered Lieutenant Sherwood, April 11, 1873, under a flag of truce.

THE TRIAL

At Fort Klamath the military court was set in a hall. A long, narrow table stood in the middle of the room. Here, July 5, 1873, the trial started. At the head of the table sat Major H. P. Curtis, Judge Advocate, and, nearby, Dr. E. S. Belden, shorthand reporter. At the other end of the table was Lieutenant-Colonel Elliott of the Ist Cavalry; to his right, Captain Hasbrouck of the 4th Artillery and Captain Pollock of the 21st Infantry. To Elliott's left were Captain John Mendenhall of the 4th Artillery and 2nd Lieutenant George Kingsbury of the 12th Infantry. Seated on a bench to the right of Elliott were Captain Jack, Schonchin John, Black Jim, and Boston Charley. Lying on the floor were Barncho and Slolux. Back of Major Curtis were Frank Riddle and Tobey. At another table were newspaper reporters and at either end of the room was a detail of soldiers with bayonets fixed. Hooker Jim, Bogus Charley, Shacknasty Jim, and Steamboat Frank, unfettered and unguarded, stood idly near the open door among the crowd of spectators.

The several members of the court, the interpreters Frank and Tobey Riddle, and the official reporter were all duly sworn and the prisoners were arraigned.

Two charges were preferred against each prisoner. The first was "murder in violation of the laws of war" and referred, of course, to the killing of General Canby and Reverend Thomas. The second charge was "assault with intent to kill in violation of the laws of war" and "assault on the Commissioners," referring to the attempt to kill A. B. Meacham and L. S. Dyer. To both charges all prisoners pleaded "not guilty."

The Court then began hearing testimony, T. F. (Frank) Riddle being the first witness. His testimony consumed the remainder of the day and part of the next, July 6th, when he was followed on the witness stand by L. S. Dyer.

On the third day, July 7th, the Court heard the testimony of Shacknasty Jim, Steamboat Frank, Bogus Charley, and Hooker Jim, in the order named. Then another Modoc, known both as William and as Whim, was called and while he was testifying A. B. Meacham entered the court room. Less than three months had passed since he had been desperately wounded. Meacham was called as a witness.

When court adjourned for the day Meacham inquired of Elliott whether it was a fact, as the proceedings indicated, that the prisoners had no legal representative, and upon being answered in the affirmative, Meacham volunteered to serve as their counsel rather than see the trial conducted in an ex-parte manner. Meacham told Elliott that he would decide definitely by the following morning. However, upon advice of his friends and the professional advice of an army surgeon, Meacham was persuaded to forego the idea as a menace to his recovery.

On the fourth day of the trial, July 8th, Lieutenant H. R. Anderson of the 4th Artillery, was called as a witness, chiefly in regard to General Canby's relation to the Government, the Army, and the Commission. He was followed by Assistant-Surgeon Henry C. McEldery, who testified about the examination of the bodies of General Canby and Reverend Thomas.

The Government rested its case and only three witnesses were called for the defense, Scarface Charley, Dave, and One-eyed Mose, all Modocs. Captain Jack then told the court that he had no further testimony to present. The Court informed him that if he wished he could make a statement. Jack arose hesitatingly and made a speech and was followed briefly by Schonchin John, after which court adjourned for the day.

Next day when the verdict was announced it recited that the death penalty had been fixed for Captain Jack, Schonchin John, Black Jim, Boston Charley, Barncho and Slolux, and October 3, 1873, was designated as the day of execution. The Judge-Advocate also ruled that no others would be placed on trial and, since that was his prerogative, several Modocs equally guilty with those condemned, were saved by that act of Major Curtis.

The rest of the Modocs were confined in a stockade near the fort except the traitor scouts who were at complete liberty. Occasionally the condemned were permitted to visit the stockade, and in turn their families visited them in the guard house.

At the conclusion of the trial A. B. Meacham left Fort Klamath, first visiting the prisoners and shaking hands with them as evidence of his forgiveness. Captain Jack told Meacham that but one side of the story had been told and that he had no one to speak for him. Meacham assured Jack that the trial had been honestly conducted but that he, Meacham, would write a fair statement of all the facts for everybody to read. Jack expressed a great dread of being hanged and held Meacham's hand till the moment of Meacham's departure.

THE EXECUTION

On October 2, 1873, the long scaffold had been completed on the open level of the meadow. Six ropes dangled from the beams.

Also on that day General Wheaton, accompanied by Father Huegemborg, the Catholic priest who was Post Chaplain, Oliver

Applegate, and Dave Hill who was a Klamath Indian acting as interpreter, visited the prisoners for the purpose of officially notifying them of the sentence. The Chaplain offered a prayer to which the condemned men listened attentively. General Wheaton then asked the Chaplain to inform the prisoners of their fate. The six condemned men listened with traditional Indian stoicism. Then Captain Jack spoke briefly saying that when he had surrendered that he had expected to be pardoned and live with his people in Klamath Land. He also said that he felt that Bogus Charley, Shacknasty Jim, Hooker Jim, and Steamboat Frank had triumphed over both himself and the Government.

General Wheaton then asked Captain Jack whom he wished to select to rule the tribe in his stead and Jack replied that he could trust no Modoc—not even Scarface Charley. Slolux and Barncho both spoke, each denying responsibility for the crime. Black Jim, who was Captain Jack's half-brother, said that he was anxious to live so that he could lead the tribe, to which suggestion Captain Jack shook his head in disapproval. Then Jack asked that the execution be postponed until his story could be submitted to the President of the United States because of the belief that the President did not know who had instigated the murders of General Canby and Reverend Thomas.

The request was denied and then Boston Charley made a stirring speech in which he confessed his part in the crime; that the murderers suspected the Commissioners of treachery. Schonchin John was the last to speak. He was most dramatic, ending with the words, "War is a terrible thing. All men must suffer—the best horses, the best cattle, and the best men. I can now only say, 'Let Schonchin die'. "

Then the Chaplain said another prayer, which Oliver Applegate translated into Chinook jargon to Dave Hill, who repeated the words in the Modoc tongue, whereupon General Wheaton terminated the interview.

Sheriff McKenzie of Jackson County, Oregon, arrived with warrants for the arrest of the four traitorous scouts and certified copies of indictments, together with a letter from L. F. Grover, Governor of Oregon, addressed to Jeff. C. Davis, Commanding the Department of the Columbia. The letter recited that Judge Prime of the Circuit Court of Jackson County had issued a writ of habeas corpus commanding that those named be brought before the Jackson County court for trial. The efforts of the Oregon authorities were futile, ending with a communication from E. D. Townsend, Adjutant-General of the United States, to the effect that all other Modocs except the condemned were by concurrence of the President to be sent to Fort E. A. Russell and that no further action was necessary.

The morning of October 3, 1873, dawned to find the roads leading to the fort lined with many onlookers. At 9:30 A. M. a detail of soldiers took position in front of the guard house and the Officer of the Day, Colonel Hoge, entered and unlocked the cells. A wagon drawn by four horses drew near the guard house. In the wagon were four coffins. The six prisoners mounted the wagon. The blacksmith then cut the chains from the prisoners. Captain Jack, Schonchin John, Boston Charley and Black Jim were then directed to mount the scaffold. Slolux and Barncho remained in the wagon.

Captain Jack was placed at the extreme right, next to him was Schonchin John, then Black Jim, then Boston Charley. Corporal Ross, of Company G, 12th Infantry, adjusted the rope to Captain Jack's neck. Corporal Killien performed that duty for Schonchin John, Private Robert Wilton for Black Jim, Private Anderson for Boston Charley. The Adjutant read two documents, one calling for the execution of the six condemned men and the other a commutation of sentence to life imprisonment for Slolux and Barncho, by order of the President of the United States. An axe flashed in the sunlight, severing the rope which held the trap and four Modocs swung into eternity. Their bodies were placed in the coffins and Slolux and Barncho rode back in the wagon with the bodies of the dead as cries of anguish arose from the stockade.

Note: A. B. Meacham says in his book, *Wigwam and Warpath,* that an offer of $10,000 was made to General Wheaton for the body of Captain Jack, which offer was indignantly refused. Meacham does not say who made the offer.

Note: The author has a letter dated March 24, 1949, from the late N. H. Atchison, Office Representative of the Masonic Service Bureau, Portland, Oregon, as follows:

"In reply to yours regarding Captain Jack's skull, would say that on the death of Col. Robert A. Miller, who lived at 235 N. E. 16th Ave., Portland, Ore., his will left all his effects to the Grand Lodge AF&AM of Oregon. On going over same we found in the basement several boxes filled with old copies of Oregon papers, rocks from mining properties, and in one of them we found three skulls, one of which had a label on it reading "Captain Jack." We had a representative from the University of Oregon come up and go over these effects and some of them, including the skulls, were sent to the University. If this gives you anything you can use you are at liberty to do so."

THE NEZ PERCE WAR

BATTLE OF THE CLEARWATER

YOUNG JOSEPH—Chief of the Nez Perces—was greatest of all chiefs. His father, Old Joseph, was himself a great chief, and, no doubt, by precept and example contributed much to his son's later greatness. Today, when reference is made to "Chief Joseph," it always means Joseph, the Younger, and this text will follow that precedent.

The Nez Perces were predominant among the native races—intelligent, strong and cleanly. Their country comprised Southwestern Idaho, Southeast Washington, and Northeast Oregon. The Wallowa Valley in Northeastern Oregon was home to Old Joseph. Here was a garden spot and life was good. "Wallowa" means "Winding River." The old chieftain was aware of increasing numbers of white people and sensed the day when his tribesmen would be asked or told to move elsewhere. On his deathbed he called his sons Joseph and Ollicut to him and admonished them never to give up their land in which their father's grave was to be. Young Joseph, two years older than Ollicut, was hereditary chief, and the mantle of leadership fell on his shoulders. Primarily he was not a warrior. His preference was for peace, and he strongly desired to be left strictly alone with his people in the land they loved. Government decided otherwise. In 1873 a conference was held at Lapwai, Idaho, between various chiefs and government representatives. Joseph refused to move either to a reservation in Northern Idaho or to the Umatilla Reservation in Eastern Oregon. His refusal was reported to the Secretary of the Interior who decided that the Nez Perces could remain in the Wallowa Valley for the following summer and autumn. Then a Presidential order set apart the Wallowa and Imnaha valleys for Joseph and his non-treaty Indians. That arrangement continued until 1875 when increasing pressures from settlers persuaded the President to rescind his order and a commission was appointed to negotiate with Joseph and his people.

Joseph seems to have had two Indian names, Hallakallakeen, meaning "Eagle Wing" and In-mut-too-yah-lat-lat, meaning "Thunder traveling over the mountains." He, himself, said that his name was the second of those mentioned and that he was Chief of the Wal-lam-wat-kin band of Chute-pa-lu, or Nez Perces. He was of magnificent physique, dignified, passionately devoted to his followers, and would have been great in any company.

The Nez Perces were generally considered to be divided into three groups. In addition to the Wallowa branch under Joseph there was the Idaho branch, the largest. They lived in the fertile valleys of the Clearwater River and its tributaries, with their principal center at Kamiah. The third important group was that under Chief White Bird who lived in the Salmon River country. The main section of the tribe centered at Kamiah remained completely aloof from participation in hostilities. A smaller, struggling unit, under Chief Lookingglass, consisting of about 60 warriors and their families, ultimately joined Joseph, and is sometimes described as a fourth branch.

Early in May of 1877, the Government ordered General O. O. Howard, who was then in command of the Department of the Columbia, to call a council of all branches of the Nez Perces at Fort Lapwai in Northern Idaho. Here the Nez Perces congregated, including those under Joseph. The Government urged Joseph to move to a permanent home to be set aside on the Clearwater. Several days were spent in discussion and argument without persuading the Indians to make the move. General Howard, at length, decided that enough time had been spent in negotiations and decided to issue an ultimatum. There is much reason to believe that General Howard personally felt that Joseph's band should be permanently established on a Wallowa reservation but his orders read otherwise. Accordingly, he told Joseph that 30 days would be allowed him for the removal of his people and their belongings from the Wallowa country to the Clearwater. Joseph explained that his live-stock was scattered and that 30 days was insufficient in which to comply with the order without loss to the tribe in personal property, but General Howard would not modify the terms. Moreover, the whole situation was not aided by the arrest of Too-hul-hul-sute, a principal orator for the Nez Perces. General Howard had announced at the opening of the council that every Indian present was requested to express his opinions freely in reference to the Government's offer. The council had convened on May 3rd but Joseph had requested postponement until Chief White Bird and his band could arrive. The request was granted and the next day White Bird and his people arrived and the council started. Too-hul-hul-sute was the principal speaker for the Nez Perces that day, the substance of his argument being that God had created the earth to be as it is and that it was wrong to cultivate the soil or to build churches and schools upon it and that white settlers should be kept out of the Indian lands. General Howard replied that the non-treaty Indians, such as Joseph's band, were in the minority and that they would be well advised to follow the example of the more numerous treaty Indians. Howard realized that the Indian orator was a person of influence and decided that another postponement was advisable in order to dissipate the effect of Too-hul-hul-sute's speech.

So the council was again postponed until the following Monday. When it re-assembled Too-hul-hul-sute again appeared in the role of principal speaker. He said, "The Great Spirit Chief made the world as it is and as He wanted it, and He made a part of it for us to live upon. I do not see where you get authority to say that we should not live where He placed us."

This questioning of authority irritated General Howard, who ordered the speaker to stop any further talk in that vein and said that if the Indians did not move as suggested, that he, Howard, would "take the matter into my own hands and make you suffer for your disobedience." To that statement Too-hul-hul-sute made a strong reply, in effect asking General Howard if he had made the land, the rivers, the grass, and that if he had, then, without doubt, he had to speak to the Nez Perces as if they were boys. Howard, further irritated, said, "You are an impudent fellow and I will put you in the guardhouse." Howard thereupon ordered the arrest. The Indian made no resistance, merely saying that if that was Howard's order that, at least, he, Too-hul-hul-sute, had availed himself of the opportunity to speak for his people.

The arrest caused a great stir. Joseph knew that if he did not immediately bring about a change in the Indian sentiment that all of the white men would be killed within a few minutes. So Joseph advised his warriors to be calm and then arose, saying, "I am going to talk now. I don't care whether you arrest me or not." He then faced his people and continued, "The arrest of Too-hul-hul-sute was wrong, but we will not resent the insult. We were invited to this council to express our hearts and we have done so." Joseph then walked among his people quieting them and to that prompt action and his quieting words may be ascribed the reason for no hostile act at the council.

The next day General Howard invited Chiefs Joseph, White Bird and Lookingglass to ride with him in search for new lands for the Nez Perces. The chiefs accepted the invitation. In the course of the day they crossed beautiful country occupied by both Indians and white settlers and Howard offered to remove all residents and give the land to the Nez Perces as their reservation. In "Joseph's Own Story" he says that he replied as follows to General Howard's offer, "No. It would be wrong to disturb these people. I have no right to take their homes. I have never taken what did not belong to me. I will not now." No unoccupied land which was good could be found. Next day General Howard issued his ultimatum.

Joseph wanted more time, knowing that 30 days was insufficient for his people to locate and move their live-stock and gather supplies for the coming winter. Howard refused to extend the time, telling Joseph that should he not be within the reservation within the time specified that all cattle and horses outside the reservation would fall into the hands of white men.

In his own narrative, Joseph says that he made up his mind then to avoid war even though it meant giving up his beloved Wallowa country wherein his father's body reposed. He also expressed the opinion that General Howard began at once to prepare for war and said, "I have been informed by men who do not lie that General Howard sent a letter that night telling the soldiers at Walla Walla to go to Wallowa Valley and drive us out upon our return home." Returning to Wallowa, Chief Joseph found his people greatly excited. Soldiers were already in Wallowa Valley.

Joseph immediately called a council and almost wholly because of his influence the tribe decided to submit quietly at once to General Howard's order. However, while a majority agreed, the decision was far from unanimous. Too-hul-hul-sute had been released after five days in the guardhouse and was outraged at having been arrested for merely expressing his opinion as he had been requested to do by General Howard. He urged the tribe to go to war and persuaded a number of the younger braves to his point of view. He argued that only blood could erase the disgrace of his arrest. It is said that Joseph then rode among his people, pistol in hand, and asserted that he would shoot any warrior who dared to defy the soldiers when they arrived.

Joseph's Nez Perces began rounding up their live-stock but with their time limited they left many horses and cattle on the Wallowa. As the tribe moved across the swollen Snake River more live-stock was lost.

From the Snake River the exodus continued in and out of the

General Otis O. Howard

"After the scouts had located the Indians, General Howard, himself, rode to a high point from which he could see the hostiles in force and apparently working themselves into a frenzy by war dances and much waving of blankets and brandishing of weapons." (page 235)

General Nelson A. Miles

"The Nez Perces . . . were unaware of the presence of General Miles until almost at the moment that Miles' troops charged the Indian camp. It was the first week of October, 1877." (page 220)

Scout John W. Redington

"General Howard sent Scout Redington with an order to Colonel Miles to do an about-face and by forced marches try and head off the hostiles. . . . Redington succeeded in reaching Colonel Miles though it took him most of the night to accomplish the mission." (page 234)

Chief Paulina of the Snake Indians

". . . in 1851 the Snakes went berserk, making life miserable for immigrants, killing 34 of them, wounding and outraging many, and stealing $18,000 worth of immigrants' property." (page 50)

Note: It is said that when Chief Paulina posed for this picture he didn't know what the camera was. He thought it might be some kind of gun. He knew he had "plenty coming to him" from the whites and he "suspicioned" he might be about ready to get some of it; so when they said, "Hold still," he instinctively closed his eyes and put his hand over his heart. This picture was taken at Fort Klamath sometime in the early 1860s, when Paulina was there under safe conduct to talk about him and his band going to the reservation.

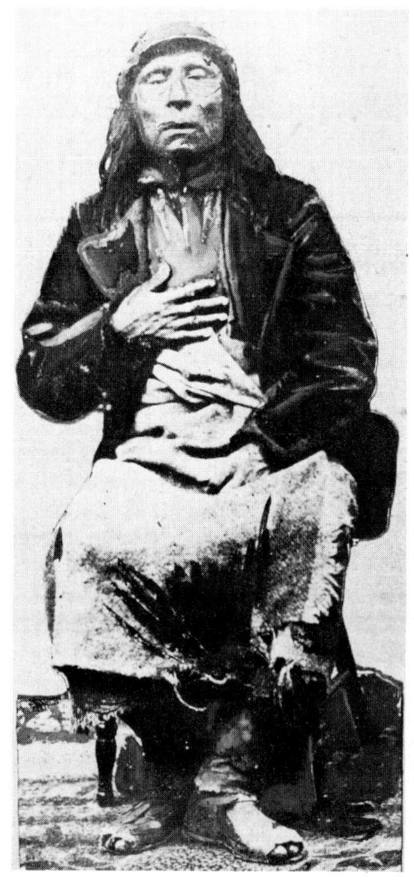

Salmon River canyon and northward to the Clearwater River. This latter stream was the northern limit of the land set aside by the government for Joseph and his people. Joseph moved westward about 16 miles to White Bird Creek, a tributary of the Salmon River. Nearby was Lake Tepahlewan, about the banks of which the Nez Perces set up their tepees and began a council which lasted ten days.

Among the younger warriors who always argued for war was one whose father had been killed by white men several years earlier. This young brave called upon the council to support him in revenge. But Joseph never wavered in his argument for peace because he truly wished peace and further because he knew the weakness of this tribe in comparison with the strength of the United States Army. So sure was Joseph that his people would follow his advice that he left the council to butcher beef for his family. On the night of the tenth day of the council, June 13th, the young brave previously mentioned, enlisted several other young warriors and left the council, going to nearby farms and killing four white men. Returning to camp the young leader rode up to the council and shouted, "Why do you sit here like women? The war has begun already."

In his own story which he related on his trip to Washington, in 1897, Chief Joseph says that he would have given his own life if, by so doing, he could have undone the killing of those white men by his tribesmen. Yet, he places only part of the blame on his young warriors. The rest of it he fastens upon General Howard for not having given enough time to get their livestock away from the Wallowa Valley. Further, 20 years after the event, he did not acknowledge the right of General Howard to order the removal from Wallowa. He emphasized his belief that had he been given time to round up his horses and cattle and had Too-hul-hul-sute been treated like a man, that there would have been no war.

Joseph said that it was his intention to move away from White Bird canyon but that the soldiers attacked before his preparations for leaving had been completed. That circumstance arose from the fact that news of the murders of the white people had been carried to the small settlements of Mt. Idaho and Cottonwood as well as Fort Lapwai. Mt. Idaho was about 20 miles north of Joseph's location, while Cottonwood was about an equal distance northwest of Mt. Idaho. Fort Lapwai was approximately 50 miles northwest of Cottonwood. Colonel David Perry was in command of the fort and, at the time, had about

120 soldiers of the regular army. News of the murders came to Colonel Perry immediately after the arrival at the fort of General Howard from Lewiston. Howard at once ordered Perry with 90 soldiers to go to White Bird Canyon. At the same time, Howard sent messengers to the nearest telegraph station 120 miles away with dispatches ordering more troops from Walla Walla and Fort Vancouver. Before the war was ended, additional troops came from five other forts in the Pacific Northwest, from California and Arizona, while the 2nd Infantry was sent from far-away Georgia.

Joseph, of course, knew that soldiers would be sent to avenge the murders, and while he did leave White Bird Creek he concentrated his people at a point in the canyon where the creek joined the Salmon River. Meanwhile alarmed settlers fled to Mt. Idaho where earthworks were erected and other preparations made to meet possible Indian attack.

Perry's command was joined by eleven volunteers from Mt. Idaho and two friendly Indians who acted as scouts. Perry rode hard and on the morning of June 17th came in sight of Joseph's camp in the broad canyon below. To Perry it seemed that there was little activity at the Indian camp and he started his troops down the trail. Chief Joseph, his brother Chief Ollicut, and Chief White Bird were aware of the presence of the troops at the top of the escarpment and Joseph explained his strategy to the other chiefs. White Bird with his braves crept up a narrow lateral ravine to a point beyond which the troops would have to pass. While the soldiers were mounted troops, most of them, at the time, were walking, leading their horses. A single shot was heard, evidently a signal, upon which the Indians opened a devastating fire. The soldiers, many of whom were having their first taste of Indian warfare, were routed. Perry and his officers tried desperately to reorganize the command but to no avail. The men fled in panic and the troops were not reformed until the summit of the gorge was reached. They then began a retreat to Mt. Idaho, followed by the Indians until within two miles of the town. Perry lost 33 killed and seven wounded. While the Indian casualties are unknown it is probable that they were very light, if any occurred at all, in view of the complete rout of the soldiers. Only 60 Nez Perce warriors took part in the fight. Joseph had fought and won his first battle.

Panic seized the entire area. Settlers and friendly Indians hastened to Fort Lapwai, the settlers for protection, the friendly Indians by their presence at the fort showing that this particular war was not theirs. Reinforcements began arriving. A small detachment of artillery returning home from duty in Alaska was diverted to the pursuit of the Nez Perces. Troops of volunteers were being recruited everywhere within a radius of 200 miles. Within a few days General Howard had an additional 200 men ready to send into the area of trouble. This additional force was a mixture of regular artillery, cavalry, and infantry and some volunteers. The artillery had two Gatling guns in addition to other weapons. This force moved, establishing a base of supply at Cottonwood, where a small detachment under Colonel Perry was left as a guard. The main body of reinforcements recently arrived continued to the scene of Perry's battle. The dead were buried and the troops were ready to take up the pursuit of the hostiles. But Joseph's location was unknown. The Nez Perces had somehow crossed the swift waters of the Salmon River and were somewhere beyond in the rugged country.

General Howard moved into the mountains beyond the Salmon River hoping to pick up Joseph's trail but Joseph had outsmarted him and was moving toward Kamiah on the Middle Fork of the Clearwater River, the ancient home-territory of the Nez Perces. Enroute some of his warriors strayed to the neighborhood of Cottonwood where Perry was in command of the small garrison at the temporary supply base. Perry became alarmed at the sight of so many hostiles and sent a mounted messenger by a circuitous route to Mt. Idaho asking for help to reinforce his small command. It will be recalled that Mt. Idaho was the rendezvous for all the frightened settlers from all parts of Camas Prairie and that the only armed men at Mt. Idaho were volunteers.

In spite of none too many of these citizen guards, after the message from Perry had been debated, it was decided that help should be sent. The decision to go was left to the individual will of each man, and 17 offered to ride to Cottonwood 20 miles away. D. B. Randall was in command; 18 miles of the journey were covered without incident, but when about two miles from their objective they noticed several mounted Indians about midway to the village. The white men headed for Cottonwood as fast as their horses could run. The number of Indians increased as if by magic to about 100, who with equal speed started to intercept Captain Randall and his men. Randall rapidly calculated his chances and decided that the odds were on the side of the Indians' likelihood of intercepting him. To his right about a quarter of a mile was a knoll, not high enough to be called a hill, but rising somewhere above the general level of the terrain, and Randall ordered his men to reach it if at all possible.

The Indians had deployed with a view to surrounding the 17 volunteers. But Randall and his men spurred their horses and rode directly at the Indians, which seemed to be an unexpected tactic as far as the hostiles were concerned. Immediately the melee was man-to-man and the Nez Perces gave way with casualties on both sides. One volunteer was killed and several wounded, among them Randall himself, who was mortally wounded. The volunteers gained the knoll, taking their wounded with them as well as those of their number whose horses had been shot. Using their horses as barricades the white men met every recurring charge of the Indians with deadly fire, killing many of the hostiles and finally forcing the enemy beyond rifle range. As usual the Indians removed their dead. Apparently Joseph was not with this war party.

The fight had been within plain sight of the garrison at Cottonwood. Perry's men wanted to go to the relief of the volunteers but he ruled that the men would have little chance of getting through the Indian lines. However, when the Nez Perces retired out of range of Randall's men, Perry could no longer hold his soldiers back. They rode to the knoll and returned with the survivors and the dead. That night the Indians departed.

On Independence Day, 1877, two civilian scouts attached to General Howard's command, William Foster and Charles Blewett, were ordered to scout the whereabouts of the Nez Perces. They ran into an ambush. At the moment the two men were some distance apart and Foster yelled to Blewett that they would be well advised to get away from where they were. Blewett replied, "I am going to get one shot first," and dismounted, firing at an Indian. Blewett's horse stampeded. Foster unsuccessfully tried to head off the horse and called to Blewett to hide in the thicket, and that he, Foster, would try to bring aid. Foster observed that Blewett was injured, evidently from a leg wound. The last sight of Blewett by Foster was when the former was limping toward the underbrush along the creek. Foster took off for Cottonwood. There Foster, fully stressing the dangers, nevertheless prevailed upon Perry to send a detachment to attempt Blewett's rescue. All of Perry's men volunteered for the mission but all could not be spared so Lieutenant Sevier M. Rains with ten men, including Foster, undertook the task.

They left at once and had gone only a few miles when they were ambushed. All were killed, Foster being the last to fall while trying to escape on foot after his horse had been shot from under him.

Meanwhile the Nez Perce Chief Lookingglass had decided to cast his lot with Joseph and brought about 60 warriors with him. The Nez Perces were moving about somewhat but a few days later General Howard's scouts located them east of the Clearwater River and southeast of Kamiah. Howard awaited reinforcements and on July 10th came in sight of the Nez Perce position. Joseph had selected a most favorable site to do battle. In front was a vast open space over which the troops would have to travel before coming to grips with the Indians. Back of Joseph's position and laterally were wooded canyons into which the Indians could retreat should the trend of battle go against them. With Joseph were Chiefs White Bird, Lookingglass, Black Eagle, other lesser chiefs and about 300 warriors, all armed with the most modern breech-loading rifles. With their women and children the Nez Perces numbered, perhaps, 700 souls. Rifle pits and barricades of logs had been prepared. Howard waited till noon on July 11th before beginning the attack. The reason for the slight delay arose from the fact that additional detachments were arriving and Howard needed to fit them into his battle plan. His force now numbered about 400 men. At noon Howard threw out a skirmish line and intensive firing began from both sides, the troops supplementing their rifle fire with bursts from the Gatling guns. The skirmishers suffered from the accurate marksmanship of the Indians. Forward progress was almost nil, but some of the soldiers' bullets also found their marks. At nightfall the shooting ceased. The troops could hear the chanting of the squaws wailing over the Indian dead.

Next day, July 12th, Howard opened the battle with heavy firing from field guns and Gatling guns. After this preparation the troops attacked. The fighting was terrific and after the Indians had suffered about 60 casualties in killed and wounded and the troops 40, the Indians retreated into the canyons. Howard ordered pursuit discontinued, fearing an ambush. However, at daylight on the 13th the chase was resumed, the troops not stopping until they had reached Kamiah, which, as previously described, was the center for the principal branch of the Nez Perces who had never joined in Joseph's war. From Kamiah it could be seen that Joseph had taken a new position to the east on the high ridges which marked the beginning of the Lolo Trail leading over the Bitter Root Mountains into Montana. From his new location Joseph could watch all the troop movements.

Thus ended the battle of the Clearwater.

With the prospect of Joseph retreating over the Lolo Trail, General Howard knew that he was confronted with a long and difficult pursuit. On July 17th, Joseph and his Nez Perces started the long trek which was to lead him over two major mountain ranges toward the traditional buffalo hunting grounds of his tribe.

THE GREAT TREK

General Howard had a real task imposed upon him by Joseph's retreat. Hundreds of miles lay ahead even under the most favorable circumstances. All supplies and ammunition had to be transported by pack animals. The army's pack-train, already large, had to be augmented. Additional provisions had to be brought from supply depots. The process was time-consuming, but at the end of ten days Howard ordered his men to take up the trail.

Meanwhile Joseph was clicking off the miles. The day following that on which General Howard had started into the mountains, Joseph emerged from the eastern end of the pass. There at a vantage point where the trail reached the Bitter Root Valley, the Nez Perce chieftain found the pass in possession of a group of armed settlers. They were above the defile and Joseph was fully aware of the danger to his column. He tried bargaining and a bargain was made. It was agreed that in return for Joseph's free entry into the valley that the Nez Perce would not molest the settlers in any degree. Both sides strictly observed the pact; in truth there was much trading between the settlers and Joseph's Indians, as a result of which Joseph's people came into possession of fresh supplies which were greatly needed.

Joseph then sprung a surprise on his pursuers, but in so doing may have formed the basis for untimely lack of success. Had he continued northeastward, using the old Lewis and Clark trail, he probably could have reached Canada before being intercepted. Certainly he must have still had the idea of joining Sitting Bull, then in Southern Canada, if only as a last resort. It may well be that Joseph still cherished the hope of a satisfactory settlement with the United States authorities. At any rate, he moved in a southerly direction, slightly southeasterly, and in the forepart of August was encamped in the Valley of the Big Horn River on the Montana side of the Bitterroot Mountains and about 75 miles south of Missoula.

THE BATTLE OF THE BIG HORN

HERE Joseph planned to rest his caravan for a day, believing that General Howard was far in the rear; and here Joseph was to have a new type of experience resulting from a new type of enemy, the telegraph. Howard had wired General John Gibbon, in command at Missoula, telling of Joseph's probable location. Gibbon left Missoula with about 200 soldiers, only 32 of whom were volunteers, and soon picked up Joseph's trail where it emerged from the pass. Gibbon lost no time. He rented animals and wagons from settlers and moved fast. On August 8th his scouts spotted the Nez Perce camp. Gibbon kept his caravan in concealment until nightfall. Then under cover of darkness and as quietly as possible he moved his men into position and waited for daybreak. At dawn he attacked. Having some open meadow to cross, the troops were seen by some of the Indians who gave the alarm and immediately began firing. Everything was confusion. Squaws and children poured out of the tepees. The mounted soldiers were everywhere, as were the Indians, the women and children screaming, the soldiers yelling, the warriors giving voice to their warwhoops. Hundreds of rifles flashed, much of the time without careful aiming. Indians and soldiers began falling.

Chief Lookingglass was killed. Joseph's men fled to the thickets leaving General Gibbon and his troops in possession of the camp and its carnage. Up to that moment the melees had been of only a few minutes duration. Then Joseph began organizing his braves. They poured a murderous fire into the soldiers from three directions. It was too much to withstand. Gibbon ordered his troops to evacuate this camp, cross a small stream, and entrench on a nearby slope. Gibbon himself was severely wounded. The soldiers reached their objective, the Indians following with unrelenting fire. Some of the warriors circled into a position above the troops, others approached under cover of the underbrush from below. The soldiers fought back and the battle continued in full force all day followed by occasional shooting during the night. Gibbon's force was in a serious predicament but General Howard had anticipated Gibbon's possible need of reinforcements and had detached his cavalry, sending it ahead of his main army at full speed. The cavalry met some couriers from Gibbon's command, these having been sent with news of the impending battle. As a result Howard's cavalry arrived on the scene the morning after the big fight. Gibbon had lost 69 men, Joseph a smaller number. The army officers agreed that Joseph had shown remarkable military sense in having reversed what at first had looked like a major defeat.

Howard decided to await the main body of his troops. The wounded, including General Gibbon, were sent back to Missoula.

Then the Nez Perces moved southward, crossing the Bitterroots into Idaho to Camas Meadows, just west of the site of old Fort Henry and not far from the western entrance to Yellowstone Park. This route across the mountains is still known locally as Nez Perce Pass.

On August 10th, Howard again took up the pursuit, hastened by the news that a number of settlers had been murdered and many horses appropriated by the Indians. As the troops proceeded it was evident that they were on the right course because they progressively came upon large numbers of jaded ponies abandoned by the Nez Perces. Howard's command reached Camas Meadows, there to receive news from scouts that the Indians were only 15 miles in advance. Howard was encouraged because he felt that he had out-guessed Joseph. The General had reasoned that the Nez Perces would take the trail predicted, and in furtherance of a plan to bring Joseph into battle, Howard sent a large detachment by a round-about route to head off the Indians. Upon receipt of the news of the proximity of the hostiles Howard concluded that his intercepting detachment would cut off the line of retreat east of Joseph's location. The General had the advantage and an early victory seemed assured.

That night the army, dog-tired, hurried through the evening meal and sought its blankets. The horses and mules were turned out to graze properly guarded. In the early hours of the night the sentries spotted a large troop of cavalry advancing in formation and at a trot. They rode through the herd of grazing animals and were challenged. The horsemen paid no attention and were challenged again when they were recognized as Indians. Joseph had succeeded in a ruse; by having his warriors adopt a normal cavalry formation—he had stolen another chapter from the white man's book. The alarm was sounded but the Indians stampeded the animals, driving off several hundred head. The entire camp was soon awake and enough stray animals were rounded up to equip a detachment to follow the Indians, and some of the animals were recovered but the Nez Perces retained about 250. As if that were not enough bad news, Howard learned that the expected interception by his large detachment, sent out for that purpose, had failed. The force had missed the route entirely.

The army was now in a bad way. The nights were cold, shoes were worn out, and Howard decided that his men should rest in camp for a few days while wagons could be sent to Virginia City, Montana, for supplies. This delay gave Joseph an advantage and he moved further eastward entering Yellowstone Park at the point known as West Yellowstone. Crossing the Park northeasterly he chose a route through the Absaroka Range, which brought him out of the Park and into Montana in the vicinity of the communities of Silver Gate and Cooke. The hostiles killed some tourists in the Park and committed other depredations. There remains no question but that Joseph, at that time, was beginning what he thought would be his trans-Montana lap of his planned flight to Canada. But he met an unexpected impediment to the plan in a strong force under Colonel Sturgis of the 7th Cavalry, located in a strategic position controlling a narrow pass. Joseph changed his course from northeasterly to southeasterly and crossed into Wyoming. Sturgis, of course, could not know at what point Joseph might turn northwest, but set out in pursuit. As it developed Joseph soon turned north and Sturgis, outfitted with fresh horses, made good time. He overtook the Nez Perces north of the Yellowstone River in south-central Montana and attacked at once, greatly outnumbered though he was. His attack was repulsed but Sturgis did succeed in capturing a large number of the Indians' reserve ponies. Sturgis did not renew the attack and Joseph hurried on, ever northward, for by this time he was fully aware of the need for haste if he were to reach Canada at all, much less in time to prepare for the coming winter. Sturgis kept harassing the hostiles at long range, too weak numerically to attack after his initial effort, finally reaching the Musselshell River in Central Montana.

Meanwhile a cavalry column under Colonel Gilbert, who, like Sturgis, was subordinate to General Nelson A. Miles, tried to intercept the Nez Perces. However, Gilbert's column crossed the trail of the hostiles far to the rear of General Howard's advancing army. Howard was moving fast in an effort to effect a junction with Sturgis. Gilbert, convinced of his inability to catch up with Howard, returned with his command to Fort Ellis.

General Nelson A. Miles had built Fort Keogh on the Tongue River near to its confluence with the Yellowstone in Southeastern Montana, at which place is now Miles City, named for him. The telegraph had again appeared to work its magic against Chief Joseph. Miles himself set out in a northeasterly direction, hoping to intercept the Nez Perces before they could reach Canada and also to connect with the forces of Howard and Sturgis. The latter commands had met on the Musselshell River where Sturgis received word from Miles of the latter's start and intended route.

Upon receipt of the news of Miles' start, Howard revised his strategy. Calculating the approximate time necessary for Miles to reach his objective it was decided by Howard that the tempo of his part of the pursuit should be reduced, expecting that the Nez Perces, through their own spies, would learn of the relaxed chase and also slow the speed of their flight. Thus, reasoned Howard, more time would favor Miles. So Howard left Sturgis in command of the army and, with a small escort, proceeded to a possible junction with Miles, Sturgis following at a slower pace.

Miles moved rapidly. Joseph, now believing himself secure, was traveling slowly. He had crossed the Missouri River on September 23rd, moving northward by easy stages, and was camped in the Bearpaw Mountains on Snake Creek, a tributary of the Milk River and only about 40 miles from the Canadian border. The Nez Perces, by Joseph's statement in his own narrative, were unaware of the presence of General Miles until almost at the moment that Miles' troops charged the Indian camp. It was the first week of October, 1877.

The charge of the troops was as powerful as it was sudden. The camp was bisected and almost all the Indian ponies were captured and driven away by the soldiers. Joseph met the crisis magnificently. Separated from part of his family, his stentorian voice, rallying his warriors, could be heard above the din of battle. He urged his braves to fight and to defend their women and children. The impetus of the attack drove many of the Indians into the woods and nearby ravines. The soldiers tried to follow but the Nez Perces began another of their typical murderous firings, from behind trees and rocks, and the troops had to fall back. The Indians lost 18 men and three women during the first day and night of the fight. General Miles had 66 casualties, 26 dead and 40 wounded.

The Indians were now in a desperate plight. Winter winds were blowing from the Arctic; their camp was in the hands of the troops; there was no shelter.

The next day General Miles sent a messenger under a flag of truce to Joseph, who detailed his friend Yellow Bull to meet the messenger. Yellow Bull understood the courier to say that General Miles did not wish to kill unnecessarily and requested that Chief Joseph carefully consider the situation and all of its implications. In short, Yellow Bull considered it to be a demand for surrender. He reported the conversation to Joseph, at the same time questioning the earnestness of General Miles' demand. Joseph issued instructions that his reply would be that he had not made up his mind; that he would think about the matter and send his decision soon. Shortly after the messenger's departure some Cheyenne Indians who were scouts for General Miles, came to Joseph with another message. These Cheyennes told Joseph that they believed General Miles to be sincere and that he really wanted peace.

Joseph then walked to General Miles' tent. They shook hands. The General said, "Come, let us sit down by the fire and talk this matter over." Joseph remained overnight at the General's camp.

The next morning Yellow Bull came to the General's camp to learn what had happened to Joseph. The General would not permit the two Indians to talk alone but did grant them leave to speak in his presence. Yellow Bull expressed the opinion to Joseph that since the latter was in the General's power that Joseph would never be permitted to leave, but added that an army officer was at the Indian camp and would not be released until Joseph returned. Joseph told Yellow Bull that he had no idea of the General's intention toward him but that even if he, Joseph, were killed, that in no event was the officer to be killed in retaliation.

Yellow Bull returned to the Nez Perces. Joseph made no agreement with Miles. Joseph knew how close they were to Canada and reasoned that some of his men might have gone to Sitting

Bull's camp across the border and might return with reinforcements. As soon as Yellow Bull reached his people the fighting was resumed but it was sporadic and not at all on a scale of the first day's battle. Little damage was done by either side.

The next morning Joseph returned to his people under a flag of truce and in exchange for the officer. Joseph said afterwards that his tribesmen were divided on the subject of surrender but that all of them knew that they could escape that night to Canada if they abandoned their wounded, the children and the old women. The decision was against escape on the single premise that they knew of no Indian who was wounded ever recovering while in the custody of white men.

Meanwhile General Howard had arrived. On the evening of the fourth day of the encounter, General Howard, with a small escort and a Mr. Chapman who was a friend of Joseph's, came over to Joseph's camp for a talk about surrender.

Joseph said later, in his own narrative, that General Miles had told him that if the Nez Perces would surrender that their lives would be spared and that the Indians would be returned to their reservation. He has said that had he not believed General Miles that no surrender would ever have taken place. At the same time Joseph acknowledged that he knew nothing about what General Howard and General Miles may have discussed concerning the subject of return to the reservation.

At any rate, on the fifth day Joseph went to General Miles and gave up his gun, saying, "From where the sun now stands I will fight no more."

His people were tired, cold, destitute. Joseph wanted peace. About 400 men, women, and children surrendered with him. The rest had escaped to Canada, among them Chief White Bird. Chiefs Ollicut and Lookingglass had died fighting.

Only one day's forced travel had separated the Nez Perces from security. Perhaps only the telegraph caused their final defeat.

General Howard records the fact that his command marched 1321 miles from June 27th to October 10th, and that Joseph and his people traveled much farther, either in avoiding or deceiving his pursuers.

The Nez Perces did not go back to their reservation. Years later Joseph said that General Miles told him that the General's recommendation did not prevail; that orders from higher authorities took precedence; and that to have pursued the subject further would have been possible only if Miles had resigned his commission. Only under the latter circumstances could General Miles have continued his efforts in behalf of the Nez Perces.

Instead, the captives were sent first to Fort Leavenworth and then to the Indian Territory. There many Nez Perces died. Years later Chief Joseph and the remnants of his band were moved to the Colville Indian Reservation in Northeastern Washington.

Joseph and General Miles remained friends and each had great respect for the abilities and character of the other. Joseph was in Washington, D. C. in the interest of recovering his old reservation when President Grant died on July 23, 1885. General Miles invited Joseph to ride by his side at the head of the funeral cortege in New York City, which honor Joseph accepted.

Joseph then returned to Nespilim (now spelled Nespelem) on the Colville reservation. In September, 1904, Joseph was seated outside his tepee when his great heart stopped beating. The dead Chief slumped to the ground.

Later, when time had healed some of the old animosities, the body of Old Joseph, our Joseph's father, was disinterred and moved to the Wallowa country. There he was reburied on a hill overlooking the north shore of Wallowa Lake, in the homeland of the Nez Perces.

Note: The author has talked with Nez Perces who insist that they know that the body reinterred at Wallowa Lake is not that of Old Joseph.

Buffalo Horn, Chief of the Bannocks

". . . the Chief was badly wounded and after the end of the war some of his braves said that the Chief traveled for two days and then ordered that he be hidden in the underbrush and left there to die. His order was obeyed." (page 230)

Bannock Indian Camp

"The Bannocks were a strong race, loving warfare, and resentful of the white man's coming. The main wagon trails to both Oregon and California crossed their country. They attacked immigrant trains at every opportunity." (page 225)

THE BANNOCK WAR

THE LAST MAJOR UPRISING

THE Bannocks (or Bannacks) comprised a subdivision of the great Shoshone Nation. The word is derived from their own word "Bampnack," meaning "to throw backward," which referred to the custom of their braves in wearing their hair in a lock which was thrown back from the forehead.

The center of their culture was in Southeastern Idaho in the vicinity of the modern cities of Pocatello and American Falls, but all of Southern Idaho was their range. The latter point is emphasized because, for countless years, they occupied Camas Prairie in Southwestern Idaho each summer to dig the roots of the camas plant which constituted their principal food. Camas, or quamash, is a plant which sends forth a purple bloom on a long slender stem and produces roots not dissimilar to the edible underground part of the onion. The roots were dried, then pounded into meal in primitive mortars or on flat stones, and made into a sort of bread. Venison and trout and berries supplemented the major diet. Camas Prairie is important to this history because circumstances there contributed to the Bannock War. It is a great area southeast of Boise, Idaho, and on the north side of the Snake River.

The Bannocks were a strong race, loving warfare, and resentful of the white man's coming. The main wagon trails to both Oregon and California crossed their country. They attacked immigrant trains at every opportunity. Their terrorism became so bad that in December, 1862, the people of the Mormon settlement of Franklin, in extreme southeastern Idaho, appealed to the military authorities at Fort Douglas, near Salt Lake City, for help. The town of Franklin had been founded by the Mormons in 1860, and they believed that the site was within the boundaries of Utah. In spite of foreseeable hardships, the Commandant, Colonel Patrick E. Connor, set out with about 200 soldiers. The snow was deep and the temperature sub-zero. About ten miles from Franklin and on Battle Creek, a tributary of the Bear River, is an area of hot springs. These caused the snow to melt in their vicinity and warmed the ground so that it was a favorite winter campsite. Bluffs shut off the winter wind. Most of the tribe was encamped there. Some miners were passing through that region and were fired upon by the Indians, one miner being killed and several wounded.

While Connor was on the march, an incident occurred in Franklin which was typical of the nature of the Bannocks. It was in January, 1863, and Chief Bear Hunter with some of his Bannocks rode into the town and demanded wheat. The settlers gave them 24 bushels but the Indians demanded more and became very threatening but did not actually attack anyone. The very next day Connor arrived with his troops and decided to attack the Indian camp at the hot springs without delay. The troops reached the place on the morning of January 29th. The Bannocks were ready for battle and were in a favored position behind the steep banks of the creek and screened by willows.

The thermometer stood at 23 degrees below zero. Connor assaulted the position and had to withdraw, having lost 14 killed and many wounded in a mere 20 minutes. The Colonel then changed his tactics, dividing his troops into three detachments. One section was sent to approach the Indians from the downstream side; another to move in from upstream, while Connor would attack frontally as soon as the other two detachments had been given time to get into position. The plan worked. The Indians fought desperately but they were slaughtered by dozens every minute. Two hundred twenty-four warriors were killed, 160 squaws and children captured. A very few of the braves escaped. Chief Bear Hunter died with his fighters. As a result of this terrible defeat, the raids and depredations of the Bannocks ended until the war of 1878.

In 1867 the Government completed a plan for placing the far-western Indian tribes on reservations and appointed a commission to conclude treaties. Among the many treaties completed was one with the Bannocks, which required them to occupy the regions on the Portneuf River, afterwards known as the Fort Hall Reservation, named for old Fort Hall erected in 1834, and on Camas Prairie. Through a clerical error the treaty referred to Camas Prairie as "Kansas Prairie." When the reservation boundaries were surveyed the Indians received much more land than they expected in the Fort Hall area but for some reason Camas Prairie did not fall to the lot of the Indians. However, they continued to occupy Camas Prairie each summer until that of 1878.

The Bannocks had been growing more and more restless as their reservation existence continued. One of the reasons lay in the fact that they were usually roaming their wide country and were often not on hand when the Indian Agent made his periodic distribution of provisions and clothing. Large numbers of Shoshones had settled near Fort Hall. They were quiet and peaceable and were always available when the Indian Agent passed out the supplies. The Bannocks resented this seeming discrimination. Their Chief, Buffalo Horn, was highly intelligent and very ambitious. He had commanded a group of Bannock scouts in the Nez Perce War and had served under both Generals O. O. Howard and Nelson A. Miles. But Buffalo Horn and his scouts had stolen 40 horses from General Howard, who suspected them and placed ten of their number under guard until the horses were returned. That angered Buffalo Horn who demanded permission to execute three Nez Perce scouts who were with Howard's command. As explained elsewhere, the Nez Perces under Chief Joseph in the war of 1877 comprised only one of three sections of the Nez Perce Nation and the three scouts were not of Joseph's band. Howard had confidence in his Nez Perce scouts and refused to turn them over to Buffalo Horn. So Buffalo Horn left Howard and spent the winter stirring up various Indian tribes to seek revenge upon the whites. Results of Buffalo Horn's efforts were soon observed. The younger men among the Bannocks became increasingly insolent. Two drivers belonging to a wagon freight train were killed and the murderer was most reluctantly surrendered upon demand of the authorities. The culprit was barely started from the agency to jail when an employee at Fort Hall was shot and killed. The killer was not apprehended. Depredations increased.

Chief Buffalo Horn visited the Piutes, the Cayuses, and the Umatillas. By springtime he considered that he had enough allies to defeat any force of Federal troops which might be mustered to fight him. All the tribes in Southern Idaho and Eastern Oregon were restless. Next to the Bannocks, the Piutes seemed most likely to start trouble. One branch under Chief Winnemucca was in Nevada in their country around Pyramid Lake and Lake Winnemucca, named for the Chief. The other branch had been placed on the Malheur Reservation in Oregon and it was this Malheur division which was to be troublesome, in fact very few of Chief Winnemucca's band joined in the war.

About April of 1878, settlers brought a drove of hogs to Camas Prairie to fatten on the camas root and they soon had the earth well rooted into little mounds. While the hogs were being fattened, three stockmen, George Nesbit, Louis Kensler, and William Silvey, brought in a herd of cattle and horses to graze upon the grassy areas among which the camas grew. Two Bannocks came into the herders' camp on May 27th, visited several hours, had supper with the white men, and then left, apparently in a friendly mood. Next morning the Indians returned, had breakfast with the white men and then, at an opportune moment wounded Nesbit badly. Kensler was grazed by a bullet but succeeded in badly wounding one of the Indians as the Bannocks fled. The three white men mounted their horses and started for help at the nearest stage station, which meant a ride of about three hours. Looking back they saw a large band of Indians raiding their camp, but they were not pursued.

It was later established that the Bannocks had been watching Camas Prairie while all the livestock feeding was in progress and that following the attack on the three white men a tribal council was held which lasted almost all night, resulting in a division among the Indians. However, Buffalo Horn enlisted about 200 warriors on the side of hostilities. The rest of the tribe immediately returned to the vicinity of Fort Hall where they remained entirely neutral during the war which was soon to follow.

General O. O. Howard, military commander of the Department of the Columbia, was at his home in Portland, Oregon, when he received news of the outbreak. He wasted no time in sending orders to many army posts for a quick mobilization of troops. His promptness undoubtedly prevented a larger concentration of hostiles than otherwise would have been the case, though great numbers of Indian allies did join in the war.

From all over the region reports of Indian depredations began pouring in. When Buffalo Horn and his warriors left Camas Prairie they rode to the King Hill stage station on the Snake River. Their appoach was observed by the stablemen, who fled. The Indians took everything they could use, destroyed the rest, and continued down river to Glenn's Ferry where they crossed and then cut the ferryboat loose to float down the stream. Next they came in sight of a wagon freight train. The drivers fled, the Indians looted the wagons and then kept on their march of destruction.

Governor Stephen F. Chadwick, of Oregon, sent large quantities of rifles and ammunition to Eastern Oregon. Canyon City, in Grant County, Oregon, was the center of a rich mining district. There a company of 44 mounted volunteers, known as the Grant County Guards, was organized under the command of Captain F. C. Sells. The women and children were quartered in mine tunnels for their safety.

In the Oregon counties of Harney, Malheur, Grant, Baker,

Union, Umatilla, and Morrow, isolated ranchers and their families were murdered, their houses burned, and their livestock slaughtered. At La Grande, in Union County, a force of men and boys directed by United States Senator James H. Slater prepared rifle pits around the three-story brick building of Blue Mountain University, and barricaded the building. A volunteer company was formed by General J. H. Stevens and Colonel Micajah Baker and these volunteers stood guard around the town night and day. Notice was given that in case of attack the church bell would ring and all citizens were to rush to the fortified university building. Everywhere in the threatened region fear and uncertainty reigned.

The news of Buffalo Horn's foray soon reached Boise Barracks, then commanded by Captain Reuben F. Bernard, of Company G, First Cavalry, who was a Brevet Colonel. At Boise was also Orlando Robbins, a colonel in the state militia, who headed a group of volunteer scouts. Robbins had been a United States Marshal for Idaho and a scout for General Howard in the Nez Perce War. Bernard and Robbins, with their men, set out for Camas Prairie where they picked up the trail of the Bannocks, followed it to King Hill stage station, then to Glenn's Ferry, then on down stream to the confluence of the Bruneau River with the Snake. Here they found that the trail led up the Bruneau. They crossed to the south side of the Snake and followed up its valley for 20 hours without pause until they came to a rudimentary fortification behind which the Bruneau Valley settlers had taken refuge. One man had been killed and, of course, the settlers had lost all their horses and cattle.

By this time Buffalo Horn was in extreme Southwestern Idaho and Bernard concluded that the Bannocks were headed for Southeastern Oregon, where one large division of the Piutes were located in the Steens Mountain and Malheur River district.

While Bernard was still in the Bruneau Valley, news reached the settlement of Silver City, in Owyhee County, the most southwesterly county of Idaho, that part of Buffalo Horn's hostiles were at South Mountain, which was a small mining camp a few miles south of Silver City. A volunteer company of 26 men under Captain J. B. Harper was quickly organized and, acquiring several friendly Piutes as scouts, left for that locality at once. On June 8, 1878, they encountered a force of 50 or 60 picked warriors under the personal command of Buffalo Horn. This was a raiding party, well armed, and in a strong defensive position. Greatly outnumbered Captain Harper nevertheless ordered a charge, losing two men killed and three wounded, but Buffalo Horn, himself, was critically wounded, which may account for the fact that Harper and his men were not exterminated. There are various versions of the story of Buffalo Horn's wounding, one of which was the statement by a Piute scout that he had shot Buffalo Horn and had seen him fall from his horse. It was a fact that the Chief was badly wounded and after the end of the war some of his braves said that the Chief traveled for two days and then ordered that he be hidden in the underbrush and left there to die. His order was obeyed. My reliance on the second version mentioned is based upon an article by Scout John W. Redington in the 50th Anniversary Issue of the *Hailey Times,* Hailey, Idaho, of June 18, 1931. In that account Scout Redington says that the circumstance was related to him by Paddy Capps, one of the Malheur Piute hostiles, after the conclusion of the war. Capps was with Buffalo Horn at the time. Redington, in the same article, says that Chief Egan, soon to take Buffalo Horn's place, was forced into the war by his braves; that he knew Egan well; that Egan had told him before the war that he never wanted any more fighting; that Egan was a fine man.

Buffalo Horn's death probably was the cause for several wavering tribes to decide against participating in the conflict. The number of others killed in the South Mountain fight was never known, for, as usual, they carried away their dead to avoid losing scalps, and the day after the battle headed once more for Steens Mountain in Oregon, and a union with their potential allies, the Piutes.

Brevet-Colonel (captain) Bernard, with 250 officers and men, proceeded to Silver City. General Oliver O. Howard went to take charge of the war, arriving there June 12th. General Frank Wheaton was in command of the Walla Walla District and Colonel Grover succeeded Bernard at Boise Barracks, but since General Howard had established his own headquarters there, Grover was his ranking senior officer. General Howard ordered a mobilization of troops, some of which came great distances. He was taking no chances of unpreparedness. The memories of the defeats at the hands of Chief Joseph the preceding year and the Custer two years before, were leavening memories.

The Oregon Piutes were preponderantly in favor of allying themselves with the Bannocks. Chief Winnemucca was friendly to the whites but his council did not prevail and Chief Egan became their predominant leader. Chief Winnemucca's daughter, Sarah, was even more friendly toward the whites than her father, and speaking English fluently, rendered valuable service for General Howard. Fearing for the safety and reputation of her father and his peaceably inclined followers, she, with two other Piutes, set out post haste for her father's camp. Arriving there she successfully engineered the escape of her father and about 75 others of the tribe, all of whom reached the protection of General Howard's forces.

Colonel Bernard reached Silver City two days after the battle at South Mountain and learning the direction taken by the hostiles, set out the same day, June 10th, in pursuit. His first objective was Jordan Valley just over the line in Oregon. Enroute he stopped at Sheep Ranch where he found that the overland stage was overdue. He sent Colonel Robbins and his scouts to investigate. After a ride of eight miles, and across the Owyhee River, they found the remnants of the stage coach which had been burned, and, nearby, the body of the dead driver.

The hostiles were moving fast. They effected their junction with the Piutes. Dissident elements from several other tribes joined the movement. Among them were some Umatillas and Cayuses, whose lands were to the north. This roving army headed toward the Umatilla and Cayuse country, hoping to enlist sympathetic support, plundering and killing on the way. The Indians were now under the supreme chieftainship of Egan.

Colonel Robbins and his troops finally picked up the trail and riding hard still did not overtake the Indians till June 22nd. General Howard and his command, riding equally hard, maintained the same distance to the rear of Robbins from day to day. Toward evening on the 22nd the trail became so fresh that Colonel Robbins, known affectionately by the nickname "Rube," halted his troops and went ahead to reconnoiter, fearing an ambush. He climbed a mountainside and spied the Indian camp several miles away on Silver Creek, a stream flowing from the northwest and which emptied into Harney Lake (now dry). Robbins went back to his command and late that evening Colonel Bernard came in with his men. It was decided that Robbins and his scouts should investigate the position of the Indians and accordingly they rode out about midnight. The night was clear and when nearing Silver Creek Robbins again left his men and went ahead to make observations. Well schooled in the ways of silent approach, he succeeded in getting into a position from which he could carefully appraise the campsite and so decide on the best angles of attack. Reporting back to Bernard, who was moving up as Robbins was returning, the latter estimated that the hostiles numbered 2000, more than half of whom were warriors. If the estimate proved to be correct, it meant that this was the largest concentration of warring Indians since the massacre of Custer and his troopers by the Sioux.

Colonel Bernard sent a messenger to General Howard reporting that the Indians were in sight and then held a council of his officers. It was decided that Bernard with 250 men would occupy a position downstream from the Indian camp and attack from the canyon side. Robbins with 35 scouts was to take a position above the camp. They agreed that at daybreak the Robbins detachment would charge the camp, yelling and shooting, in the hope that the Indians would be completely surprised and confused. Bernard was to attack immediately after the initial charge of the scouts. Even with the advantage of surprise the troops would have to fight hard because they were outnumbered at least four to one and the Indians were as well armed as the soldiers. General Howard was coming with plenty of help but he was at least two or three days away. Both Colonels were old hands at Indian fighting and to fail to engage the enemy now might delay a decisive action for a long time. So they would attack.

Silently the men moved to their positions. No sound came from either the troops or from the Indian camp. As the first streaks of dawn lighted the sky, Robbins and his scouts charged, their horses running. Armed with repeating rifles and six-shooters, the scouts came in yelling like mad-men. They stampeded the Indians, who imagined themselves in the midst of an onset by a huge force of cavalry. Some of the hostiles fled down stream only to be met by Bernard's men rapidly moving into action. However, after the first surprise, Robbins and his men began meeting with stiffened resistance and had to ride through the camp to join Bernard's force. The troops mowed the Indians down by scores. And then with suddenness occurred one of those combats like the knights of old, when each contesting army chose a champion. Colonel Robbins and Chief Egan each saw the other at the same moment. Within a split second each started riding toward the other. Both were veterans of many battles, both were courage personified. The Chief slid to the far side of his horse and fired from under the horse's head. The Colonel sat his horse erect. Both animals were plunging and rearing, interfering with the aim of the contestants but Robbins' position on his horse made his aim more certain. Several bullets passed through the Colonel's clothing and some grazed his body but none hit home. Then one of the Colonel's shots struck the Chief's wrist causing him to fall from his horse. As he rose, Robbins shot him in the breast. Egan's warriors carried him away. The chief was not killed but his wounds were so serious that his leadership was lost to the Indians for the rest of the war.

The first reaction of the hostiles to the wounding of their chief was intensified fighting — so intense that the troops had to retire to shelter. But the fighting waned and for the rest of the day there was a minimum of firing. The troops expected that the Indians would attack and no one knows why they did not unless it was because of the lack of leadership. The troops had lost five men killed and several times that number wounded. The Indian dead numbered more than 100 with many more wounded. That night the hostiles stole away. They had a new chief—Otis (or Oytes).

Morning came and when it was known that the Indians were gone, Bernard again took up the trail. Robbins and his scouts determined that the hostiles were headed toward the canyon of the John Day River. Indian prisoners said that a mixed band of Columbia River tribes were waiting in the John Day Valley to join the hostiles.

General Howard overtook Bernard's column two days later and assumed command. But the Indians reached the John Day River ahead of the troops and headed for the Umatilla Reservation, almost due north. The hostiles had stripped down their baggage to the bare essentials and were not handicapped by a slow moving wagon train as were the soldiers. It was rough terrain and the rigors of the wagon trail at times were almost insurmountable. Colonel Robbins and his scouts were miles ahead of General Howard and the main body of troops. The scouting party found plenty of evidence of the Indians' recent passing—a large drove of slaughtered hogs, mutilated sheep, a settler, scalped but still breathing.

On the 2nd of July, twelve scouts, under Robbins and Scout John W. Redington, discovered an ambush all set for several troops of the First Cavalry, now only two miles behind the scouts. This ambush was on the North Fork of the John Day River and on the western fringe of the forest, now known as the Umatilla National Forest.

Drawing the fire of the hostiles, the scouts were able to give notice to the troops. In the bushwhacking type of warfare between the scouts and the Bannocks, Scout Frohman was killed and Scout Jack Campbell and three others wounded. Colonel F. J. Parker rode into Fort Boise with dispatches from General

Howard. Parker told the editor of the *Idaho Statesman*, which carried the interview, that he was sad over the loss of his friend Johnnie Redington, who hadn't reported for a week after starting on a lone scout trip into the Malheur River country. But the Colonel had not reckoned with Johnnie's abilities. Scout Redington was to live a long and interesting life.

The troops came up rapidly and engaged and defeated the Indians but could not stop the progress toward the Umatilla Reservation. In fact, the troops were to overtake and fight the Indians at Birch Creek, then at Silver Creek, and again at Eagle Rock without stopping them.

Of course Chief Egan's purpose in wanting to reach the Umatilla Reservation had stemmed from the hope that he could persuade that whole tribe to join him.

Meanwhile a company of 32 volunteer riflemen had been organized at Pendleton and took the field. They encountered several hundred of the hostiles, were completely surrounded and fought for 24 hours, until the Indians, for some unknown reason, decided to resume their march. Sergeant William Lamont of the rifle company was killed, his body returned to Pendleton where it lies in what is now Pioneer Park.

Early in the forenoon of July 8th, Scouts John W. Redington and Frank Parker again located the Indians on Birch Creek, a tributary which flows north to join the Umatilla River. General Howard's troops attacked and defeated the Indians, who took refuge in the deep pine forest and continued their march toward the Umatilla Reservation.

About that time the Twenty-First Infantry, commanded by Colonel Evan Miles, was 40 miles away and marching to join General Howard, who was traveling northward faster than Colonel Miles had calculated. After the fight on Birch Creek, General Howard sent Scout Redington with an order to Colonel Miles to do an about-face and by forced marches try and head off the hostiles before they could effect a junction with the Umatillas. Redington succeeded in reaching Colonel Miles though it took him most of the night to accomplish the mission. The Twenty-First wheeled about and reached the reservation at daybreak. Tired and hungry, the infantrymen pitched camp and started to cook breakfast when, without warning, the Bannocks streamed out of the surrounding forest and down the sloping hills to attack the soldiers. In the war party were about 1000 braves, mostly Bannocks and Piutes, but also a few from other tribes, while Colonel Miles had about 500 men. His troops consisted of several units of the Twenty-First Infantry, two companies of the Fourth Artillery acting as Infantry, Troop K of the First Cavalry under Captain Bendire, and the Pendleton Volunteers under Captain William Matlock and Lieutenant James Turner.

We must now return to General Howard and July 8th so that we may reconcile events. After the scouts had located the Indians, General Howard, himself, rode to a high point from which he could see the hostiles in force and apparently working themselves into a frenzy by war dances and much waving of blankets and brandishing of weapons. Sarah Winnemucca was with the General and she told him that it was her opinion that if the General attacked that the battle would not last long because the warriors would flee to the forest. Howard decided to attack at once.

The Indians were in good position on an elevation, with the forest in the direction of flight should they be forced to retire. Howard's plan required that Bernard with seven troops approach from one flank, and a mixed force under Captain Throckmorton to attack from the other side. General Frank Wheaton was to bring his infantry up in support. Robbins and his scouts were to be with Bernard. The plan worked with precision and the Indians took to the forest. There were no casualties among the soldiers, though some horses were killed. The Indians suffered some fatalities but took their dead away with them and were soon lost in the fastnesses of the wooded mountains. There was much speculation about the location of the Indians then but no facts, and General Howard decided to go to Walla Walla, believing that he could better direct his campaign from there. He left Major E. C. Mason, his Chief of Staff, in command of the troops in the field.

Mason proceeded toward the Umatilla country, for it was certain that only the tide of war would determine whether the Umatillas under Chief Umapine would or would not join the Bannocks, Piutes, and others under Chief Otis and the wounded Egan.

In the meantime three men riding from Meacham to Pendleton were attacked, one being killed, another wounded, and the third escaping to take the news to Pendleton. On the morning of July 13th Major Connoyer with 13 men left Pendleton to rescue the wounded man and almost immediately encountered a large force of Indians. Connoyer had to flee, returning to Pendleton for reinforcements. These Indians were, no doubt, the same who attacked the camp of Colonel Miles and his Twenty-first Infantry, previously detailed.

During the engagement between the Twenty-first Infantry and the hostiles, all of the Umatillas in war paint and feathers, sat on their horses atop a hill overlooking the fighting. They were merely waiting to see which side was to be favored by the fortunes of war before joining the hostiles or returning to their wigwams. When the Bannocks and their allies fled from Colonel Miles the Umatillas negotiated with the army officers, offering to kill or capture Chief Egan. By this offer the Umatillas hoped to secure forgiveness for Chief Umapine for having led them to meet the Bannocks in the John Day country. The army officers agreed, Chief Umapine was forgiven, and he with a band of warriors and assisted by two sub-chiefs, Four Crows and Yettinewitz, pursued the Bannocks into the mountains.

The Bannocks were located and there are two stories about what then happened. One tale has it that the Umatillas pretended friendship and while conducting a pow-wow and at a pre-arranged signal, attacked Chief Egan and his principal men, killing thirty including Chief Egan. The other story recites that the two groups having met engaged in a talk during which Egan tried to persuade the Umatillas to join him; that an argument ensued, growing increasingly heated until a fight started with the aforementioned result. This incident probably occurred on July 15th, certainly not later than July 16th, and, of course, Egan was, at the time, still suffering from the wounds received in his duel with Colonel Robbins. The site of the slaughter was in the forest three miles from Meacham.

The Umatillas returned to the troops, reported the fight, and the next day a detachment rode to the scene. It is not known why the hostiles had not cremated their dead, but this time they had not. Scout Redington turned over the body of a scalped Indian and said that it was Chief Ehegante, known as Egan. Redington had known Egan well, having hunted bear with him the previous year. Colonel Robbins also identified the dead chief from his wounds. It is believed that Egan was born a Umatilla, who had been captured when a small boy, and then grew up as a fellow tribesman of his captors.

But time was running out for the hostiles. While they had thus far succeeded in escaping after each battle, their numbers were being decimated, they had successively lost two top leaders and many other principal men, yet they were not subdued. The few renegade Umatillas who had joined the hostiles were almost home on their reservation; the Piutes from the Malheur district were not too far from their country; but the Bannocks were faced with a long journey if they were to return to the Fort Hall Reservation. Apparently the Indians had decided to break up their war and go home. True, the troops had no knowledge of such a decision, knowing only that the hostiles were still at large and learning of murders and depredations almost daily.

The big news was that of a new outbreak in Idaho, to be known as the Sheepeater War. Aside from that, the fast-traveling but somewhat scattered Indian allies were killing and destroying as they were homeward bound, in no sense diminishing their reign of terror even though aware that their war was hopelessly lost.

William Lockwood, veteran stage driver of the route between the Union Pacific Railroad in Utah and Umatilla Landing on the Columbia River, was holed up in Meacham. He decided to run the risk of taking the mail to Pendleton. Loading the mail into a light carriage, he hitched four horses to the vehicle, put an expert rifleman in the back seat, and started. The distance was 25 or 30 miles. Soon after he set out, a group of mounted Indians gave chase. It was a run for life but the rifleman pumped lead and discouraged the Indians who gave up the effort when nearing some cavalrymen who were found to be guarding the road. The Fred Foster family, living on the stage route, had heard of the killing of travelers on the road and barricaded themselves in the log station house. When the stage drove up with the horses frothing and the driver's announcement that he had been chased by Indians, they decided to leave. The driver quickly loaded the family into the stage coach and started for Pendleton. The Indians came in sight and the driver lashed the horses to keep a safe distance ahead of the pursuers. Fortunately they came upon a camp of soldiers and the Indians pulled away. Later, when the Foster family returned, they found their place completely ransacked.

A wagon freight line worked out of LaGrande in Union County, Oregon. The wagons were drawn by 16-horse teams. Four drivers, Wallace McLaughlin, John Doe, A. Smith, and a fourth, known as "Whispering" Thompson were moving freight when they were attacked. McLaughlin was instantly killed and scalped. Thompson ran into the forest where he was killed and scalped. Doe hid in some bushes where he was found, tortured, killed, and mutilated. Smith, badly wounded, hid in some willows near a spring. Desperate for water he tried to reach the spring. The Indians tied him with a horsehair rope, dragging him back and forth just out of reach of the spring until he died. The teams were killed, the freight scattered, and the wagons burned.

While such acts of violence were being committed, the soldiers, from time to time, captured small bands of Indians, hanged some of them, and returned the others to their reservations.

Colonel Harry Lee Bailey, who was an aide to General Wheaton, advanced an idea which stemmed from the awe in which Indians generally held steamboats, telegraph lines, and other inventions of white men. There was some danger that the hostiles might try to cross the Columbia River and join the Yakimas in the State of Washington. Colonel Bailey suggested that a steamboat be armed and set to cruising the river where the Indians might be expected to attempt a crossing. Two steamboats were thus prepared. Actually some Indians did try to cross the river. The steamboats opened fire with their howitzers; the Indians fled southward leaving their canoes, which were burned by a landing party.

Thus the disintegration continued. The various warring tribes continued their devious homeward journeys. The Bannocks were particularly vicious. As their trek took them toward the Fort Hall Reservation they killed a stage driver named Hemmingway, who, by chance, had reached the Owyhee Ferry on the Snake River at the same time as the Bannocks. Onward they went, murdering and robbing, but hastening so that they could keep ahead of the pursuing troops. Reaching their reservation they mixed with their tribesmen who had refused to go to war and were soon enjoying the bounties of a benevolent government.

No punishment was thereafter inflicted beyond the fact that they were confined to the limits of their reservation. And thus the brief but bloody Bannock War passed into history.

The Oregon Piutes were subsequently moved to the Yakima Reservation where they did not coalesce. Later they were returned to Nevada, to join the Winnemucca Piutes on the reservation surrounding Pyramid Lake.

THE SHEEPEATER WAR

END OF AN ERA

At the time which marked the early stages of the War Between the States, the germ of a smaller and later war was planted in Central Idaho. The region is even today largely unexplored. It is a vast domain of rugged and precipitous mountains, deep canyons, cold winters, and wild game and a place of almost limitless mineral resources. There, in the early 1860's, a small band of renegade Indians began to congregate. They numbered probably less than 150 and were comprised of those who had fled from tribal punishment or who had been marked for the white man's justice. They were the scum of the Bannocks with a sprinkling of other tribesmen and were known as "Sheepeaters" because the mountain sheep, with which the area abounded, constituted their chief article of diet. Their clothing was, generally, made from the pelts of wild animals, supplemented by what they could steal. They were sneaking and venomous. The lone prospector who ventured into the fastness of the region was almost certain to lose his pack animals and supplies, and probably his life, to these low-level human beings. Gradually settlers filtered into the canyons and finding an occasional grassy meadow or a level shelf adjacent to grazing land, set up their cabin homes. Many of them, too, became the victims of the Sheepeaters.

In the summer of 1878 the Bannocks of Southern Idaho were engaged in their own war, most of which was fought in Northeastern Oregon. When it became apparent that the Federal troops were winning, the Bannocks decided to make their way back to their Fort Hall reservation in Southeastern Idaho. It was a long trip and the troops were in hot pursuit. Sometimes a few Bannocks would find themselves cut off from flight to their home reservation. These took refuge with the Sheepeaters. Others of the Fort Hall Bannocks were afraid to face the justice which would be meted out to them for murders and depredations coincident to the war. They, too, took their way to the Sheepeater country. There were also a few renegade Spokanes, Coeur d'Alenes, and Nez Perces, and an occasional discredited member of some other tribe-rejects from the native mill of life.

With the advent of the veteran warriors from the Bannock War, it was not long until the Sheepeaters, now greatly reinforced, became more bold. The first evidence of this more dangerous attitude came in the summer of 1878 when a mixed group of these Indian allies raided Indian Valley, between the Weiser and Payette rivers in what is now the Weiser National Forest. The Indians ran off five or six dozen horses. Four of the ranchers started in pursuit and were ambushed. Three of these men were killed and the fourth badly wounded, but finally escaped. Ordinarily such an occurrence would have resulted quickly in the dispatch of a punitive expedition, but attention of the United States Army was centered in the contemporary Bannock War. Also many Idaho towns had organized home guards because of Bannock depredations and those hardy souls who might have formed a volunteer force to pursue the Sheepeaters did not dare to leave their own homes unprotected.

Many raids of a minor nature, resulting in thefts of livestock and other thievery, punctuated the late summer. Winter was approaching, the tribe was being rapidly augmented by the desperate runaway Bannocks, and provisions for a long, hard winter had to be assembled. Under the leadership of Chiefs Eagle Eye, Tamanmo (known as War Jack), and another called Chuck, they spent what must have been an unpleasant winter.

In the spring of 1879 the Sheepeaters and their reinforcements swooped upon a Chinese mining camp in the Payette Forest country, killing a number of the Chinese. They continued their reign of terror by forays against other camps of miners and prospectors and lonely ranches. Word was sent to the Army and General Oliver Otis Howard, from his headquarters at Vancouver Barracks, immediately issued the necessary orders to set the military forces in motion.

Grangeville, Idaho, is about 200 miles due north of Boise, and near Grangeville was Camp Howard. Captain (Brevet Colonel) Reuben F. Bernard, the hard-hitting veteran of the Bannock War and other campaigns, with 56 men of the First Cavalry, was ordered to move into the Sheepeater stronghold from Boise Barracks, starting on May 31st. On June 4th, Lieutenant Henry Catley with 48 mounted infantrymen of the Second Infantry, left Camp Howard, moved into the hostile country from the north. It may be a matter of wonder after the Nez Perce War of 1877 and the Bannock War of 1878, why so few troops were sent into this campaign. The fact was that General Howard was unaware of the many additions to the Sheepeater ranks. He believed that they were limited to the relatively small number who had occupied the hide-out for more than 15 years and, hence, considered that the troops were approximately equal to the hostiles.

However, the General soon decided to add somewhat to the expedition. In an article published February 17, 1926, in the Pinewald (N.J.) *Bulletin,* General Howard said that he reached the conclusion that some of the Bannock refugees might have joined the Sheepeaters and that it would be a good plan to organize a troop of scouts. He ordered 2nd Lieutenant Edward S. Farrow of the 21st Infantry, a young officer just out of West Point, to enlist a company of Indian scouts and add a detachment of expert riflemen, to be selected for their endurance. Lieutenant Farrow enlisted 20 Indians from the Umatilla Reservation and selected seven soldiers as his sharpshooters, thus starting his expedition with a fighting force of only 28 men, counting himself. He had in addition two guides and six packers with 34 pack animals. General Howard designated this group as an independent command and started it on its way to hunt down any hostiles who might be found. At the close of the campaign Lieutenant Farrow had a total of 80 men in his command, counting soldiers, civilian scouts, Indian scouts, guides and packers.

From the start of the campaign Colonel Bernard and Lieutenant Catley, and their respective commands, ran into difficulties. A hard winter had been followed by a late spring. Snow still remained to a depth of six or eight feet, which is not too unusual for a region a mile high, in average elevation, above sea level.

The mining town of Warrens, now Warren, Idaho, was near the junction of the Salmon River and its South Fork. Lieutenant Catley had reached a point seven miles beyond Warren by mid-June when he was forced to go back to the town because it was impossible to get through the snow. For days the men had been tramping down the snow so that their horses could follow, and men and horses were exhausted. It was not until July 11th that he succeeded in moving forward with some degree of freedom, but from beginning to end his march was over difficult mountain trails. After back-breaking effort he reached Rains' Ranch, owned by James F. Rains, on the South Fork of the Salmon River and where there was a crossing known as Rains' Crossing. Catley was about 100 miles from his starting point. Having rested briefly at the ranch and repaired pack-saddles and other gear, Catley started eastward toward Big Creek, keeping scouts ahead and at the flanks, on the lookout for hostiles.

Meanwhile Colonel Bernard was not faring much better. On July 15th, General Howard received a report from Bernard saying that the country was rougher than that anywhere else in the United States and that to get at the Indians would be a work of great difficulty. In this latter regard he said in the report, "Should they discover us before we do them they can hide in the timbered Rocky Mountains for a long time and go from point to point much faster than we can, even if we knew where to go . . . we have traveled over much country that no white man ever saw before. Old guides and miners declared that we could not get through at all."

Lieutenant Farrow had crossed the ferry over the Snake River at Brownlee, Oregon, on July 11th. He traveled almost due east and on the 16th reported from Council Valley on the Weiser River that he had already found signs of Indians.

Of course Colonel Bernard was to assume command of all troops at the seat of war when they had all reached points near enough to each other to communicate by courier and operate in unison. The plan of approach was well conceived and, for the most part, well executed except for Lieutenant Catley's misfortune in his first encounter with the hostiles.

Generally, the territory to be combed was that now constituting Valley County, Idaho, which, in turn, is practically covered by the Payette and the Idaho National Forests. Bernard was approaching from the south, Catley from the north, and Farrow from the west, On July 17th Bernard and Catley were about 80 miles apart and Farrow was near enough to Bernard to be in touch with him by courier. Bernard's force had lost several pack animals carrying food supplies, and the men were hungry. Up to that time no Indians had actually been sighted though some signs had been observed.

Lieutenant Farrow followed the signs he had come across and upon his close approach the Indians in that band dispersed and sought refuge on the Lapwai and Lemhi reservations. Farrow then chased another band into the higher elevations of the Seven Devils Mountains, capturing several of them whom he forced to act as guides. He received a report that some Nez Perces who had succeeded in reaching Canada during the campaign of 1877, were back in the Idaho high country, and he decided to try to find them if he could. Before starting on this mission Farrow ascertained Catley's location and, already being in touch with Bernard, set out. By late July the snow had melted except in the higher elevations, streams were again at normal flow, and conditions for campaigning were propitious.

Big Creek was a major tributary of the Middle Fork of the Salmon River. There Catley's command camped on July 28th. Many signs of Indians were found, such as tracks of their horses and the remains of recent campfires. On the morning of the 29th they started on the down slope, having to travel in single file, and often using the stream bed itself as a trail. Suddenly an Indian was observed on a cliff. The Indian saw the troopers, yelled at them and disappeared behind the rocks. Indian rifles cracked and two troopers toppled from their saddles. The soldiers dismounted and began firing, using their horses as shields. But no Indian could be seen, whereas the soldiers were exposed to the gunfire of a hidden enemy who had them in a trap.

In a reminiscent article written many years later by Colonel Aaron F. Parker, another Indian campaigner, Parker notes an official report made October 28, 1879, by Lieutenant Muhlenberg, an officer of Catley's command, in which it was stated that scouts twice reported to Catley that they had seen Indians but that Catley apparently placed no credence in the reports, although a recent camp of the hostiles had been found that day. Catley had ordered the troops into camp the previous night over the insistence of Lieutenant Webster that a scouting party be sent out, but which was not done. In any event, after the ambush Catley ordered his command to turn about and go back up the trail. The two men who had been shot from their horses were not dead but severely wounded. They were carried by comrades. The troops were soon out of range because the Indians, for some unknown reason, did not then pursue.

After back-tracking for about two miles they met their pack train coming down. Catley decided to camp for the night, being in a somewhat favorable defensive position. They were not molested that night although anxiety was manifest in the entire command.

Catley decided to move up the slopes and get out of the immediate territory by using the route which had brought him in. The following morning he started to carry out that plan, the wounded being carried in hand-litters. But the command lost its way and the pack train in the rear was attacked. However, Lieutenants Muhlenberg and Webster succeeded in bringing the pack train safely within the lines just as the front of the column was attacked. Thus the troops were between two fires but since the Indians were remaining at long range, front and rear, no particular damage was done. The packs were removed from the animals and the troops barricaded themselves as best they could among the rocks and trees, with the packs filling in the exposed places. Then the Indians set fire to the grass and timber at the foot of the mountain and the updraft sent the flames roaring up the slopes.

The soldiers back-fired, thus saving themselves from being driven out of their shelter. The weather was very hot and the nearest water was in the creek below them. The men sipped vinegar from kegs carried by the pack train and from that incident their rocky ridge was named "Vinegar Hill," which designation persists to this day and by which name the battle is also known.

The Indians kept up a desultory firing from long range all day, though inflicting no casualties. It was apparent that the hostiles were in small numbers but they had the advantage of position as well as familiarity with the country. Catley decided to move on during the night. Accordingly, after the moon had disappeared behind the mountains, the cavalcade set out, moving into the ravine and up the opposite slope where they found their inbound trail.

They had abandoned much of their equipment and in addition had lost a number of pack animals in the darkness. It was Catley's plan to continue his retreat to the vicinity of Warren or to Burgdorf Springs, now called Burgdorf, which is about 12 miles west of Warren. But couriers brought news of the defeat on July 29th to Colonel Bernard, to Lieutenant Farrow, and to General Wheaton, the latter at Fort Lapwai. Things began to happen. Bernard notified General Howard of Catley's retreat and of the probable location of the Indians. General Wheaton sent Captain A. J. Forse of the First Cavalry to reinforce Catley and to turn him once again against the Indians and in support of Lieutenant Farrow. When the courier reached Farrow the latter lost no time in getting started. He cached his surplus supplies and equipment and, living off the country and by forced marches, reached Catley five days later at Rains Crossing on the South Fork of the Salmon River.

On August 24th General Howard sent word to Colonel Bernard that the hostiles were encouraged by the defeat of Catley, that the trouble was spreading, and urged that every possible effort be made to subdue the Indians. Bernard replied in optimistic tone saying that Farrow was 30 miles ahead of him and pursuing the hostiles down the canyon of the Middle Fork of the Salmon and that Farrow was so hot on the trail that the Indians had abandoned most of their baggage.

Captain Forse joined Bernard and the merged command hastened on, following Farrow's trail. Lieutenant W. C. Brown, who was Farrow's second in command, was out with a scouting party on August 19th and came in contact with the hostiles. Shots were exchanged but the scouting party suffered no casualties. Bernard heard the firing and moved up as fast as the rugged country and tired horses would permit, to find that the Indians were retreating. On August 20th Private Harry Eagan died of wounds received that day. He was shot through both thighs, making amputation necessary, and died under the operation. He was buried where he fell and today a small stone monument marks his grave. The stone was hauled 75 miles by wagon and 40 more by pack-horse, such is the nature of that country even today. Pursuit of the retreating hostiles at that time was impossible. Men and horses had reached the absolute end of endurance.

Meanwhile an incident had occurred at the Rains Ranch. As previously recited, it was on the South Fork of the Salmon River. It was in a sheltered valley and the river crossing there was known as Rains' Crossing. Here James F. Rains and his family had lived for several years. They raised livestock and vegetables, but the chief crop was hay which was baled and carried on pack horses to Warren where it was marketed. When Catley's retreat brought him to the Rains Ranch the owner was aware of the probability that the Indians might follow the retreating soldiers, so he moved out with his family to the town of Warren, leaving the ranch to whatever fate might befall. Several days later he learned of Colonel Bernard's presence in the back country and no Indians having been reported in the vicinity of the ranch, Rains decided to return with three men to help him with hay-making. The men were Harry Serren, James Edwards, and Albert Weber, the latter being Rains' brother-in-law. For several days everything was peaceful. At noon on August 15th, the men had taken a mid-day rest and then returned to the hay field, for the first time neglecting to take their rifles with them. Towards evening Weber went to the house and soon thereafter bullets began to whizz past the three men in the field. They took cover behind the hay bales and then decided to rush to the house and regain their rifles before the Indians could raid the house. They started and almost immediately Rains was critically wounded. Edwards and Serren dodged into a ravine and headed for Warren, which they reached the next day. After dark Rains managed to drag himself to the house where he died in a short while. Weber, who by that time had been wounded, then escaped. The Indians burned the buildings and ran off the livestock.

Bernard caught up with Farrow who had found it necessary to go into camp to rest his men and horses. The Colonel surveyed the situation and sent a dispatch to General Howard, which read in part as follows, "The country is so rough that animals cannot be got through it at all. All our stock except a few of Captain Forse's horses and the animals captured by Farrow are exhausted. Most of our horses and mules have given out and have been shot."

General Howard realized the pounding which nature had been administering to the troops and promptly sent orders to Bernard to use his judgment and if Bernard considered it inadvisable to do more than had been done that he pull the troops out of "that fearful country and distribute his forces to the posts where they belonged."

Bernard proceeded to act upon the order and with his own command set out for Boise Barracks. Captain Forse departed with his troops for Fort Lapwai. Lieutenant Farrow remained in camp to ward off any Indian attacks until it could be certain that no white people remained in the neighboring country. Several prospectors had been killed and signal smoke indicated that the hostiles were not far away and would doubtless attack any ranch still occupied after the troops had left.

Lieutenant Farrow's orders permitted independent action to be fitted to circumstance. He and Lieutenant Brown decided to have one more try at the subjugation of the hostiles. They set out with the Umatilla scouts and a small detachment of soldiers, leaving most of their equipment behind. They knew that with the approach of winter the Indians could no longer take refuge in the higher elevations and that fortune might smile. The very next day they met several squaws and boys whom they took prisoners and from them secured some bits of information about the movements of the hostiles. Lieutenant Brown rode ahead with a few men, Farrow being slowed by the presence of the prisoners. In the early evening Brown heard the barking of dogs and soon sighted an Indian camp. Farrow came up and the expedition surrounded the camp and closed in, only to find that the hostiles had fled, leaving a store of provisions and a few horses.

The trail was a hot one. Farrow and Brown were relentless in their pursuit. It was September and the wintry blasts from the snowy mountain peaks spoke the message that time was running out. One day they saw a lone Indian signalling to them from the edge of a thicket about a half mile away. Lieutenant Brown and Wa-tis-kow-kow, one of the Umatillas who was something of an interpreter, approached, told the Indian to lay aside his gun, which he did, and a parley ensued. It was War Jack, or Tamanmo, one of the Sheepeater chiefs. He said that he was tired of fighting. The Chief accompanied the two back to camp, where Farrow demanded unconditional surrender but promised no punishment except to those who might be proved guilty of murder. War Jack agreed to go to his people and bring them in. Farrow loaned him a horse and in a few days War Jack brought in a mixed group of warriors, squaws and children. But the recent Bannock allies were not there. They had decided to sneak back to their reservation.

Getting the prisoners out was a task. Food was scarce. The snows had started to fall. After 62 days Farrow brought his force and the prisoners to the Columbia River, eventually delivering his charges to Vancouver Barracks, where Colonel Henry A. Morrow, a brevet General, was in command, with Captain John A. Kress in charge of the arsenal. Orders were soon issued to move the prisoners to the Umatilla Agency, which was done. The following spring they were again moved, this time to the Fort Hall Reservation in Southeastern Idaho.

How many prisoners were there? A letter from the Adjutant-General, Washington, D. C., dated June 18, 1925, in response to an inquiry from Colonel Aaron F. Parker, says in part, "Nothing has been found of record showing definitely the date of surrender of the last party of Sheepeater Indians to Lieutenant Edward S. Farrow, Twenty-first Infantry, in 1879. However, the records indicate that Lieutenant Farrow and his force of Umatilla Indian scouts captured 14 Sheepeaters at Big Meadows September 21; compelled the surrender of 39 near the Middle Fork of the Salmon River October 1, and compelled the surrender of 12 on October 6, 1879, near Chamberlain Basin."

In the Thursday, May 13, 1909, issue of the Asbury (N.J.) *Evening Press* is a lengthy account of a talk delivered by Major Edward S. Farrow, United States Army, about his experiences in the Indian campaign of 1879. That account credits Farrow with the statement that his command captured 388 Indians in the campaign and also that it was the largest number of Indians ever captured at any time by any United States troops.

For their accomplishment, Lieutenants Farrow and Brown received brevet promotions. Later, Lieutenant Catley was tried by a general court martial and found guilty of misbehavior in the presence of the enemy and sentenced to be dismissed from the service. The sentence was not carried out because the Judge Advocate General recommended clemency and President Rutherford B. Hayes set aside the sentence. Catley soon withdrew from the army.

Much later when W. C. Brown was a retired Colonel he wrote a book titled, *The Sheepeater Campaign,* compiled from official sources in which he says that the guides and couriers should be held in grateful remembrance; that they had to carry their food and bedding on the saddle; that travel was restricted to trails which the hostiles could watch in safety and attack in safety; that the couriers often had to travel at night; and then lists those who took part in the Sheepeater Campaign, as follows: "Orlando (Rube) Robbins, John S. Rainey, George Shearer, Bright, Josh Falkner, Calvin R. White, Levi A. White, David R. Monroe, Johnny Vose, the Parker brothers, J. W. Redington, Jake Barnes, John Corliss, Alexander Foster, Harry Serren (Lemhi), and Uncle Dave (Cougar) Lewis."

The last of the Indian wars of the Pacific Northwest ended. Each year for the past three had generated a separate war. There were many people who wondered whether some other outbreak would continue the series in 1880. But the Indians had finally decided that they wanted no more punishment from the troops. Resentment still rested in the breasts of the tribesmen but the futility of several efforts to keep the land for themselves was evident. They submitted to reservation life, and a new era of expansion and development spread across the old hunting grounds and battlefields.

INDEX

Index

T

Y